D1559108

Burning Money

BURNING MONEY

The Material Spirit of the Chinese Lifeworld

C. Fred Blake

HAWAI'I

University of Hawai'i Press
Honolulu

Library of Congress Cataloging-in-Publication Data
    Blake, C. Fred.
    Burning money : the material spirit of the Chinese lifeworld /
C. Fred Blake.
    p. cm.
    Includes bibliographical references and index.
    ISBN 978-0-8248-3532-3 (hardcover : alk. paper)
    1. Spirit money—China. 2. Rites and ceremonies—China.
3. China—Social life and customs. I. Title.
    BL1812.R57B53 2012
    393'.90951—dc23
                                            2011021429

Designed by Josie Herr

Printed by Sheridan Books, Inc.

the last rose of summer

Contents

ACKNOWLEDGMENTS

Over the course of years that I have been working on this study, I have benefited enormously from the hospitality and help with logistics, data collections, translations, and criticisms from my kin, students, friends, and colleagues, none of whom are responsible for shortcomings in my interpretations or conclusions. These include Wang Li, Ginger Harris, Terry Blake, James Leong, Tian Chenshan, Wang Lian, Yuan Tongkai, Ding Yuling, Gao Bingzhong, Cai Weirong, Zhu Jiangang, Lei Hongji, Yang Shengmin, P. Steven Sangren, Vu Tu Ahn, Shihlun Chen, Margaret Boedemer, Tian Yongxiang, and anonymous reviewers of the manuscript for this book.

Introduction

In my dream a few nights ago, I visited my granny and granddad, as I often did in my youth. I knocked at the familiar door of their frame house on Old Orchard Avenue in Webster Groves, and after a longer-than-usual wait, the door swung open. I was immediately taken aback. Instead of opening onto the cheerful living room, I had before me a little windowless cell with bare cement walls against which my granny and granddad were propped; their expressions were pale and disconsolate; the scene was vivid, and I woke with a troubled heart.

I simply walked away from this experience with a heavy heart and the consolation that it was, after all, "only a dream." As an anthropologist I am familiar with the notion that dreams of deceased loved ones are a common experience among people around the world and in many places are treated as actual communications, for dreaming is an experience the reality of which cannot be denied. Many Chinese will tell me that this was a message entrusted to me from the spirit world. They have an idiom for it. Deceased for these many years, my granny and granddad "entrusted" me with "a dream" (*tuōmèng*)—they contacted me during my dreamtime, which is their waking time, to entrust me with the knowledge of their grim situation. Chinese not only have an idiom, but also provide a remedy for my grandparents' dreadful plight and my feelings of regret, which I can choose to ameliorate by sending them something—money, clothes, even a new house—made from paper and easily transmitted by the ancient magic of fire. Over the past millennium and across the length and breadth of China and beyond, people have been replicating their material world in paper in order to provend and avail their deceased family members, ancestors, and myriads of imaginary beings by an act of immolation.

There are countless names for this "empire of paper things"—every locale has its own nomenclature. The most common and irreducible reference is simply "paper" (*zhǐ*), which is usually predicated with "burning," as in "burning paper" (*shāozhǐ*). Slightly less common in everyday talk (used more in writing), but altogether unambiguous in Chinese vernaculars, is "paper money" (*zhǐqián*).

Across China, a prodigious amount of paper is burned for every ritual occasion, not just for dead souls at wakes and funerals and memorials, but for all the problems associated with coming into this world and prolonging the stay as far as fate allows. Today, over ten centuries after its advent, the inventory of paper items is prodigious and growing. From unofficial numbers and countless vignettes, the amounts manufactured and burned defy imagination. In 1980s Anxi County, Fujian, one Overseas Chinese ordered that two truckloads of paper money be burned for his mother's funeral, at a cost of ¥20,000. Although this act was considered extravagant (Dean 1988:28), even this extravagance begins to pale against aggregate expenditures calculated on estimated averages. For example, a report from the *Chengdu (Sichuan) Commercial News* (Xiao, Zhang, and Lei 2008), based on stated assumptions, estimated that Chengdu residents burned a hundred tons of paper during the 2008 spring equinox or Qingming festival for sweeping the tombs, and this only included the traditional paper replicas. From Shenyang, Liaoning, we read that every year several tens of millions of yuan worth of real money in the form of paper monies goes up in smoke. Even after a single event like the Ghost Festival of 2003, the burning paper turned into 60 or 70 tons of "black trash" (ash), making the work of cleanup crews extremely arduous (Wang Xinling 2004). There is nothing special about Chengdu or Shenyang. Comparable amounts spent on burning paper money are reported from Dalian to Swatow, often around the major ghost festivals. The *Guangzhou Daily* estimated that during any given Qingming festival, people in China spend more than ¥60 billion for the paper and incense offerings. "Adding in expenses for transportation and meals, the cost is unimaginable" (Yin 2006). These estimates are typical, although there are to my knowledge no official numbers. The custom has always been denigrated as a waste of paper, and in particular a waste of the labor it takes to make paper simply in order to burn it, to say nothing of the nonsense that rationalizes such waste. Today, opponents add the environmental detriments (air and water pollution and wildfires) that burning paper causes.

My task in the following chapters is to narrate the ins and outs of this custom, beginning with the extent to which it is embedded in the everyday lives of the vast multitude of people who use it: that is, how people talk about it, conceive of it, and interconnect it with the other materials that signify the spiritual side of daily lives. This is the focus of chapter 1. Chapter 2 surveys the galaxy of papers that are cut from an endless scroll that stretches back a thousand years and canopies most of continental east Asia from Lanzhou to Taipei, from Harbin to Hanoi and its diasporas. I emphasize the word "survey" because there is no way a chapter, even a book, can do justice to all the items in the galaxy of paper. The paper monies available in a single metropolitan locale are more than can be comprehended in a single book (e.g., Hou 1975; Scott 2007). The third chapter looks for the origins of the paper money custom. The quest for origins is an adventure that goes down different paths. The first pathway is ethnology, which reveals the panhuman aspects of paper money in the offering customs around the world. The second pathway is folklore, which narrates the peoples' own sense of how paper money came about. Folk stories are entertaining, and it is here that the ludic spirit of the burning money custom wraps its wisdom in a sense of humor. Third is history, which tells the story from the fragments of written records left by a not-so-amused literati.

While the first part of the book is devoted to a description of the custom, the second part of the book considers three ways to explain the meanings and motives behind the custom. Each combines anthropology with a particular theoretical or philosophical foundation: structuralism, historical materialism, and phenomenology. The first is a structuralist analysis of the semiotic role of paper money in the common ritual service. In this analysis I employ a well-known ethnological theory of the ritual process in tandem with a well-known Chinese theory of cosmic change (*yīnyángwǔxíng*) to comprehend the alchemy of ritual fire by which worldly materials (one of which is paper money) are sublimated into the numinous aspects of the human psyche. This structural analysis brings forth the implicit liturgical meaning, or, at an even higher level of abstraction, the canonical meaning of paper money in the common ritual service.

Next, historical materialism brings to light the function of paper money under different historical formations. Under the premodern conditions of a highly developed centripetal-oriented feudal formation, paper money rituals enabled petit producers and tradespersons to participate in the mysteries of imperial/cosmic order that were more or less in concert with the rites of imperial sacrifices. But unlike many other customs—even some close companions to the paper money custom, such as footbinding—the paper money custom survived the collapse of the feudal formation in its encounter with the modern European cum global economic system by augmenting the forms cut from the endless scroll of paper in concert with the modern (capitalist) ideology. I thus draw a dotted line between the modern system of capital formation and the "precapitalist" formations, or what I prefer to call *social economies*. For me, a social economy is better understood as "lifeworld" than as "culture" to the extent that social economy is predicated on an all-encompassing world constituted in the connectivity of intersubjective experience and thus has much to do with the way value is produced. In drawing this line between the modern or capitalist economy and the social economies of human history, I do not mean to suggest that the precapitalist social economies were simple, homogeneous, or idyllic. On the contrary, each had its way of representing (and hiding) the sacrifice by which the lifeworld was materially, laboriously sustained and reproduced.

Chapter 6 concludes the middle section of the book by shifting from the historical formations to the structures of the lifeworld in which the consecrative handling of the papers is concerned with producing value, a thing of value, in the form of a sacrifice. The question that vexes us here is, what is actually sacrificed in burning paper money? I try to formulate an answer by *describing the experience* of consecrating—touching, handling, folding—the paper for the flames. This description is based on an intuitive or phenomenological method, which is "wary of the mere substitution of symbols for what is symbolized without returning to the full intuitive presentation of the phenomena thus symbolized" (Spiegelberg 1975:58). To get at this intuitive level of presentation, Edmund Husserl developed a transcendental procedure, the phenomenological reduction, the suspension of our beliefs in the existence of the phenomena, which to my mind bears an uncanny likeness to the logic of paper money itself. In other words, Husserl's transcendental phenomenology and devotees burning paper money share a similar goal: both seek a "reduction" of the mundane phenomenon (an object of concrete experience, in one case, and a tangible treasure, in the other) to a purer form, an eidetic form of essential meaning and true value, respectively. One uses brackets, the other uses fire, to transcend the finite world of things—to get to the "irreal," as Husserl (1962:40) characterized the eidetic form. This brings us to another striking similarity in that both methods of eidetic reduction (phenomenological intuition and burning money) agree on the necessity for an *attitude of plenitude.* In phenomenology this is a kind of "thick description," which takes us behind the world of symbols and into the structure of the lifeworld to see how that world is put together in conscious experience. The spirit of burning money likewise requires a thick treasure trove of paper, an uncountable largesse. This attitude of plenitude runs against the prevailing attitude of efficiency and thrift in the positive sciences and capitalist economic behavior, respectively.

Thus, "what" exactly is sacrificed is hidden in the modality of being that we call "sacrifice." To get at the "whatness" of the sacrifice requires shifting Husserl's phenomenology onto an ontological foundation where we gain access to phenomena that are not directly perceived—that is, going behind the Confucian a priori of "becoming human" to the meaning of human existence, the existential of being-*in*-the-world (Heidegger 1962) and *beyond*-the-world (Binswanger 1941) and *at* or *of* the world (Merleau-Ponty 1968). Here I argue that the sacrificial mode of giving up a part for the good of the whole is the experiential foundation of the historical mode of production. Or to put it another way, the modes of being-in-beyond-and-of-the-world, which is *experiential,* and production, which is *historical,* are mutually grounded in one another.

From the dialectic of experience and history, we move into the third and last section of the book, where our narrative rejoins the symbol-dependent world of positive realities, now in the modernist dross of simulacra, where simulations of reality have displaced their originals, leaving only "the desert of the real" (Baudrillard 1994). Thus, the final two chapters tell how modern times have changed the paper money custom in ways that conform to the ideology of realism and, in the process of changing it, have turned its traditional ludic or "unruly" spirit (Shahar and Weller 1996) into a burlesque. The ludic spirit is inherent in burning money. The idiom *yìzhuāngyìxié* expresses the idea that opposing moods of "gravity" and "jest" become one another just as *yīnyáng* do. We see this in the common ritual service, which begins in solemnity by lighting candles to open the way into the spirit world and ends in jocundity by lighting crackers to restore the mundanity of the here and now. The argument from chapters 1 through 8 follows this dialectic.

The paper money custom is dramatic and colorful; waxing rhetorical, I often call it a potlatch for the spirits. As such, it is photogenic. It lends itself to visual imaging and representation, representations of representations, via mechanical reproduction, to which our modern lifeworld is hopelessly addicted. The colorful, often dramatic imagery is a distraction from what I take to be the important lessons about money and value that this custom has to teach. To avoid the distraction, I have included only a few images (at the insistence of the editors) to illustrate some of the paper monies described in the text. Images of the papers and rituals I describe are, however, readily available on the Internet (e.g., Taobaowang, at www.taobao.com), in the back of your local Chinatown grocery, and in other books cited here, notably Hou 1975 and Scott 2007.

The materials assembled for this study and the process of writing about them are spread over many years, beginning in the 1960s, when my youthful research project was focused on other matters (Blake 1981). My way of approaching the present study has been more casual and protracted than formal. I did not seek financial backing from research foundations, although I have accepted academic posts teaching anthropology at several Chinese universities during the course of my endeavors, and otherwise traveled around the country visiting friends, colleagues, confreres, and former students while encountering others for the first time (on my walks, on my bicycle, on the train) who simply showed me the kindness of strangers. My friends often helped me find neighbors to ask questions of using the local vernacular. As language is the key to ethnographic fieldwork, I have always preferred to work in or with local vernaculars, even if, as in this project, it meant working through local sponsors, spokespersons, and interpreters who in many instances were already helping me with logistics and establishing the chain of responsibility for my inquiries. In China, you can do research well enough in many areas by using the "common language" (Pǔtōnghuà, a kind of modern Chinese Esperanto), but the conversations often fall flat, hesitant and accented, even when the conversation is between persons from different parts of China—sometimes the differences in verbalization interject themselves as the topic of discussion—until the talk shifts into the regional vernacular, or, even better, one of its local dialects, in which case the speakers' eyes noticeably brighten, even glisten a little, because the vernacular is where the Whorfian concomitants of being-in-the-world come to life.

Finally, my idea of anthropology is conceived in a materialism founded on a sensibility of the aesthetic and the ethical, that is, the way of being-in-the-world, the way we insinuate ourselves, our cares, our works, into others' lives. It is a materialism I have long pursued in an imaginary seminar with the likes of Maurice Merleau-Ponty, György Lukács, Mikhail Bakhtin, Walter Benjamin, Gaston Bachelard, Ivan Illich, and Kenneth Burke, among others. I believe this pursuit also brings us to an encounter with Chinese ways of thinking, an encounter that can be felt in every chapter of this book but is most explicit in chapter 4. I think to understand Chinese culture history we must employ its ways of thinking in concert with European analytics. Any hope of drawing fresh insights depends on developing the kind of "conversation" that Evans-Pritchard had with the Azande, in which the presuppositions of Azande witchcraft were disclosed in a way that made their beliefs and practices coherent on the everyday level and also questionable on the epistemological grounds that underwrite modern European thought (Evans-Pritchard 1976; Douglas 1980; Feuchtwang 1992). Only a little less explicit in Evans-Pritchard's descriptive analysis was the extent to which Azande witchcraft called into question the grounds of European thought. On the European side, I give special regard to the older Hegelian and Marxian theories of production and reproduction (especially as updated for our time in works by Amin [1980], Harvey [1982], Saad-Filho [2002], Fine and Saad-Filho [2004], Robbins [1999], and others) and as they encounter Chinese cultural history (e.g., Sangren 2000).

It follows from this that I am less smitten with the recent turn in American anthropology toward a politics and poetics of consumption expressed in a pathos of resistance, identity politics, and a "deconstruction" that abjures the older possibilities of human enlightenment, emancipation, and reconstruction. This politics/poetics of consumption, emblematized in "styles of resistance" and misplaced relativism, *is the obfuscation of an economic system that views its own historicalness as the realization of human nature* (with its emphasis on "nature" in the Darwinian sense of the word). To compound the irony, this "turn" would rather deconstruct Malinowski's *Argonauts* as a literary product of European colonialism than view it (i.e., *Argonauts*) as the instrument by which that colonial project in its theory of economics was in effect and in fact "deconstructed." This politics and poetics further equates theorizing imaginative and critical holistic concepts and essential reasoning with a Euro-centered rhetoric of empowerment, and thus turns all values and identities into contested expressions of an omnipresent "power" that resonates through every quotidian institution and relation (see Spiro 1996; Sahlins 1999; Sangren 2000; and Graeber 2001 for insightful and critical discussions of this orientation). Trite and banal though it has become, the politics/poetics of consumption, in some of its original inspirations, produced pertinent critiques and conceptual insights, which I think should have *built on* the past, should have augmented the older theories of production and reproduction, of labor value and use value, of intentional consciousness, of essential meaning, and of holistic analyses. Thus, my broad purpose is to contribute to an anthropology of value by sketching out a materialist aesthetics in the tradition of Western Marxism married to a Husserlian descriptive phenomenology with both of its transcendental and ontological legacies. In short, I seek to comprehend the connections between the modes of production and the modes of being-in-the-world: that is, how under varying conditions of material history, we humans as persons produce the value that becomes us.

Chiasm

Yīnyáng is separated by a piece of paper.
—Common saying

Many people in China burn paper effigies of things to send to the world of spirits. The paper effigies are often accompanied with burning sticks of incense and offerings of real food, although an offering may be composed of any one of these three items or any combination of the three. The ostensible purpose is to circulate worldly goods on a cosmic level in order to include beings, spiritual beings, who reside outside the mundane world of the here-and-now. These offerings are especially important in funerals and the major ghost festivals, but also other festivities and countless personal occasions. The paper effigies are replicas of everyday items, utensils, valuables—a virtual inventory of things that constitute the effects of Chinese civilization, both old and new. Much as in the real economy, the effigies of socially valuable things center on replicas of money, and the whole galaxy of paper replicas is generally glossed as "paper money" (*zhǐqián*). Chinese have been making and burning these paper effigies and replicas for over a thousand years, and the tradition has lost little of its popularity despite opposition to it. Many cultures use real money to ease the passage of the dead (China does this too), and other cultures (e.g., Japan) use paper for ceremonial purposes, but none to my knowledge substitute paper for money in ritual offerings, at least not to the extent that the Chinese do.

This inquiry describes and explains various aspects of this custom. This is not a conventional ethnography. I do not focus on a single local expression of the paper money custom. The conventional ethnography focuses on a particular organization of materials, which does justice to the local social organization but not to the galaxy of materials as a whole. My focus is on the social formation of a material culture itself, the galaxy of papers with its own emergent characteristics, which I call a common custom (Thompson 1991). So I began by simply wanting to see, perhaps record, possibly collect, what all is "out there." Were the materials in places I was most familiar with (Hong Kong, Honolulu, and Taiwan) the same as those in other places? And what about these other places that were long under the rule of Maoist iconoclasm? My focus on the material culture plus these questions were best approached by a multisited ethnographic methodology, which, according to George Marcus (1995:96), examines "the circulation of cultural meanings, objects, and identities in diffuse time-space." This approach not only allows more focus on the phenomenon of the burning papers in geographic and historical space-time; it also allows us access to a broader stretch of the life-world in which paper-burning practices are experienced and interpreted by variously committed and situated participants, by diverse voices, including nonconcurring and opposing voices. This is a key point: *naysayers always have a voice in my work.* The paper burning custom is not simply the product of people who use it "religiously" or whose livelihoods depend on its manufacture and distribution—these two sites form a chain of values from the commodity to the sacrament—but is constituted in a manifold of discursive practices that extend from remote villages to urban apartment blocks, from ritual manuals to the mass media, from groups to individuals, from the multitude of devotees to legions of scoffers, and every position in between, each with as much say as the other in what the custom means.

Matter-of-Fact Attitudes

The paper money custom is embedded in the matter-of-fact world of many Chinese to such a depth that when I broached it as a topic of study, a university student in Hong Kong repined: "I came to know *jīn* [paper replicas of gold, i.e., paper money] before I learned how to talk. . . . I never paid attention to *jīn* as I am very familiar with it, so familiar that I regard it as a non-issue." Others have responded similarly to my inquiry. Two physicians on the train from Hunan to Sichuan in 2007 assured me that burning paper money is not a superstition but merely a way to show respect; both were unusually upfront about their own practices and organized a spontaneous discussion group, a focus group of sorts, among the other passengers in the car. A few people have wondered why I find the practice interesting, since everyone in the world does it. Early European travelers and missionaries mention paper money in almost perfunctory terms; if they found it remarkable, that was usually because of the incredulousness of its devotees. Lucy Soothill (1931:45–46), a missionary in Wenzhou, Zhejiang Province, of the 1880s, described her most trusted convert as having "been a maker of the gold and silver paper money, which when burned at the grave, provides money for the use of the departed in the next life." She went on to remark: "One cannot tell which to admire most, the ease with which the spirit world could be deceived, or the credulity of the devotees." The misgiving of a foreign missionary in the nineteenth century is not exclusive to that class of persons. For centuries, the Chinese literati dismissed village customs of offering paper money to spirits as vulgar and wasteful, while the twentieth-century intelligentsia attacked the custom with a new, European locution, "superstition" (*míxìn*) (see Feuchtwang 1989; L. Liu 1995). Today, many devotees acknowledge the "superstition" label, and most are aware of the stigma attached to the practice. We can cull countless stories and documents as evidence.[1]

Some devotees wonder, in a purely traditional vein, whether what they are doing is effective or whether what they are sending is getting through to the intended recipient. They take any number of measures to set their minds at ease on these matters. One thing everyone does is to consciously "touch" the papers being offered, an act we explore in chapter 6. Many will write names and addresses of senders on packages containing the paper monies: in places such as Zunyi township, Guizhou, people entrust the skill of addressing the packages to a local spirit master. In other places, devotees include hair or nail clippings in the package so that the recipient may recognize his possession by the scent of the burned body part; this is an expression of what I call a piety of the flesh. A more common practice is for the sender to scrawl the surname of the intended recipient on the ground where the paper treasure is to be burned, or draw a circle around it that prevents the uninvited from crossing. Some add a special charm to guarantee a speedy delivery. Especially to higher divines, many supplicants add the charm of nobility (*guìrén fú*), a patron of honor and high rank to help convey the treasure from its worldly abode to the divinity. Some folks read the ash of the burned offering, if they know how, to tell whether their paper treasure got to the intended recipient; and on special occasions some senders employ the oracle power (second sight or clairvoyance) of children to see the apparition that walks off with the burned offering. A lot of other folks express a sense of indifference to these matters and simply say there's no way of knowing whether or not the paper burned in this world can get to the other side.

But until questioned, most devotees seem uncurious about their paper money offerings. It may be superstitious; it may be that the treasures they are sending don't get to the intended recipients; but the bigger question of why people bother to do it in the first place is one many people never think much about, since the specific reasons for doing it seem self-evident. When asked, outside specific contexts, to explain why they burn money, most persons simply say that the tradition is passed down from the older generations, which in the traditional lifeworld is quite sufficient as an explanation for a thing's existence.[2] Even within a specific context, reasons may be difficult to come up with: Asking rural folks around Yu County in Hebei why they burn paper shoes for the divinity they call *Niángniang* (the mothering spirit), Dr. Wang Li was simply informed that this is their custom. But eventually one older woman, Liu Laotai, pondered the question and offered a rationale in what for her was an epiphanic moment: it must be, Liu reasoned, because *Niángniang* is constantly walking here and there to deliver babies and wearing her shoes out.

Many devotees imply that a level of well-being, a feeling of relief, of expiation, the lifting of a burden, comes with sending a gift of paper monies to spirits. Quite a few express fear of the consequences were they to quit the practice—that is, from their point of view, to renege on an obligation. Once you have begun, you create expectations among the spirits; you cannot forget an anniversary or just quit without being put on notice via a stomachache or worse. The practice of offering paper monies is embedded in the lifeworld by means of the ritual process, where, in the final analysis, it tends to get lost among all the other props in the frisson of some larger ceremonial. Even for anthropologists, who came late on the heels of missionaries but were less taken aback by the foolishness of it all, the pattern of paper offerings is so pervasive "that even a trained observer soon takes it for granted" (McCreery 1990:1). For instance, listening to National Public Radio's Melissa Block (2008) describe so movingly the horrific scene at Juyuan Middle School during the 2008 Sichuan earthquake, I was struck by her uncontexted reference to "paper money," as if her American audience, even those among the better-informed strata of the American public, would know what she was talking about. Here is the print version: "Parents built makeshift shrines and placed the bodies of the dead on pieces of cardboard or plywood as they grieved over the small lifeless forms. Some lighted red candles or burned paper money to send children into the afterlife. Others set off firecrackers to ward off evil spirits. The grim ritual played out by dozens and dozens of families as they kept watch over their babies one last time." In the days following the quake, Internet viewers could see makeshift altars and piles of paper money among the rubble. A Reuters news caption read, "Stacks of Chinese religious 'money for the dead' are sprawled on a floor in the earthquake-hit area of Hanwang, Sichuan, May 22, 2008." The picture shows whole cartons of paper money ripped open and simply dumped unburned; and the paper money is all one kind, facsimiles of the ¥100 RMB bill.

Previous Studies

Although Europe's first encounter with Chinese paper money was likely from a note in the travelogue of Marco Polo, it wasn't until the mid-nineteenth century that Chinese customs became a sustained object of European curiosity and study. Among the first European observers was the Reverend Justus Doolittle, who included terms for paper offerings in a glossary of Chinese terms at the front of his book on social life in Fuzhou, a treaty port in Fujian Province. Doolittle ([1865] 1966:xv) described the principal types of paper offerings. The first was "mock clothing": depictions of various kinds of clothing stamped on sheets of paper, and sheets of paper of various colors representing pieces of silk, satins, and cotton goods. The second was "mock money": sheets of various-sized papers laminated with tinfoil to represent silver or colored yellow to represent gold and sheets with rows of perforations to represent cash. In addition, there are pieces of pasteboard that in size and appearance resemble Carolus dollars.[3] Today we have in many places a similar pasteboard facsimile impressed with the early-twentieth-century "big head" of the Yuan Shikai silver dollar. When burned, "these [different kinds of paper] are believed to become . . . silver, gold, cash, or dollars, according to color and shape, which may be used by the divinity or the deceased person for whom they are designed" ([1865] 1966:xvi).

From these early accounts we can infer several general points. One is the continuity and change in the form of paper monies over time. From the descriptions provided by Doolittle alone, we can study how and the extent to which the paper monies have changed. Here, we note that Doolittle's description 150 years ago is entirely consonant with what we have today, with but two exceptions: (1) most of the change has amounted to introducing new symbolic content (e.g., the change from replicas of Carolus silver dollars to replicas of Big Head silver dollars, i.e., from use of money that simulated a foreign monetary system to money that simulates a native Chinese monetary system); and in keeping with this principle, there has been (2) an expansion of types of replicas, in addition to already-noted symbolic content, to keep pace with shifts toward a global consumer-based economy. One of my purposes in this book is to show how in recent years the paper money custom has exploded in every direction, but most notably in the hypertrophy of signs, a process that parallels if not converges with the economy of brands and sign-values that followers of Jean Baudrillard say characterizes a postmodern world of hyperrealism. I take this up in the penultimate chapter.

After Doolittle, other studies extended our knowledge of the paper money custom across historical time and geographic space. Toward the end of the nineteenth century in the Treaty Port of Amoy in southern Fujian, J. J. M. de Groot (1969) described how different kinds of paper monies were used in the cadences of local funerals. His description drew heavily from an archive of historical documents. For instance, the papers described by Doolittle that are laminated with tinfoil to represent silver or colored yellow to represent gold and that are to this day a mainstay of the paper money custom along the southeastern coast can be traced back a thousand years. Other studies along China's southern coast soon followed (Dore 1914; Hunter 1937). Dard Hunter brought out a limited-edition volume on the craft of paper making in Zhejiang Province that featured specimens of the actual ceremonial papers. Hunter did not limit his survey to the Zhejiang workshops, however. He followed the paper money trail into the regional, national, and international markets, which led north to Beijing and across the South Seas to Bangkok and on round the earth.[4]

With these studies plus ones that followed, a picture of the geographic spread of the paper money custom began to take shape. I don't know of any studies that attempt to trace the custom's historical diffusion. Although southeastern coastal China has long been the area of its greatest efflorescence, at least in the sheer production of the material corpus, we find paper money everywhere we care to look for it. Even in remote places like the Ordos Plateau, sinicized Tu have a complex tradition of paper monies. I think it is fair to surmise that from the Tang dynasty the paper money custom extended across nationalities, language stocks, and kingdoms in a contiguous culture area stretching from the trans-Ordos Plateau to the southern littoral, where it runs from Shanghai to Hanoi and beyond to settlements of Sinitic and sinicized peoples across Southeast Asia and on around the earth. Cambodians who claim some Chinese ancestry and who survived the Khmer Rouge terror revived their paper money custom soon after the terror ended. With few exceptions (notably the world religions like Islam and Christianity), the peoples of this vast area burn paper money as a matter of custom. The horizons of the paper money custom thus exceed the transnational Chinese cultural sphere, or "cultural China," as Tu Weiming (1994) calls it. It is not entirely accurate to limit the custom to the "Chinese." No single cultural formation characterizes this broad area so succinctly as does the paper money complex, although there is only a vague collective consciousness of its existence beyond particular localities. It does not evoke an identity. There is no "paper money people." Its limiting factor is not so much the development of a commercial way of life; its limiting factor is simply the availability of low-grade paper joined to an anthropological notion of money.

Most earlier studies of paper money merely included paper money in larger contexts of material cultures. For Doolittle, the context was social life; for Groot, it was mortuary customs; for Dore, it was Chinese superstitions; for Hunter, it was the paper craft itself, which a later work by Roderick Cave (2002) augmented with an emphasis on paper charms ("paper horse," or *zhǐmǎ*). For Clarence Day (1940), it was the New Year pictures ("paper gods," or *niánhuà*). Hou Chien-lang (1975) was the first to concentrate exclusively on the paper money custom itself. There, for the first time, we have a systematic inventory of paper monies restricted to a single locality—Taiwan, which at the time possessed the most impressive array of paper monies. This was a salient point in 1975, the year of Hou's publication and the penultimate year of the Cultural Revolution on China's mainland. Hou intimated, without putting too fine a point on it, that while the mainland communists were busy smashing ancient folk customs such as paper money, Taiwanese were faithfully preserving theirs as a point of *national Taiwanese* identity. Having collected 200 kinds of paper monies, Hou limited his study to the 31 types that are destined for circulation through the Celestial Treasury (*tiānkù*). Several anthropological studies emerged from Hou's work, among the most provocative of which was one that posed Chinese gods as bankers (Gates 1987, 1996), a proposition I address in chapter 5.

Part of the impetus for my book is to meditate on at least two predicates that undergird Hou's landmark work. The first, contrary to what Hou (and I at the time) thought was the demise of the paper money custom on the Chinese mainland, is the degree to which it revived and reinvented itself after the demise of Maoist rule. Even more, in reinventing itself, is the extent to which it has accommodated our modern notions of money (see chapters 7 and 8). I say "accommodate" because my second point is that wherever we find the custom, taken as a whole, it is not reducible to a modern notion of a general-purpose currency. Rather, it exhibits ancient notions of "money" as special-purpose monies, as valuables in kind, as gifts, charms, décor, and the like. As such, there is not a single form of expression. It is an endless scroll of paper forms that extend from recognizable replicas of monetary values through continuous, imperceptible gradations into replicas of other forms of value (e.g., bolts of cloth and finished clothes), shifting here and there into other media of replicating value (e.g., edibles). As we unroll the paper scroll, the shift from "money" to, say, paper-pasted objects and paper bindings (*zhǐzhā*), paper cuttings (*jiǎnzhǐ*), paper gods (*zhǐshén*), or New Year pictures (*niánhuà*) depicting the reign and influence of particular spirits (including the new sages Mao Zedong and Zhou Enlai) over the domicile, is mostly a difference between ritual burning and ritual decoration. And although fire is an irreducible element in the paper money custom, it is a matter of timing, since even replicas of monetary forms are used to decorate the tomb or the domicile. I will give an example of this below. The shift from paper to other media may seem discrete, but in northern China there are places like Yu County, Hebei, where the peasants make replicas of money and things out of paper and also make their counterparts out of flour dough called "flour flowers." The paper and flour replicas of monies and utensils from shoes to combs are offered in various combinations and permutations depending on the ritual occasion.

Most of the studies that have appeared since Hou's have been aimed more at theorizing the paper money custom. These studies explain the ostensible notion that paper money extends a monetized notion of value to the spirit world. For Gary Seaman (1982) paper money preserves the multicentric aspects of premodern economies; for Hill Gates (1987, 1996) it is a folk ideology that reflects a peasant mode of production; for John McCreery (1990) it codifies a ritual performance; for Janet Scott (1997) it is the expression of a Chinese identity in Hong Kong. And in a recent book that complements Hou's work, Scott (2007) provides a detailed description of the paper offerings available in Hong Kong. For me, the study of paper money raises questions about, to put it as succinctly as I can, how value is realized and produced. In its most elementary form, the paper money custom facilitates communion with spirits—first, family and familiar spirits—and this can be accomplished with a single scrap of paper, for I have heard a lot of people say, contrary to the spirit of largesse that animates the custom, that it's not how much you burn, it's the thought that counts, so long as the thought is wrapped in something that can be burned. Toward the end of the Cultural Revolution a friend of mine dreamed that her much-missed grandmother was cold and destitute, and, paper being in short supply, she burned a small scrap of paper, a gesture that gave respite to her sad feelings. In a similar case, a friend of mine awoke from a dream in which his recently deceased mother was feeling cold. Being highly educated, he reasoned that his dream must have been occasioned by the fact that he had left his arm outside the heavy quilt and that it was the cold sensation in his arm that he was aware of when he awoke with the feeling that his mother was feeling cold. But an older woman who had cared for the mother, and whom the family called Auntie, had the same dream. In this case, the family members, although divided on what to do or not to do about it, sent their mother her old nightgown by burning it. The traditional explanation for the son experiencing his mother's cold is based on what I call the piety of the flesh. Burning paper (or in this case a piece of clothing) belongs to this reasoning. This is the foundation of the custom. It reverberates in the folktales and folk psychology we will come to in chapter 3.

The Lifeworld of Paper Money

Now I want to show how this foundation resonates with other symbols that gird the reality of everyday lives. On a visit to a village in rural Hubei in 2000, my friends and I talked with a woman we addressed as Zhao Dasao.[5] Our discussion took place along with some of her cohort who were visibly jammed in the little room, with its low ceiling and packed earthen floor. The most vivid parts of this conversation revolved around entrusted dreams (*tuōmèng*) that Zhao's deceased mother conveyed to her children shortly after her funeral. The mother first appeared to Zhao's younger brother, complaining that she had no place to stay; the family then burned spirit materials for her on the third seven-day interval after the funeral, although they did not invite her to eat "because we didn't believe in offering food." Zhao continued:

> Later mother entrusted her dream to me telling me . . . she had
> nothing to eat. She was carrying a sorghum stalk to gnaw. I said,
> "Ma, how can this be gnawed?" Mother answered, "I have nothing
> to eat at all. What can I eat if I don't eat this?" Asking again, "Even
> if you gnaw this you still cannot be full. How can you have nothing
> to eat?" Mother answered, "Nobody gives me anything to eat!" The

next day, I asked other people. They said I should burn money paper
(*qiánzhǐ*), make a grass torch and then get a bowl of rice. Then burn
the grass torch in the middle and spread a circle of rice around the
periphery, in this way she can get something to eat on that side.
When it got dark, I did what I was told, burning money paper,
grass torch, and the lit incense. So mother became untroubled and
untroublesome. She no longer complained that she had nothing
to eat.

At this point a discussion ensued among our gathering that brought in
the entrusted dream of a deceased neighbor, who had given Zhao's mother
half his food but who suffered from having gone to his grave improperly clad
and thus needed shoes.[6]

The transcriptions of Zhao's responses to our inquiries, as with any inter-
view, are difficult to fathom, much less appreciate, without situating them in
a larger discursive context of the local vernacular—local history and politics
and other symbolic systems. The first point of interest is how the entrusted
dreams sent by spirits to the living are intertwined with stories exchanged
by neighbors; the entrusted dream is part of an ongoing conversation, full
of complaints and requests, that takes place in a community where ritual
services are less routine (due to recent historical happenings) and the disembodied and the embodied communicate among themselves, more or less ad
hoc, with those on either side. It turns out that one reason Zhao's family did
not believe in making food offerings is that the mother had been a Christian
and, "believing in religion" (*xìnjiào*), did not allow food offerings, or, in local
vernacular, "calls to eat"; the mother said just before she died, "You're busy
all day long, how can you find the time to make offerings?" "She also said
that she believed in religion, she was about to go to heaven (*tiāntáng*); there
was something to eat in heaven. But whatever anyone thinks, it turns out
that there's no food to eat when you get to heaven."

To Zhao, relying on the evidence of her own experience, the aura of her
mother's entrusted dream (a piety of the flesh) seemed more original than her
mother's avowal of Christian faith. The experiential evidence of the entrusted
dreams challenges the veracity of Christianity, which in recent years had
regained a toehold in the vicinity in the form of an unregistered Bible study
group. One real benefit, sometimes a selling point of Christianity, is that it
relieves survivors of the burden to make offerings; countless persons have told
me as much, although there are Christians who would argue that sustaining a

Christian faith is the greater burden; but Christianity cannot guarantee that the survivors will not be the recipients of entrusted dreams, which, after all, as an experience is as real as it gets (I vouched for this in the introduction), although generally regarded as an unpleasant experience; to be the recipient of an entrusted dream is rather dreadful, sometimes frightful, to say nothing of burdensome. As a phenomenon, the dream experience is vivid and real, unlike the abstractions of Christian promises. When the mother returning as a spirit complained to her son that she had no place to go, the son answered, "Since you came back, don't scare the kid." The mother answered: "I won't scare him, I will leave at the crack of dawn." Zhao continued, "Just because of this, we made spirit materials." In other words, the mother's ghost kept hanging around making a nuisance of itself, which caused the son and daughter to burn paper to coax the ghost to depart.

In discussing how this communication is possible, Zhao Dasao explained: "As for the departed, we have heard it said from the older generation that [our] evening is their daytime." Zhao went on to explain that this is how we [the living] can be together with the departed through dreaming. This raised more questions: for instance, being intertwined as night and day, how different is the *yīn*-world from our here-and-now? Zhao's answer: "Uh, it's definitely different from our place." Beyond this intimation, Zhao did not venture; it's definitely different, but how different, not really that different, we surmise from Zhao's talk about her mother's entrusted dream.

We asked this question of many persons in different parts of China, and the responses were similar to Zhao's. In a survey of thirty adults in different parts of central China, every respondent had a different way to phrase it, but I think none of them would have found the others' opinions disagreeable. A middle-aged farmer from Hunan summed it up by asserting that the *yīn*-world was pretty much the same as the *yáng*-world, but asked about the specific nature of the *yīn*-world—whether the *yīn*-world is a purgatory, a paradise, just more of the same, or nothingness—he replied, "There's no *yīn*-world. If you believe, [then] there is; if you don't believe, [then] there's none—this is the best answer to the question." Almost half the folks in our survey chose "nothingness" as the most likely alternative; this was followed by the ever-popular "purgatory," then by "just more of the same," and lastly, just one person chose "a paradise." These results strike me as odd given all the wealth sent over to the other side plus the paradisiacal imagery depicted on paper monies. An answer to the question "Why don't more people think of the next world as paradise?" might be that the other world is a pilgrimage that begins closer to home in a purgatory of dematerialization (disembodiment) and becomes one of increasing etherealization. This rationale is implicit in the hierarchy of metallic qualities that the different kinds of paper monies replicate.

The opinion that the *yīn*-world is nothingness would also suggest that it is not a place from whence the living might be receiving an entrusted dream. Yet, to the question about entrusted dreams, almost half the respondents indicated that they or members of their family burned paper money after receiving an entrusted dream; and half of these had indicated they envisioned the *yīn*-world as nothingness. Whatever their beliefs about *yīn*-world, the vast majority lived in families that also burned paper money on the various festivals. Twenty-nine of thirty respondents indicated that their families burned paper money for Qingming. There is thus a certain disjuncture between individual "beliefs" of a so-called religious nature and the complex of notions that entail ritual practices of burning paper money, a point I follow throughout the course of the following chapters. With emphasis on the reality of the social and discursive, most folks readily hold to the commonsense that the hereafter is a continuation of the here-and-now; in both spheres of time-space people need money to live, but here-and-now worldly money is no good to spirits in the *yīn*-world. The point has often been driven home to me by people in different parts of China. A close-knit cohort of working-class women in Shanghai in 2000 chimed in at once that "it is hard to circulate [real money] universally!" "Oh, [it] cannot circulate universally." "This [real money] is circulated in your place, that [paper money] is circulated in their [spirits'] place." So in one sense, paper money is the counterpart of real money; it fulfills the ideal purpose of money by extending its circulation to the *invisible realm* of the macrocosm. "People use paper money because money can achieve everything," intoned an undergraduate student at Jishou University, where I was teaching anthropology, in 2007. All of this talk leads to the inevitable question concerning the nature of the intersection of the *yīn*-world and *yáng*-world.

Responding to this question, our working-class cohort in Shanghai offered conventional metaphors: "People say there's a river between *yīn*-world and *yáng*-world, whatever." Another woman laughing: "But you've never seen it!" Persisting with the first woman, we asked, "In your view, what do you feel the boundary is like between living and dead people?" She answered: "*Yīkǒuqì* [one breath]. . . . Hey, one breath." "Persons are nothing but a single breath, are they not? Without it, everything is 'fine' [i.e., finished]." The

same question on the survey of thirty persons around central China elicited
other tropes. While most mentioned obvious things like change from day to
night, or being covered by earth, a few mentioned legendary figures, such
as "the legendary gate guarded by ghosts." A couple of respondents came
up with the trope we were pitching for: that is, "paper." A middle-aged Yao
farmer from southern Hunan listed "a piece of paper because when people
die, the face will be covered with a piece of paper." A Tujia farmer from
western Hunan said simply, "It's separated by a piece of paper." Years earlier,
an elderly lady in Hong Kong had spontaneously told me it was a piece of
paper; and then Zhao Dasao in rural Hubei responded with what by then I
understood as a traditional phrase: "There is a piece of paper between *yīn*-
world and *yáng*-world. . . . Oh, yes, it is divided [*shì fēnkāi de*] by a piece of
paper." There are other ways of phrasing this notion, but whichever trope
is used for "separation," it conveys the sense of an interruption, a reversal
that sustains the continuousness and vitality of a larger living whole, such
as breathing (inhaling/exhaling) or burning (visible *yáng* / invisible *yīn*), in
which "the coincidence eclipses at the moment of realization," to borrow a
phrase from Maurice Merleau-Ponty (1968:147). This moment of the dialectic, this moment of realization, is the sensibility of the "chiasm" or "the flesh
of the world," which Merleau-Ponty philosophized and which bears striking
resemblance to the Heraclitean or even "Zhuangzian" sense of reality, of life,
of being in a state of continuous change, which transposes into social and
ethical sensibilities of the Confucian emphasis on how persons *become "human"*
in the way they cultivate relationships, that humanity is a *relationship* of form
and substance, a kind of "intercorporeality" (Cataldi 1993:69) that makes
possible a way of being-in-the-world—of receiving entrusted dreams, for
instance. If this is a mouthful, I would submit that it is how ordinary persons
like Zhao live in a world where a piece of paper, a man-made artifice, "separates" living persons from spirits of the dead.

There are other points of coincidence in Zhao Dashao's lifeworld that
must be mentioned, for with Zhao, we became aware of the rather narrow
scope of spirits that she and others seemed particularly concerned with in
terms of making offerings. When speaking in general terms about local paper
money practices, Zhao insinuated an equally general belief in the pantheons
of ancestors, spirits, and demons; but when the questions came around to her
own personal beliefs, she declared: "As for me—I depend on—I depend on
the country," and lapsed into the local vernacular. My colleague, host, and
local spokesperson queried leadingly, "What did the country give you?" "Uh,

country, if the country isn't good, and your current condition . . . [is] . . . just like the past, how can you be this way [so well off]? How can I not believe in the country? I don't believe in gods [*shén*], I believe in the country."

Zhao thus separated the whole business of tending to the needs of recently deceased members of her family from patronage of exalted spirits—more distant ancestors, divines, and demons, which in other venues (possibly even for her, and definitely for other people), especially in southeastern China, takes up an enormous portion of offering papers. There was no necessary contradiction here. Zhao's rhetorical point was cogent given the local social structure and historical horizons. In Zhao village, the temple for the patron deity and the Zhao ancestor hall had fallen into disrepair during the Great Leap Forward (1960–1962) and into complete ruin in succeeding decades.[7] The architectonics of spirit offerings had retreated to the domestic sphere, where the communists insisted it belonged; it was also here, in some of the entrance halls of Zhao village domiciles, that large colorful reproductions of Mao Zedong and Zhou Enlai were enshrined, in effect replacing the altars for ancestors. One of these shrines superimposed the figures of Mao and Zhou on the huge red graph *fú* (fortune) to signify their blessing; they were flanked by emblems of longevity and traditional eulogies.[8] Here was a kind of large paper charm within the scope of New Year pictures (*niánhuà*) (see Day 1940). They eulogize the great leaders of "this generation," who, like the soaking of a spring rain or the illumination of sun and moon, bring the common people untold blessings. It seemed to answer the rhetorical question uttered by Zhao Dasao: "How can I not believe in the country?" The whole composite was covered in crystalline plastic and pasted on a peach-colored mat that was mounted on the whitewashed adobe wall. The high table below the portrait, traditionally an altar, held vases with flowers, bottles of wine and distilled spirits, a stack of tumblers, a teapot, two hot-water thermoses, and a partly opened umbrella drying after days of downpour (just outside the door was a sea of mud). The assemblage in some way mystifies and in others reifies Mao and Zhou as a force of history, a force of nature, or even a cosmic force, and while it flirts with the apotheosis of the two leaders, whose demonic power might be harnessed for personal benefit by lighting candles and burning incense—even by offering food and paper money, as is done in other places— there were no signs of these things here.[9] More than other such displays in Zhao village, or other places for that matter, this one moved me with the splendor of its earthiness and the secular style of its hegemonic message.

Thus, if the souls of ancestors and the spiritual power of gods were more or less replaced by a veneration of legendary heroes Mao and Zhou, the souls of deceased family members continued to need attention, and the paper money tradition served these needs. As already intimated, we could also extend the paper money tradition to include the paper charms bearing the images of the great leaders and simply say that for some villagers, at least, the paper money tradition is oriented more toward the recently deceased members of the family than toward the more remote ancestors (zǔxiān) or patron deities (shén), whose places on the altar are in effect filled by a new set of venerable spirits, Mao and Zhou.

Thus does a village-level paper money custom interact with other powerful symbolic systems such as religion (Christianity) and historical legends (Mao and Zhou) and of course its own purview of the recently deceased. We can briefly compare this with the Yu County, Hebei, custom of "perpetuating money" (chángqián) pasted over invisible domestic divinities located on the interior walls of a house. Here a local type of paper money is used as a lucky charm to protect and decorate the inhabitants of the house. Here the prophylactic purpose is conflated with aesthetic purpose; but this same region enjoys a special reputation for making paper cuttings (jiǎnzhǐ) to decorate paper-paned windows (chuānghuā), and in important ways, these are endowed with a certain numinosity. Increasingly they are used as gifts and to decorate objects other than windowpanes. At the Changsha, Hunan, Kaifusi (Buddhist) temple, the gold paper is framed with red decorative paper cuttings. However the line is drawn, the papers of the offering tradition extend to decorative functions and other practices, like the decorative paper cutting tradition and the New Year pictures tradition, to mention two. The multitudinous paper craft traditions overlap each other, without clear-cut external or internal boundaries.

Conclusion

The paper money custom is widespread, common, and more or less taken for granted across the length and breadth of China and beyond. Although the custom exhibits remarkable commonality, each locale has its own traditional forms. Some are materially elaborate; others are simpler. From the time Europeans encountered the paper-burning custom in the nineteenth century, they have subjected it to a major academic study about every thirty years. These studies show the remarkable historical continuity that characterizes this custom. The custom is contiguous in space and time; it is also enmeshed with other symbolic systems of the ongoing system of social relations. In this

chapter, I have shown, among other things, how the custom bears a complicated relationship to the other symbol-wielding systems. Some of these
depend on the same endless scroll of paper (e.g., paper charms and paper cuttings). Others, such as communist iconography, are being incorporated into a
papery apotheosis. And still others, such as Christianity, with its unfulfilled
promise of personal salvation based on the evidence of a dream, are contro-
verted by the burning of paper. In one family, the mother who has accepted
the Word of the Christian Bible tells her children not to waste their time and
money calling her to eat and burning paper after she is gone, for she will be
in Heaven; what a relief! Whereupon the children receive a dream from their
mom, who has found no home and is wandering around ill-clad and hungry,
so they call her to eat and burn paper for her. The dream, or at least its possibility, is enabled by posing the family as chiasm of flesh and spirit or what
I call a piety of flesh. The dream is only one, albeit a most widespread, commonly accepted, explicit, and agreeable (though at the same time ominous
and unpleasant) means by which the disembodied supposedly communicate
their needs to the embodied; just as burning paper is one way, a widespread
and accepted way, in which the recipients of requests respond. Of course,
devotees do not wait for requests to be submitted via dreams; they are careful
to make offerings at every memorial appointment. Once devotees begin to
remember the dead in this way, missing an appointment can induce in them
a state of high anxiety. If this is not enough, the paper-burning custom and
Chinese religion, although grounded in the apotheosis of family relations,
is easily extended to encompass the gamut of spirits, from the most exalted
Buddha and native and Taoist demigods to debased and disinherited demons.
We will encounter examples of these in the following chapters. The next
chapter examines some of the material forms of paper money.

CHAPTER 2

Endless Scroll

Increase Increase Increase
  —epigraph on a Little Heavenly Gold

My plan to collect all the different paper monies ended very quickly years ago. Trying to grasp the whole galaxy of paper monies soon becomes a bewildering and endless task. Simply walking into a store specializing in paper monies in any sizable city in China is a daunting experience. Some Tian Jiu chain outlets in Hong Kong even provide shopping baskets. Although such shops import paper monies from other regional markets, no one shop can possibly retail the whole corpus of commercial manufactures, not to mention the vast sea of homemade paper monies that extends from Harbin to Hanoi.

Then there is the question, paper money for what? Paper replicas of worldly things are burned for every passage fraught with danger or crisis or anxiety that attention to ritual helps resolve: pregnancy, birth, travel, washing hair at the risk of losing whatever little fortune one possesses, coming of age, marriage, marital estrangement, divorce, dealing with a harasser or other nuisance (or, conversely cursing or harassing an adversary), exorcising a demon, mourning a death or helping the deceased through the hellish ordeal of ridding the body of its worldly corruption, remembering the deceased, giving thanks, opening a business, responding to an entrusted dream, leaving on a trip, taking an exam—the list is endless. Each ritual occasion in different places may entail a different ensemble of papers.

Along a busy boulevard in Guangzhou on a summer afternoon in 1995, I happened on a wheelbarrow outside a construction site in which an older worker was feeding a fire with sheets of gold-foiled papers in a nonchalant manner. The giant sheets of yellow-brown tissue were stamped with a wood block of red emblems for longevity and monetary fortune; below these was an incantation that read, "Giving thanks for the kindness bestowed by the divines" (*chóudá shén'ēn*).

There is considerable overlap in the ensemble of papers appropriate for different occasions, and knowing which papers to use is usually a matter of family tradition or consulting a spirit master or a vendor. Much of the business of assembling papers for maximum communicative effect is a combination of implicit rules of thumb, common sense, individual style, ingenuity, purpose, and sense of aesthetic. This includes the physical motions and gestures that cannot be separated from the papers.

A mother and pregnant daughter-in-law laid out an elaborate offering on the floor of the Wong Tai Sin temple, Hong Kong, on a brisk fall morning in 1999. The food offerings included a small roast pig resting in the long paper shopping bag in which it was transported, while the two women folded the Longevity Gold papers (HK$5 packs) in a novel style. Working in unison, each took a pack and turned each leading edge of a leaf back to its opposite edge, creating a kind of puffed-up tube and giving maximum exposure to the gold foil. Then into each "coiled" pack was inserted the red paper charm of a "noble benefactor" (*guìrén fú*), and the whole reconfigured pack was placed snugly against a previous pack to create a sea of gold. Then in a manner that was out of the ordinary for this place, the mother and, close behind, her daughter-in-law got down on their knees, upon which the two turned to face away from the main altar and bowed deeply from the waist in a kneeling position to praise the sky. It was a grand gesture and lovely to behold. They did not actually touch their heads to the pavement, but as their folded hands came down with the downward motion of their bodies from the waist, the hands separated, spread down and to the sides, with the palms open to the sky but never touching the pavement. The way they did it was as sweeping as it was graceful and their bodies and offerings became the flesh of the world. After beseeching the firmament, the two turned around and did the same for Wong Tai Sin.

Taxonomies

Although a lot of paper money is made by family members for home consumption, most paper money is manufactured and retailed by countless little family-based workshops and hand-labor paper money makers scattered around China. There are also entire village economies that rely on paper money making, one of which I describe at the end of this chapter. Increasingly there are small and medium-scale industrial firms machine-manufacturing increased types and amounts of paper monies, some of which is advertised directly to retailers and consumers online. Not only is a complete inventory of Chinese paper monies impossible, as already noted, but beyond a local system, a particular manufacturing firm or retail outlet, even trying to discern an agreed-upon, formal taxonomy of paper monies is frustrated by the fact that labels use terms that are sometimes literary, other times of a local or regional vernacular, and still other times the same terms as used for the real thing. Once you think you have the labels in hand, there is the *protean structure* (endless in-between, overlapping, and hybrid varieties and purposes) of the paper replicas and facsimiles. Any attempt to stay true to the spirit of the paper money custom must guard against the tendency to reify its terms or in any other way stop the unrolling of the endless scroll, which bears an uncanny likeness to time itself. Even more, the edge of the paper money corpus is frayed and entangled with other media for simulating value—for example, the offerings that peasants in Yu County, Hebei, make to their ancestors juxtapose replicas of valuables made from paper with replicas made from wheat dough. Or, as we saw in the last chapter, the tradition of pasting "perpetuating money" in Yu County, Hebei, and "new year's pictures" in Jingshan County, Hubei, and red paper cut frames for gold offering papers in Changsha, Hunan, mixes decorative and magical purposes. The decorative purpose of paper money is manifest when it is offered or displayed unburned, which we have traced to the very beginning of the custom. The example that has always arrested my attention from the time I encountered it in 1992 was on a gravestone in Wan'an cemetery in a western suburb of Beijing. Draped over the shoulders of a large gravestone was a thick shroud of white diaphanous tissues cut to simulate string upon entangled string of the old copper cash. The finesse that went into making this resplendent shroud was as delicate as it was conspicuous—it was the perfect convergence of ritual magic and visual poetry.

This protean structure is further exacerbated, especially nowadays, by the *hypertrophy of forms*—the sheer replication of forms with minute variations, thus exhibiting something of the nature of fashion, which, to the extent that this may be so, seems remarkable for a thousand-year-old custom. The scroll of paper from which paper money is cut is for all intents and purposes endless. Although a neat taxonomy is impossible, Chinese discern as a rule of thumb four big overlapping categories: (1) the monetary forms of paper (*zhǐqián*), (2) replicas of cloth and clothes (*yīzhǐ*), (3) paper bindings or sculpted objects (*zhǐzhā*), and (4) every sort of charm (*fú*). These are not mutually exclusive, of course—this is China. Each object is in some sense a charm, and everything is in some sense money—the corpus of offering papers straddles the chrematistic and the ceremonial.

Replicas of Money

Chinese history is replete with the varieties of materials used for real money: shell, precious stone, bark, woven fabrics (especially silk), metal, and paper. The prevalent and longest lasting have been metallic forms of money (*qián*). Three forms of metallic money have been used in the real world. These are base-metal cash, mostly copper or bronze, and also the more precious metals silver and gold. These three forms represent different levels of corruptibility and thus of concentrating wealth and communicating values in the real world. From the advent of paper money, these metallic forms have been replicated in paper and used as offerings to the world of spirits. The replicated metallic forms shape a hierarchy of value that corresponds more or less with ways of ranking the world of spirits based on various and related criteria such as their closeness and familiarity with the living donor and their different phases of etherealization. As a rule of thumb, copper cash is for common ghosts, including the familiar spirits of the newly deceased; silver bars are for the longer-deceased and more distant ancestors; and gold treasures are for the even more distant spirits and divines. Thus "closeness" and "distance" as told in paper replicas of metals are where time and space intersect in a social and material "chronotope" (Bakhtin 1981). This fits with the notion that with death, the soul begins to separate its heavier more finite material and earthy aspect (*pò*) from its lighter more infinite ethereal aspect (*hún*). The recently deceased are often imagined, with the help of funeral rites conducted under auspices of Taoist or Buddhist spirit masters, as having to be purged of their worldly corruptions, a purging that rives and rends the *pò* of flesh and bone in the most gruesome ways imaginable; thus, with the passage of time, the ethereal *hún* is rarified as pure spirit. Rendering the worldly body into pure spirit is signified in the hierarchy of metals from copper to gold, from base to precious, from that which is tarnished and corrupted to that which does not tarnish but purifies. I argue below that in some places the gold treasures are further elaborated to dignify the ranks of divinities differentiated by sumptuary rules. This general scenario of paper-replicated metallic signifiers for different time-space horizons of spiritual being(s) is never so explicit nor exact in a native exegesis; it is more an implicit rule of thumb inscribed in customary practice to the extent that the spirit world is a *continuum* of entities open to people's imaginations, and it is with these imaginations that the protean structure of paper monies resonates.

Paper Money

The basic paper money, found in every locale, is simply sheets of coarse paper usually with the natural color of the vegetal fibers. Marked only by its grainy texture, it is often called "grass paper" (*cǎozhǐ*) or "money paper" (*qiánzhǐ*). Converted into paper money, it is usually modified (incised, perforated, impressed, embossed, or imprinted) to appropriate either by imitation or contagion the value of real money. No matter where you go in China, you are bound to find people making their own or using commercially manufactured versions of this paper. In most places the paper is modified with rows of perforations to imitate the strings of cash that were the everyday currency of dynastic China. The perforations may be made by folding and cutting with scissors or knife, or punched with a hand-held nail or with a specially made metal punch that is hit with a wooden mallet, or they may be machine punched, printed, or embossed by a family workshop or commercial firm.

One such family workshop is in Yaxi district of Jishou city, western Hunan. This workshop in an old multistory wooden building supplies the surrounding neighborhoods with its paper money, a square sheet of perforated papers. Once a paper mill fed by natural springs, now engulfed by urban sprawl, it imports large sheets of coarse paper, hand-feeding them through an electric punching machine (made by a local machine shop). After they perforate enough papers, or when they have received an order from a local retail outlet, they cut the large papers into the regular 16.5-by-15-cm square pieces, each with three rows of seven perforations (figure 2.1). They call these "*yīn*-world money" (*yīnqián*) and sell it by weight. Every 500 grams of finished papers sells for ¥1. Two big stacks bundled together with a ribbon goes for ¥6. These are the bundles we see sitting in Yaxi retail shops. The operation takes up several rooms in the lower part of the domicile and is accomplished by stay-at-home female members of the family as adjunct to daily household routines. Each district in this area has the same kind of workshop making the same paper money. Although I do not know how extensive this mode of manufacturing is, I have encountered this particular form of paper money from Hunan to Guizhou and Sichuan. In the towns and villages where this particular form of paper money is the only one, it serves all the ritual needs for a paper money.

Ordinary folks of my acquaintance across China can't explain much about what the perforations signify beyond the recognition that they resemble old-fashioned cash on a string. Various kinds of spirit masters elaborate the meanings according to their own local and liturgical traditions and idiosyncrasies. For example, while walking through the Rongjiang river market in Qianzhou city (southwest of Jishou, Hunan) on an autumn morning in 2007, I happened on the combined City Temple and Guanyin (Buddhist) Temple, which was established in 1672, according to the earliest stone inscription. Inside I encountered the caretaker, a retired textile worker turned Buddhist nun, who, among other things, explained the liturgy of the local paper money to me. The first point was that this paper money has an obverse side—the

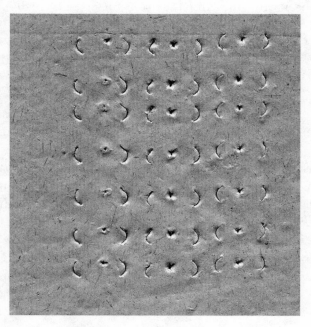

Figure 2.1 Perforated money paper replicating strung cash from Yaxi, Hunan

yáng-side—and a reverse or *yīn*-side. This is important because the *yáng*-side must face upward (outward) when the donor offers the paper. The *yáng*-side is the surface struck by the perforator such that the edges around the perforations are pushed in, whereas the reverse or *yīn*-side has the edges splayed outward. Thus the *yáng*-surface takes the hammer blow, and the *yīn*-surface takes the flame. This distinction has a certain social salience locally, because a few days later a young Miao minority woman at a remote temple in Shangjiang, Hunan, spontaneously told me that the only thing she knew about this paper money is that it must be offered with the *yáng*-side facing up. The rest of the nun's explanation was enveloped in the mysteries of odd numbers. She explained that the basic unit of offering is made from three leaves of paper in three sheaves, that is, nine leaves. For higher divines such as the Jade Emperor, the sheaves of three are folded in half with the *yáng*-side facing out. For the Ghost Festival a whole stack is separated into five sheaves and put into an addressed envelope (*bāo*). More arcane is the meaning of the perforations, which in this particular paper are aligned in three columns and seven rows. The three and seven are obvious indexes of divinity (three) in the form of the seven manifestations of Buddha (*Rúlái*).[1] The nun went on to explain how the perforations are like a rosary, counted to prevent the catalog of human misfortunes, all of which left me with the impression that the simplicity and plainness of the paper money in this locale in no way limits its liturgical complexity. I noticed, for instance, that this plain perforated paper was used in this temple in the same way that people in Quanzhou, Fujian, used their gold-foiled paper to suspend sacred altar objects from direct contact with the world of profane things (to be discussed below).

Almost three hundred kilometers southwest of Qianzhou is Zunyi township, Guizhou, where we find several different replicas of stringed cash distinguished by two criteria: the distinction between papers that are machined and handmade, and the distinction between "Short" and "Long" forms. According to my friend who is from there, Wang Lian, the higher-valued paper monies are handmade in Zunyi homes from long strips of grass paper or money paper purchased from local peddlers who are often connected by family ties to local spirit masters (*fǎshī*). These long strips of money paper are folded back and forth into layers and perforated by a handheld punch struck with an all-wooden mallet. There is a belief afoot in many parts of China—I have found it mainly among folks in the remoter, western parts of the country—that "paper monies touched by iron lose their soulfulness [*líng*] and are ineffective." This belief ignores the fact that an iron punch may be used to simulate the metal cash; but the metal punch is a locally made tool, fashioned with the labor of skilled hands, and when used as a tool to make paper money, it is a hand-held tool, or, as Ivan Illich (1973) would say, a "tool for conviviality."

But most of these paper monies are machine-perforated, cut and stacked in one of two forms: the "Long money" and the "Short money." These are different-sized pieces with different combinations of odd and even perforations for different ritual purposes, although the numerology of the perforations receives scant attention from many if not most users, and consequently, different specimens of these paper monies exhibit numbers inconsistent with the so-called traditional ideals. These ideals were conveyed to me by my friend, whose regard for the local paper money custom was implanted in him by his grandfather and uncle, a spirit master (*fǎshī*). As he put it: "My grandfather is not superstitious, but kind and good natured, and always teaching children to be pious." From my friend, I learned that the Short money uses odd numbers, preferably seven, for perforations per leaf and leaves per offering sheaf. The Short money I encountered had three parallel lines of five or seven perforations. It was used for all spirits (*shén*), divinities, and ancestral souls and is most important during the funeral of a family member. The Long money is more compatible with even numbers: for example, it may use two leaves per sheaf, each leaf having three or four lines of nine or eleven or twelve perforations. Some people also refer to this Long form as "scattering-money" (*sǎnqián*) in reference to its principal use in showing gratitude for the gifts bestowed by the divinities. In Zunyi households, the divinities that receive this Long form of gratuity are the ones that guard the entrance to the house (*ménshén*) and the one that watches over the stove (*zàoshén*), ensuring ample fuel for the stove and guaranteeing that the fire will start when ignited, without which life would be miserable indeed.

The liturgical function of these different paper monies, much of which revolves around the numerology of pieces and perforations, is steeped in complicated mystical reckonings that are the specialty of the spirit master. He is able to command the spirit world by the way he handles the paper monies; as my friend says of his uncle, "He does something subtle to the paper that changes it in ways that ordinary people cannot see." My sense is that ordinary people are uncurious about what they cannot see so long as the mystery is complicated and, putting it to practical use, it achieves the intended effect. (Of course the intended effects are only achievable to the degree that the laity remain "uncurious" about the actual author of these effects. Sometimes, as in the next chapter, they become curious and find answers in folktales.) My point in all this is that the comparatively simple material corpus of paper money in Qianzhou and Zunyi places no necessary limits on the complexity or elaboration of its exegesis in cosmological or liturgical terms. In both Qianzhou and Zunyi we have only elementary elaborations of materials that make up the ensembles of paper monies, but each of these elementary forms is amenable to the elaborate exegesis of spirit masters.

Every place has one or more versions of this elementary form of paper money. In rural parts of the northern plains (e.g., Hebei Province), people buy large sheets of grass paper or money paper, fold it back on itself in multiple layers, and cut incisions with a scissors to simulate the strings of cash when the paper is unfolded and burned for the souls of dead folks. Along the southeastern littoral, where the paper money industry produces a vast array of different kinds of paper monies, there are more varieties of the simulated strings of cash. For instance, In the southern Fujian circuit, including Taiwan, these are called "treasury money" (*kùqián*).[2] When I visited Quanzhou in 2000, these were also called "white paper currency" (*báichāo*). This white paper currency (20 by 13 cm) is white tissue with a coarse reverse side and smooth obverse side machine-perforated to simulate three undulating columns of eight cash each. Of course, they can also be made at home with a scissors and strips of white paper. They are used mostly for unburied souls, scattered and burned for three days before burial, pasted to bridges across which the funeral procession passes. As such they are also called "tollway money" (*mǎilùqián*), a concept that traces back to the medieval custom of making a bamboo and paper "god that clears the road" during funerals, which itself can be traced to the ancient use of "demon quellers" (see Ebrey 1991:115 n. 153).

In Hong Kong and its regional and global hinterlands, the strips of coarse white papers (6 by 18 cm) with three perforations in a single line are commonly called "stream money" (*xīqián*). I noticed recently in Honolulu (2009) that the red characters stamped by the manufacturer on the edge of large packs let the buyer know that these are "fuzzy-edged stream money" (*máobiān xīqián*), guaranteeing that these papers are hand-cut rather than machined. This distinction is important for later chapters. Of course, "fuzzy-edged" (like odd numbers) also connotes continuousness, the endless flow. The term "stream money" plays on another ancient word for coins, which is still used: "spring money" (*quánqián*), or just "spring" (*quán*), an endless flow of fortune from an unseen underground source. The "stream of cash" are also tollway cash, a customary payment to the demonic forces above ground that might otherwise obstruct the path of a neophyte soul to its new home under the ground. This includes using the "stream of cash" to tender the fire at a wake or to ignite a graveside holocaust.

It gets simpler and more generic: the one paper money that I have found littering the roadsides leading to cemeteries, from Hong Kong to Beijing, is a simple disk of white paper with a square hole cut in the center. This type of money can be made at home by folding a piece of square paper in half and cutting an inverted V in the middle of the fold and rounding off the outer corners. There are people who don't waste time and paper doing this, but simply toss real money on the way to the cemetery. Suffice it for now that paper cash figures prominently at funerals. It is thought that the neophyte soul must pass through numerous checkpoints, to pay off the demonic spirits that man those stations, on the way to rarefaction and redemption and possible rebirth, or, perhaps some happier place of repose. The neophyte souls, still heavy with corruption, must carry plenty of this small-denomination change to pave the way. Enormous amounts are burned, but I hasten to add that these large amounts are also the effect of a ritual practice that keeps a fire burning (the signifier of transition) during the phases of the wake, which last for several days and nights.

But tollway money is not used only for those passing *from* this world; it may also be used to protect the souls passing *into* this world as children. Souls passing into the world are even more vulnerable as they seek embodiment. From inside the womb until adolescence the souls of youngsters may be conceived as residing in a kind of uterine limbo or flower garden (*huāyuán*) in which the soul of a boy is seen as a white flower and that of a girl as a red flower (Schipper 1993:51–52); they are safely shepherded by guardian spirits of the bed (*chuángshén*), who are known more familiarly in some places as "flower granny" and "flower grandpa." Thus the incarnation and maturation of progeny happen in parallel spheres: while parents nurture the physical bodies of their children, the flower spirit watches over and helps the corresponding soul to pass obstacles on its way to adulthood. Parents, especially mothers, patronize the flower spirits with a rich ensemble of folk stories, paper charms, and ritual practices (see, e.g., C.-B. Tan 2006). One such charm, the first in an ensemble of four "overcoming impediment charms," that I found under a pile of other more conventional paper monies in a Chinese general store on Maunakea Street (Honolulu) is dark magenta in color and inscribed with the words for "passage money" (*guānqián*). Below this are three rows of the old-style copper cash, each row depicting the same motif of crossing borders and overcoming impediments, but with a different design.

Thus, the flower garden where souls are embodied is the counterpart to purgatory where souls are disembodied; and just as the dead use tollway money on their passage to the *yīn*-world, the coming-alive use tollway money on their passage to the *yáng*-world. Tollway money may be used to pave the way for an infant passing between *yáng*-world domiciles. The reasoning is the same as for one passing between an above-ground and a below-ground domicile: to purchase a safe journey from the demonic spirits that control the shadowy or invisible nooks and crannies in the alleyways and along the sides of public byways. In the documentary film *Small Happiness* (Gordon, Kline, and Sipe 1984), two women from Long Bow village, Shanxi, in the 1980s carry an infant along the road while scattering paper money.

The Charm in the Cash

The symbolic power of the square-holed copper cash surpasses its use in replicas of paper money. However trite and kitschy it may be, its ongoing function is neither simple nor superannuated, for it is the most ubiquitous and generic symbol of "fortune" in Chinese culture today. The old square-holed cash is used to tell fortunes; it has been used from ancient times as a therapeutic talisman in China and among non-Chinese in Southeast Asia;[3] it provides a template for talismans and lucky charms made from paper or made into plastic baubles; it is a rebus; it is an advertising logo, a corporate logo (e.g., Bank of China), and an architectural decoration.[4] One of its most striking uses was as a charm nailed at each of the two joints in the keel of a medieval cargo ship excavated from the harbor near Quanzhou (Fujian) and restored at the Kaiyuan temple complex. (When I saw this, my thoughts went to Malinowski's descriptions of Trobriand voyaging canoe magic and his theory of how magic complements science at critical junctures where lives depend on things we make.)

Although during the millennia of its actual use, the hole in the cash was used to string the cash for easier transport and counting, some people say the shape of the cash signifies something more original than the utility of having a hole with which to string it. They say that the old cash replicates the shape of the cosmos and continuous movement, a thing that rolls on forever. The outer, round shape of the cash is the cosmic macrocosm in its infinite, continuous motion; the square hole or "eye" at the center is the world of square things, of finite things, of utilities.[5] The circular motion and square shape are *yáng* and *yīn* becoming one another: a common idiom is "Square and circle are mutually inclusive" (*fāngyuán hùyù*). Squaring the circle and circling the square is a continuous process. In the passage charm described above, the third row of cash depicts the corners of the square hole fusing with the outer circle; this suggests the union of *yīnyáng* at the peak of vitality and productivity, perfect balance, harmony, motion, and flexibility in all manner of things, from cosmic order and sexual union to a flexible personality.[6] The square-holed cash is not only preserved at all levels of ritual architectonics[7] and in numerous idioms and euphemisms rich in sarcasm and irony;[8] it is so embedded in the everyday discourse that it pops up in ad hoc conversations, for example, a question-and-answer session with a woman in rural Hubei: "Why do you burn incense?" "We burn incense because it gives out smoke like a string going through the eye of the cash." In other words, like the string that connects and multiplies cash, incense smoke is a connector and a multiplier of worlds. The string through the eye of cash is also consonant with the notion that the cash is a wellspring (*quán*) of wealth; and in one charm we see how the depiction of two cash (*quán*) is a rebus for the word *quán* meaning "both" or "complete" where the cash connect a bat rebus (*fú*) or "fortune" with the graph for "longevity" (*shòu*). In other words, the cash rebus signifies "both" luck and longevity.

Alternatively to imitating strings of cash by perforating the paper, many people simply impress the "money paper" with the monetary value of a real RMB note. They simply roll the RMB note over the surface of the money paper, "infecting" the money paper with the value of the RMB. This is not imitation of cash, which perforating the paper accomplishes, but the contagious power of modern bills to transmit their value, their spiritual value, by contact.

People in northern China use large sheets of coarse, yellow-brownish paper, called "grass paper" (*cǎozhǐ*) or, just as often, "money paper" (*qiánzhǐ*), which they may modify using their own homemade devices as just described, while people in south China may be more apt to purchase the commercially made papers cut into smaller sizes. However, in Shijiazhuang, Hebei, in 2006, I came across the large sheets of "money paper"—the vendor called it "burning paper" (*shāozhǐ*)—which was embossed by a pressing machine in the neighboring city of Baoding. The embossed pattern consists of four rows of cash inscribed with "heaven and earth circulating treasure" (*tiāndì tōng bǎo*) interspersed with three rows of Golden First Treasure (*jīn yuánbǎo*).[9] So here we have the generic money paper impressed with the lowest coin of the realm in even-numbered rows, for common souls heavy with corruption, alongside the most exalted treasure of the realm in odd-numbered rows, for the higher divines.

Paper Silver

Silver was part of the common monetary system of dynastic China; it concentrated exchange value in the form of jewelry, ingots, and coins, especially useful for long-distance trade and tax remissions. Replicated in squares of paper either by bleach or appliqué of a tin and lead alloy, silver also signifies higher concentrations of monetary wealth for special purposes, large expenses, endowments, savings, and so on. In many places, silver is thus used to indemnify ordinary spirits, beginning with the souls of deceased family members. Large amounts are traditionally burned at wakes and death anniversaries.[10] Silver is also burned for the ghosts of nonfamilial spirits. Silver, like copper cash, is distinctly monetary and common but, unlike cash, is a more concentrated form of wealth and thus ideally represents a more advanced level of etherealization.

Silver (and gold) papers are known from the medieval advent of the custom and is simulated in different ways depending on region. Along the southeast littoral, silver papers are generally made by pasting a small leaf of tin onto a larger piece of coarse paper. In late-nineteenth-century Amoy, southern Fujian, many families living in easy circumstances preferred to use sheets of good white paper to make "white money" (*báiqián*), since these were more expensive than the tinned laminated paper and consequently were more valued by the spirits (Groot 1969: 1:154). In Shanghai the leaf of tin completely covers its paper base. In Yu County, Hebei, two tiny leaves or chips of silver paper or foil (2 by 2 cm) and two gold-colored chips are folded into two sheaves of white paper to simulate silver—the peasants simply call it "white paper" (*báizhǐ*) and offer it to deceased ghosts. In many other places and in different historical periods, sheets of bleached white paper represent silver offerings. Each locale has its way of replicating silver. In regions served by the Hong Kong and Taiwan manufacturers, the foil-laminated papers come in various sizes in order to signify the different ranks of ghostly recipients.[11]

In Quanzhou, Fujian, in 2000, I found three silver papers; these were referred to variously as "silver," "silver paper," or "white gold." Each was a coarse, thick yellowish bamboo paper (13 by 17 mm) with a small, off-center square of tinfoil pasted on it. The first leaf of each pack was stamped with a current epigraph. One kind was stamped with a big character for "longevity," topped by a "fortune" and flanked by epigraphs: "Lighting incense with great auspiciousness" and "Making everything safe and sound." A second kind was stamped with four large red characters in the center wishing for "increasing wealth and security" (*fācái píng'ān*); down the opposing margins, smaller characters framed this wish in "auspiciousness" (*jíxiáng*) manifesting itself in "wealth and honor" (*fùguì*). A third kind was an unadorned paper pasted with a square of stannous for common, otherwise unfamiliar ghosts. These silver papers were variously offered on the three ghost festivals in southern Fujian to secure the release of souls suffering in purgatory.

Perhaps the most novel silver paper tradition belongs to Wu-speaking people in regions around Shanghai. It is novel for its prevalence, ubiquity, unadorned simplicity, and singular purpose. Here the silver paper is called what it is, *xībó* (tinfoil). The foundation paper is traditionally a yellow ceremonial paper (*huángbiǎozhǐ*), which is cut to 7.5 by 11 cm and completely covered by a sliver of tin alloyed with lead to give the metal a silvery sheen. The *xībó* is glued to the paper. The more expensive *xībó* uses pristine foil, while the less expensive uses a flakier foil that has been reconstituted from burned and recycled residues (He 1997); to my knowledge the difference in worldly cost has no liturgical significance. Women spend hours folding *xībó* into auspiciously shaped "First Treasures" (*yuánbǎo*) in the sanctuary of Buddhist temples in order that the objects of their labors be blessed by Buddha, *not ostensibly as offerings for Buddha* but for the benefit of deceased family members. This configuration of unadorned foils, blessed by Buddha for the deceased members of the family, is by far the prevalent focus of the paper money custom in the Shanghai area, even though there are other paper monies increasingly available in local paper shops, from gold-tinted stannous-leafed papers imported from Wenzhou to a series of charmed sutras from the Buddhist canon printed from woodblocks on yellow-brown tissue papers to be burned on special occasions with the *xībó*. The availability of the papers from other regions is due in part to the presence of people from those regions residing locally. This is also true for places such as Hong Kong, where Shanghai people can purchase their preferred *xībó* (Scott 2007:127, 212).

To summarize so far, both silver and copper cash are paper simulations of monetary wealth in the form of common currencies, although silver is the more concentrated form of wealth and thus becomes increasingly appropriate as the soul of the deceased becomes fully fledged spirit, often thought to be undergoing rarefaction (disembodiment) in the slicing and dicing chambers of purgatory or the less sanguinary process of simple decay; and as the spirit becomes more ethereal, so do the materials, whereupon ever more concentrated and rarified forms of wealth like gold become increasingly appropriate.

Paper Gold

Gold is the most concentrated form of monetary value. Rarely used as a common currency in China, it was (and still is) a ritual currency, often fashioned in the form of jewelry for personal adornment to meet ritual obligations like dowries (Seaman 1982). Gold paper is the only appropriate form of monetary value for addressing personal concerns or making promises to the higher divinities. Neither copper nor silver, as common currencies, would be appropriate. Many people, including devotees and scoffers, say the higher divinities have no need or desire for money or even the food that often accompanies the paper offerings. On the other hand, if gold paper does not simulate a common currency, it clearly simulates a monetary value, but a monetary value of such density that its value seems to take on its own emergent properties. Thus it may serve as a prophylactic charm against the impurities encountered in ritual passages, which include attempts by common mortals to gain access to divinity (see Seaman 1982). Because it is not a common currency, gold is not burned much at funerals; it is not the kind of value that the newly deceased can carry and spend on his passage to the other side. Nor does it fit the image of the newly dead whose carnal corruptions are palpable. A leaf of gold paper may cover the face of a corpse, but this is a prophylaxis for the living against the defilement of death. Likewise, gold papers are used to purify ritual instruments and passageways (see Hou 1975:20–21) and to separate the sacred from the profane; for example, in Quanzhou I noticed household altars where the statue of Mazu (goddess of the sea) was set upon a pile of gold papers. Of course, the altar is a likely place as any for storing paper money, or it could be a simple expression of how much members of the household treasure the presence of Mazu; but more than this, the pile of gold is a ritual gesture that the spiritual purity of Mazu is preserved by separating her from the mundane surroundings of a common domicile. The same function was observed in the Qianzhou (Hunan) temple, where the oil lamps rested on stacks of perforated money papers—as the reader will recall, these were the only paper monies in this region—to separate the lamps from the ceramic tile surface of the altar. This is my interpretation; the nun told me that the paper money was to keep the lamps from slipping off the table; this kind of rationalizing a ritual act typifies explanations in the paper money custom, as we will see throughout the rest of this book. I wondered why the lamps rested on stacks of paper money rather than a single leaf, and why only the oil lamps were thus suspended, and wasn't it significant that the lamps were wreathed in petals simulating the immortal lotus?

A more significant but less apparent example of the purifying function of gold paper comes by way of solving a puzzle noted by Hou (1975:25–26) in Taiwan, where a wife who lives with and serves her husband's people customarily presents her husband's forebears with silver paper but when visiting her natal home and ancestors carries gold paper. The facile observation that she makes a gesture of valuing her natal ancestors above her husband's ancestors only deepens the puzzle. I think the solution lies in the cosmology of marriage, which "preordains" that daughters defile the most sacred of obligations (filial piety); that is, instead of serving her own forebears, a daughter is "fated" in marriage to serve her husband's forebears by bearing their progeny, hence their posterity, their immortality. This separation from her own family forebears is especially problematic in the Chinese cultural context (see Blake 1994; Sangren 2003; Stafford 2000:28). In the abstract, the "separation" of embodied being from itself is the fated experience of women: footbinding, menstruation, marriage, birthing, and affiliation of the progeny (footbinding prepared a little girl to live in a world of "separations"). In my view, the seemingly insignificant gesture of returning with gold is a way to transcend the stain of "separation" from her own family and forebears to facilitate a reunion.

A second and related characteristic of paper gold is that whereas paper replicas of common cash, silver, and gold differentiate the rank of the recipient, as along the southeastern coast, the paper gold tends to be the most differentiated in reference to the identity of spirit recipients. These distinctions are typical of archaic and feudal social formations where the exaltation of a figure's status, authority, and power is made to seem right and just by the kinds of valuables that his position entitles him to receive and display. These sumptuary entitlements are designed to maintain the mysteries of dominion, although historically they are not easy to enforce and became altogether unenforceable against the rising tide of the capitalist formation in which a common currency became the universal signifier. Against this tide, in places such as southeastern coastal China, the paper money custom holds to a feudal order of exalted spirits that are differentiated by sumptuary constraints as signified in the different gold papers, although there is a lot of play and pending breakdown even at this level of signification.

The presence and elaboration of gold papers in the various paper money venues around China is highly variable. Outside the southeast littoral, replicas of gold are either absent, or ambiguous, or simple and uniform. In most northerly and interior places gold may be represented by yellow paper, and in many places a particularly soft, course "yellow ceremonial paper." Whether deemed "gold" or known by some other cognomen, clearly they are considered appropriate for offerings within the sanctuaries of the highest divines. In Chengdu, Sichuan, the Wenshuyuan Buddhist temple provided, until a few years ago, a larger-than-life-sized stone elephant, a Buddhist icon, whose belly served as an oven for burning these yellow papers. I first saw it in 2000, before it was removed to discourage burning paper. At the time I saw it, the elephant stood on ground of packed gray ash across which drifted all day, every day, new ash from burning yellow paper. The stone elephant plus two other larger-than-life stone figures (Mílèfó, the all-forgiving happy laughing Buddha, and the Taoist stellar spirit of Longevity) were scorched black by the continuous burning of candles, incense, and yellow papers. The elephant had square holes on either flank and butt-end through which persons placed offerings to feed a seemingly continuous fire, while most other worshippers hunkered down and burned their offerings in the mound of ash along the feet of the elephant. The only papers I saw burned were sheets of yellow paper and yellow ceremonial paper. The same paper was used almost everyplace I traveled from the Sichuan basin, through the great lakes of Wuhan, and the plains of Shijiazhuang.

In Yu County, northwestern Hebei, the distinction between silver for ghosts and gold for divinities is simple; each is known by the color and fold of the paper that holds the little pieces of silver and gold papers or foils. The "white paper" described above constitutes an offering of "silver"; the "yellow paper" (*huángzhǐ*) that is folded in the shape of an envelope constitutes "gold." Each folded paper contains small squares of silver- and gold-colored paper or foil, two of each for the white paper and three of each for the yellow paper. The "two" and "three" are widespread signifiers for, respectively, the ghostly spirits still attached to worldly corruption on the finite side and the pure spirits (from house spirits, or *jiāshén*, e.g., the stove spirit, to more exalted spirits, such as Guanyin) on the side of infinity.

Around the Kaifusi Guanyin temple in Changsha, Hunan, vendors sell a yellow paper (20 by 21 cm) with a shiny golden square near the center and printed with a red décor. Because the paper's reverse side was coarse and the obverse or printed side was smooth and the shiny gold square was printed rather than a pasted-on foil, I surmised that this was one of the newfangled machine-milled forms of gold paper, in effect, the simulation of a simulation.

I take this up in chapter 8. Nonetheless, if one is not too finicky about its manufacture, this is an impressive assemblage. Along the top of this paper runs the epigram "The five roads [manifest] the spirit of wealth." The bottom epigram is "Day and night bringing in treasure." The two flanks were in the shape of an imperial edict commanding that the order to convey wealth along the five roads by the marshal of wealth, Zhao Gongming, be executed! The five roads are the five cosmic forces of *yīnyángwǔxíng* (water, metal, earth, wood, and fire), which are depicted in humanoid form, each regaled in marshal dress, at the center of the paper. They are situated around an incense burner over which a First Treasure (*yuánbǎo*) and five cash are rising. This sheet of a simulated gold-foiled paper is folded over three leaves of coarse yellow paper fanned and folded in the shape of a lotus blossom, and this whole ensemble is wrapped by a red cut paper depicting the "great and noble benefactor" (*dà guìrén*) who, by virtue of his connections with the divinity to whom the appeal is addressed, helps to facilitate the realization of all the desires for good fortune, increased wealth, offspring, safety and good health, and so on and so forth, inscribed thereupon the body of his charm and within the underlying folds of gold. Although I found this paper in Changsha, all the indications of its manufacture, assemblage, and décor indicate that its provenance was the southeastern coast.

There, along the Fujian and Taiwan littorals, all paper money is simply called "gold" (*jīn*). In 1975, Hou collected and described in detail sixteen types of gold paper on top of eight types of silver and seven types of treasury cash. As the forms of value are increasingly concentrated, they are increasingly differentiated for sumptuary purposes. Hou (1975:19) sorted the sixteen types of gold papers into three subcategories: triad gold, decorated gold, and undecorated gold.[12] In 2000, I visited Quanzhou, across the straits from Taiwan, where paper money production was coming back after the ebb tide of the Mao years. Here, the local manufacturers were making at least eight kinds of gold paper divided by size and decoration in a hierarchy reminiscent, but only barely, of the Taiwan gold. Top-of-the-line Big Heavenly Gold (*dà tiān jīn*) depicted the personified forms of the three stellar divines (figure 2.2). These roughly parallel Hou's top of the line Triad Gold. They depict in humanoid forms the three stellar spirits of Emolument, Happiness, and Longevity. The central figure overseeing the other two is the spirit of Happiness or Good Fortune, holding his sacred mushroom-shaped scepter (*rúyì*), a rebus for "as you will." Second in line is the spirit of Emolument or endless stream of wealth wearing a cap and holding an infant signifying the promise of offspring and fertility; he is fronted by the image of a deer (*lù*), a rebus for emolument (*lù*), in case you don't recognize him as the spirit of Emolument. In the third position is the balding white-bearded spirit of Longevity, with his long knotted staff and pumpkin gourd in one hand and immortal peach in the other. To digress a bit, it is worth noting that the spirit of Emolument holds an infant to signify connectedness across the generations and thus how closely intertwined are wishes for an endless supply of material wealth with having progeny. Not only do children—the means of immortality—guarantee the flow of material wealth as parents grow old and pass on; in addition, having an emolument or endless supply of monetary wealth without posterity is pointless. Hence, the spirit of Emolument rather than the spirit of Longevity holds the infant. The one only makes sense in relationship to the other, and together they become the spirit of Happiness.

Figure 2.2 Big Heavenly Gold from Quanzhou, Fujian

The Quanzhou Big Heavenly Gold figures were encased in auspicious graphs and epigrams auguring good fortune, longevity, increasing wealth, tranquility, more sons, a respectful and submissive family. At the base we read "Forever smoothing the way paper stannous" (*yŏng shùn zhǐbó*), which is likely the name of the shop that manufactures or merchandizes the stannous paper, although the name also means that offerings of paper stannous can be counted on to make one's life go smoothly. Aside from its imposing size (34 by 43 cm), this paper is distinguished from the other gold papers in this set by having a picture of the stellar divines, epigrams that command deference, plus some unconventional (i.e., truncated and seal-like) graphs to give the mystique of high office, thus making it appropriate for beseeching a celestial divinity.

One of my Quanzhou interviewees pulled out several leaves of the Taiwan top-of-line Triad Gold from a chest of drawers as if she was storing some great heirloom; the way she handled it, I could scarcely imagine her burning it, although burning it is the proper way of storing its value. She had purchased it from a new Taiwan-owned factory in the port of Amoy. It was a double-paneled mirror reflection (72 by 38 cm) on a tissue-thin coarse paper. Each panel depicted the three star spirits framed by two dragons and the "fortune" graph centered above the spirit of Happiness, plus the graphs for "blessing the family with unity and tranquility" emblazoned across the bottom. The gold pigment against which the red-inked pictures and graphs were printed glistened like gold is supposed to. Laid next to the Quanzhou product, the comparison was stark. The Quanzhou Big Heavenly Gold (figure 2.2) was on thick, heavy yellowish bamboo paper, and the red-pigmented ink gave the whole paper a cheesy reddish and orangey countenance. Plus, the Quanzhou paper was encased in epigrams, as already described.

This brings up an important point that is a constant theme throughout this book. Although the gold papers from Taiwan and Hong Kong exhibit a remarkable refinement, perhaps because they are more machined compared to the rugged-looking fuzzy-edged images and orangey-colored "gold" papers of Quanzhou, devotees of a certain region are usually wedded to the papers they have grown up with—what Clark Wissler (1906) called a "psychophysical at home feeling" to explain the persistence of a regional cultural pattern. Plus the fact that as I have found in various places there is a sense that handmade monies, or those that appear to be such, are more genuine and more effective.

Space does not allow a full description of the panoply of Quanzhou gold papers from my visit in 2000. Suffice it to say that they all bear the same manufacturing technique and homey effects (described above), and while they are configured in different patterns and cut to various sizes, they all come in sheaves of nine leaves bound by a grass cord at the top right corner. Only the top leaf is stamped with a red-pigmented design of frames, pictures (lanterns, lotuses, and such), and epigrams; the other eight underleaves simply contain the gilded foil. Differentiated by size of paper and foil— the bigger, the more icons and epigrams, and the more intended for higher realms of divinity, although those realms are deeply intersecting. For example, the Little Heavenly Gold (the source of this chapter's epigraph), which is the larger type of Middle Gold (17.5 by 21 cm), is presentable to heavenly masters (*tiāngōng*), deities (*shén*), Buddhas (*fó*), native place spirits (*tǔdìgōng*), and ancestors (*zǔxiān*) who have completed their stint in purgatory by undergoing a rite of redemption (*chāodù*) that gives the soul permanent repose in the world of pure spirits or on the road back to a future incarnation.

Also, there is little or no detectable difference in the content of the epigrams from one gold paper to another. Here is a comprehensive list, beginning with those on the Big Heavenly Gold papers for the big divines and ending with the smallest paper, simply called "gold" for the ancestors: "security and increasing wealth," "good fortune," "double happiness," "adding sons and bringing in wealth," "having a safe journey through life," "fortune," "all around safe and sound," "increasing wealth and security," "auspiciousness," "wealth and honor," "increasing wealth in gold," "increase increase increase," "everywhere safe and sound," "daily increasing wealth," "longevity," "safe and sound," "the whole family safe and sound," "daily appearance of wealth."

The epigrams of these papers, along with all the other aspects of design, vary over time and space; one of the features of the modern hypertrophy of paper monies is the turnover in design. But whatever variance there is in design, the motif remains steady; they may be interpreted as wishes, petitions, prayers, urgings, declarations, or promises that describe the good life, the way things ought to be. These didactic messages are redundant, repetitious, and trite, here and in countless other charms; but they are not irrelevant. On the contrary, they bear the central message of the paper money custom, which unabashedly aims to "increase, increase, increase" the good things in life beginning with life itself in the form of adding progeny, bringing in wealth, and adding years to one's lifetime, all in the spirit of family togetherness in a pervasive and secure tranquility. They paper over the differences between the common currencies and the magical charms.

Manufacturing Paper Gold

China is dotted with countless workshops producing paper monies. These range from individual operations to family businesses to small and large-scale industrial firms and whole villages. This is the way it has been from the beginning of the custom, and although it cannot last, it is still this way in many places. Some villages such as Huang village near Nanchang and Xu village near Quanzhou base their economies on the production of paper money. A report in the *Jiangnan Metropolitan News* (Xie and Jin 2004) tells us that Huang Village got its name "Paper Money Village" not because the people there are preoccupied with sacrificing for their ancestors but because they make the paper money that is sold to others for this purpose. When I visited the southern Fujian village of Xu in 2000, I was struck with the same sense of irony: the folks making the stuff had no special regard for any other aspect of the operation than the fact that they were "making money." Both villages showed off signs of marked prosperity since the early 1990s. In Huang village the road that had been little more than a path became known as the Street of Paper Money; and in Xu village the rows of old peasant cottages made of brick were giving way to paved roads and multistory stone mansions.

Both villages have a fairly large population: Huang has two hundred households, and Xu around eighty. And in both places, almost every household has gotten into the trade. The primary market for Xu village is the city of Quanzhou. This is where my colleague and host introduced me to a young woman who made these papers in her city apartment at night and sold them in the early morning market of an apartment complex. Every morning she sat at her makeshift table selling her gold along with a few other paper monies and accessories. She made the gold in her apartment, and she made it while sitting at her little table waiting for customers. For her, the work of production and of marketing were incessant, contiguous tasks. She used the same technique and materials as those of villagers in the region, including her natal village of Xu, going back to at least the 1920s, when the trade was not so lucrative.

Space allows only an outline of the process I observed in Xu village, a single-surname village that belonged to a township outside of Quanzhou. Most of the eighty or so small and large households each constituted a workshop (*zuòfang*) in the production of paper money.[13] Although most household workshops produced the finished product, there was a division of labor within each household-based workshop and among the village workshops at large. Not all shops made the finished product; some shops specialized in other parts of the process, such as importing and cutting paper,[14] or manufacturing paste and dye.[15] The finishing unit, which I was able to observe most closely, produced the variety of gold paper locally referred to as Middle Gold (zhōngjīn), although the village as a whole produced a small variety of other gold and silver papers.

Xu village was surrounded by a vast plain of rice fields in full production, and according to traditional agrarian standards, this was a prosperous village; but in the last twenty years, making paper money had become the primary occupation of the inhabitants and the economic base of a new prosperity. Before liberalization, making paper money had been a perennial craft open to villagers who had no other means of support. During the Cultural Revolution, a few people in the village continued to eke out a living making paper money, but it was done furtively (tōutōumōmō). With the Opening and Reform of the early 1980s, however, paper money making became the primary industry. My principal host, a Mr. Xu, came of age during this period and got into the business by hanging around and watching other families in the vicinity. By the 1990s, it proved to be a lucrative trade. The contrast between the old low-roofed brick houses that were now used as dormitories to house the imported labor and the new three- and four-story high-ceilinged stone mansions was stark. The investment of capital was heaviest in the infrastructure of new houses, but many of these units were sufficiently spacious that they were used to house the production process. Xu's mansion doubled as a residence and a manufacturing site. The front entrance, with its carved marble posts and lintel, opened into a large high-ceilinged hall backed by the obligatory table and mantel serving as altar. High on the walls hung a few portraits of ancestors. The altar seemed perfunctory and, on closer inspection, unkempt, with the few devotional objects lying on their sides, fallen over, covered with dust. There were some pieces of the paper manufactured on the premises, as if for the purpose of display, but otherwise they looked out of place. The hall was a magnificent shell, redolent with the air of manufacturing and the nouveau riche (bàofāhù). Xu made clear that his concern was the proverbial "bottom line."

The money-making operation was divided by task; each task was a work station that occupied a room or hallway. The first station was down a dark corridor from the entrance hall; the turn of a doorknob revealed a dimly lit room where five girls sat around a large table, each pasting the metallic foil onto sheets of paper (figure 2.3). Each girl had a big bowl of yellow paste, stacks of tinfoil,[16] and a pile of coarse yellow papers anchored at the top by a brick to enable the worker to flip the paper after each pasting. The girls' principal tools were the fingers on their two hands: they daubed a sheet of paper with paste, peeled off a leaf of silver foil, and pressed it onto the paper with a squeegee. Separating the foil by blowing on it and pasting it on the center of the papers required the most skill, because a poorly handled or poorly pasted foil ruined the piece, and pieces of "ruined money" (*pòqián*) lost most of their ritual value; in the old days they could be offered as extras to the main offerings, and were thus sold at a low price.

The paper had been cut into squares at the village cutting shop. Once the foils were pasted onto the sheets of paper, they were carried out the front door to dry in the sun-baked courtyard. When dry, they were carried up the broad staircase behind the entrance hall to an open corridor that was divided between two work stations. At one end several girls under the supervision of a matronly relative of Xu paddled gobs of reddish dye onto boards from which, using rubber rollers, they applied the dye with a single swish across the silver foil. The reddish dye gave the silver foil what passed for a "golden"

Figure 2.3 Pasting stannous onto paper in Xu village workshop, southern Fujian

sheen. From here, the papers were carried back to the central staircase to continue their journey to the roof, where once again they were left to dry under the sun. When dry, they were carried back down to the other end of the second-story corridor, where a man and woman hand-printed the covering paper on each stack with a carved wooden roller. The roller was rolled over a palette of vermilion pigment and then across the golden-foiled yellow paper, leaving a pattern of icons and epigraphs. Where the vermilion pigment rolled over the paper, the print left a clear and distinct image; where it rolled over the foil, it dulled the gild and obfuscated the overlying pattern. At the time of my visit, the pattern was a configuration of epigrams. The four big graphs in the center formed the popular saying "A favorable wind in the sail makes for plain sailing from beginning to end" (*yīfānfēngshùn*), which is something like the Westerner's "God speed you." This message was framed by three popular epigrams: "Let the whole family be safe and sound" (*héjiā píng'ān*); "let wealth from its eternal source flow in abundance" (*cáiyuán guǎngjìn*); and "let the business prosper" (*shēngyì xīnglóng*). The bottom of the message was framed with three characters: *zhèng zhuāng jīn* which tells us (or, better yet, the spirit recipients) that this "gold is genuine," which obviates any question about its "realness" (more on authenticity in chapter 8).[17] Between the dyeing and the printing, and then once again after the printing, the papers were carried on poles back up the flight of steps to the flat roof, where they were laid out to bake under the spring sun. From Xu's roof I saw every nook and cranny on surrounding roofs and courtyards covered in drying yellow papers.

Compared to the architectural infrastructure, capital investments in the production process seemed modest. Three principal resources were imported from outside the village: labor, tools, paper, and tinfoil. Most of the labor power was supplied by young women from other provinces. The girls doing the pasting impressed me with the speed of their fingers and the tedium of their piecework. Xu, the owner-boss, and his relatives supplied occasional labor power. Their single workshop consumed ten rolls of paper per day. The paper is trucked in from northern Fujian, where the bamboo for making the thick, coarse, yellowish paper is grown. The rolls of paper are hauled on a trailer behind a tractor to a small building near the village entrance, where the paper is cut by heavy-duty electric machines. Also, the supply of metallic foils is bought from outside, while the pastes and dyes were made in the village. The dyes were made by cooking a combination of plants mixed with ochre. The carved wooden rollers (*mò* or *tuīzi*) were made in a workshop located in the market town about two kilometers from the village. The wood carving was, like the village money making, a household-managed operation, set back from the busy thoroughfare under some shade trees. When I visited, there were four young men sitting at a work bench with chisels, mallets, rulers, pencils, and paper stencils pasted to the wooden cylinders in the vice. A middle-aged boss worked in a rear room, where she entertained and dickered with clients and customers. My survey focused immediately on a clip of white papers, the stencils for the wooden cylinders being carved out front. Hanging on the back wall, stored in sacks and boxes, were the finished rollers. I was mainly interested in tracing the genealogy of the patterns inscribed on those stencils, but was more frustrated than gratified with the kinds of answers I got. At every turn in the process of paper money making the bottom-line mentality was impressed upon me. In the case of designs and design changes, I gathered that in recent years a host of new designs had been introduced, and that their longevity was governed by their popular appeal (i.e., the market). But I was unable to put an active voice on the new designs. Suffice it to say that none of my interlocutors expressed any awareness of, much less interest in, liturgical influences on their designs. It was a money-making operation, in both senses, from start to finish. More than this, some other researcher will have to pick up the ball

Conclusion

My survey of the monetary end of paper money assemblages touched on the major species of monetary forms, leaving the newest one, paper facsimiles of paper banknotes, for the chapter on "ghost bills." In keeping with the spirit of the custom, we need to keep reminding ourselves of the labile and protean nature of this or any paper money taxonomy. Also, I have deferred the vast oceans of charms (*fú*) and paper clothes (*yīzhǐ*) and all the other material blessings, from combs to cars, replicated in pictures and in the round (*zhǐzhā*), to anecdotal treatment in other chapters. Very generally, every part of China uses a version of paper money that replicates in simple ways the ancient strings of copper cash. These are generic and multipurpose monies burned or not burned for common souls in early phases of disembodiment and dematerialization. The old-style copper cash is a ubiquitous, trite, but powerful ritual icon in the nexus of Chinese civilization. It is the essence of emolument (*lù*) and wealth (*cái*). Next are paper replicas of silver, which are burned as a means of indemnifying souls somewhere between disembodiment and etherealization. Silver is sometimes represented in coins, but more often in ingots or First Treasure (*yuánbǎo*), as is the stuff of pure treasure, gold. Gold paper is for souls whose etherealization is being consummated in a state of spiritual purity and who are thus more completely removed from the carnal world of the devotee. As we move from the plain copper to the pure golden forms of paper money, the iconographic and epigrammatic messages increase, and these messages all augur an increase in the things that in both this world and the other make life worth living. The language is that of agrarian small producers living in an ancient or feudal society.

The elaboration of different kinds of monies characteristic of southeastern coastal China raises historical questions. The assertion that this area is the historical core of the custom needs more research to establish. There are several historical factors around which such a discussion could take place: first is the early location of paper mills in this region (Hunter 1937); second is that this region, far from the imperial centers in the north, developed a commercial infrastructure, but just what part the paper money custom played in this development provokes other questions, which I address in chapter 5. As a prelude to that chapter, in brief, and in the context of the present chapter, I have observed that the ostensible hierarchy of paper monies is fairly fluid and, in effect, rhetorical in the way it finesses the ranks of spirits, but it also implies a hierarchy of spirits based on sumptuary privilege that is characteristic of ancient and feudal social formations. This hierarchy of spirits fits well with all the iconography and ritual action of the paper money custom. Just what this imagined world has to do with the material world of social relations is a bread-and-butter issue in social anthropology (A. P. Wolf 1974; Ahern 1981; Feuchtwang 1992; Gates 1996; Sangren 2000), and it will continue to dog us throughout the rest of the book. Suffice it for now to say that there is a major disjuncture between the material relations of the world today and the feudal predicates of the traditional paper monies outlined in this chapter. The question is whether this disjuncture is being papered over by the advent, proliferation, and now hypertrophy of a new and different kind of currency, the modern "ghost bill," which takes the form of a general all-purpose currency (the modern banknote) but still observes the distinction between common spirits among whom it circulates and the more exalted divinities: for instance, the Jade Emperor as the "bank president" who supposedly manages that circulation (see chapter 7). The question is whether or not these general purpose forms will one day replace all the older traditional forms and transform the *yīn*-world from a feudal image to a modern capitalist image. Speculations aside, one thing seems certain: making money is a good business these days. The idea that making money for the dead is a profitable business is actually built into one of the popular folk stories that purport to explain the origin of paper money. I discuss this story in the next chapter.

CHAPTER 3

Origins

Beyond city gates, earthen mounds;
Cold food festival—someone's weeping;
Wind blowing over desolate fields, paper money flying;
Ancient graves—another and another, green grass of spring.
  —Bai Juyi (772–846), "On Beholding the Wild on the
    Festival of Cold Food"

Sending valuables (including food and money) to accompany the dead on their journeys to a netherworld, or presenting such things to the visitors from the shadowy regions, is neither novel nor unique to China. There are at least three ways that people in China and people in other parts of the world send valuables to the netherworld. The first is to place the thing of value— Chinese often refer to it as a vessel (*qì*)—in a ritual venue and invite visiting spirits to partake of its essence. This method may also retain the offering's utility for the living. A second way of transmitting valuable things to the netherworld is to inter the valuable with the dead or as a hoard for one's use in the afterlife.[1] In China interred things lose their usefulness to the living until they are excavated by geomancers, grave robbers, or archaeologists. The third means of transmission is to destroy the vessel by immolation or by exposure to the elements of wind and water (as in the ninth-century poem cited above), but especially to the element of fire (cf. Heesterman 1993:10).[2] Destroyed things lose their utility permanently—it is often deemed a sacrifice—although the process may leave certain traces in the form of an animal carcass, or the ash of a burnt offering, to be used commensally or as a talisman. In China, the ash from certain paper charms may be wrapped in a bag and kept as an apotropaic charm or dissolved in water for use as a prophylaxis or an antidote.

Down through the ages, Chinese have used all three modes of transferring things of value to the netherworld, and often in the same ritual venue, as we will see in the next chapter. Chinese ways of transmitting value to the netherworld are comparable to those of other peoples. The modes of transmission are an ethnological commonplace. Where the Chinese offering tradition begins to stand out from the ethnological commonplace is the elaboration of valuables specifically for use by the spirits. These replicas were anciently referred to as "bright vessels" (*míngqì*), which emphasized the numinous nature of things belonging to the spirit world. (Many different peoples associate the phenomenon of shining with a life force or spiritual presence.)[3] Later, the character for *míng* meaning "bright" shifted in common parlance to the character for *míng* meaning "otherworldly." With the development of paper in ancient China, the idea of making bright or otherworldly vessels from paper began to take hold. Paper goods were also transmittable directly by fire (a kind of numinous luminescence) without being interred. By the early Song dynasty the custom of paper money was widespread, and today, a thousand years hence, it seems more elaborate than ever. How this came about is the topic of this chapter.

Attempts to explain how the money burning custom came about are divided between the oral-based tradition of current folktales and chronological accounts based on datable documents. These two streams of the native literature interact and borrow from each other to produce a rich diversity of originating narratives. My task as interpreter is to situate each piece of narrative in a culture-historical context. Aside from the sheer delight we take in reciting or reading the folktales themselves, retelling the story with an eye to how it is put together reveals the particular lifeworld design and human intellect that gives vitality and the oft-missed ludic spirit to the custom of burning money. Likewise, with the chronology of documents we call history, we require a material context to appreciate the story.

Folktales

The number of folktales devoted to the paper money custom seems out of proportion to what I said in chapter 1 about how people take the paper money custom for granted.[4] This is not the case when it comes to asking how the paper money custom began in the first place. Any person asking this question can find ready answers that are witty and waggish in any one of numerous folktales transmitted in oral tradition, some of it collected and published in written anthologies. Based on a limited survey of some present-day anthologies, the most ubiquitous answer to the question of how the custom began is that it started as a subterfuge to sell more paper.

A popular figure or point of reference in origin tales of paper money is Cai Lun, who is officially credited with the invention of paper or, more precisely, with basic refinements in the craft of paper making.[5] History marks him down as a palace eunuch who occupied an important post under the Han emperor He Di (89–106). This reputation is reinforced by his accession to patron deity in the pantheon of paper makers and stationers, plus the fact that traditional paper makers were heavily involved in supplying the papers for offerings and other ceremonial uses.

But the stories of how Cai Lun invented paper money depart from the historical figure of Cai Lun as a palace eunuch. The folk stories tell us that he was married, a tradesman, and, in the end, a trickster. Of course, this might explain why he became a palace eunuch, but thus far I have not encountered a tale with such an ending. When Cai Lun invented paper, there was little demand for it, and the unsold stocks of paper were piling up in the inventor's workshop. Wrestling with what to do with their oversupply of paper, Cai Lun and his wife invented a ruse to convince people that when burned, the paper becomes money in the spirit world. There are numerous variations on this theme. The principal variation substitutes another couple for Cai Lun and his wife, which not only places the onus of tricking the public onto someone other than the illustrious and historical Cai Lun but also explains why paper money is made from poorer-quality paper.[6] The figure that shoulders these onuses most often is Cai Lun's older brother, Cai Mo, and sister-in-law, Hui Niang, who are unknown to historical accounts. A typical version of this story, entitled "The Origin of Burning Paper," comes from Sheqi County, Henan, as told by Yang Wanshang to Yang Donglai (Xue 1994:406–407):

> In ancient times, a person named Cai Lun invented paper. People were anxious to buy the paper to use it to write on. His business flourished. Cai Lun's sister-in-law [Hui Niang] noticed how profitable his business was. She asked her husband Cai Mo to learn how to make paper from his younger brother. As he was leaving to study his little brother's trade, his wife enjoined, "Just study for a short while, then come back to start making money as soon as possible." Cai Mo went to Cai Lun's home. Three months later, he came back and

opened a paper store. Because the paper he and his wife made was too coarse, they could not sell it. The paper piled up all over the place. The couple looked at the paper and they were much worried.

Hui Niang was an astute person. She came up with an idea. She whispered in her husband's ear and asked her husband to follow her plan.

That night, Cai Mo wailed loudly. Neighbors did not know what happened to his family. They came over and found that Hui Niang had died. She had been put into a coffin. When Cai Mo saw that all his neighbors had come, he cried for a while and carried a bundle of grass paper (*cǎozhǐ*) indoors. He lit the paper in front of the coffin. He cried, addressing the coffin: "I learned the paper-making skill from my younger brother, but I was not so earnest, and the paper I made was not so good. This made you so angry and you died as a result. I will burn the paper into ash to quench your hatred." He burned paper while he was crying. After he had burned the whole bundle, he carried in another bundle and continued to burn. He burned and burned, suddenly there were sounds from inside the coffin. It seemed that he did not hear the sounds, for he kept burning and crying. Suddenly, Hui Niang shouted from inside the coffin, "Take off the lid quickly, I came back!" All of the people were startled, they tried to be brave as they took off the lid.

Hui Niang sat up. She put on an act and sang, "In the *yáng*-world money can be used everywhere, but in the *yīn*-world business is also transacted; were it not for my husband's burning paper, who would let me return home?" After the song, she tried to collect herself saying, "Just now I was a ghost (*guǐ*), now I am a human. When I got to the *yīn*-world, they had me push the mill to torture me. I suffered a lot. My husband sent me money. Little ghosts struggled to help me push the mill just for a little money—it was just like the proverb: with money you can buy the ghost to push the mill. The judge (*pànguān*) knew I had money so he asked me for it. I gave him a lot of money. This was the money my husband was sending to me. Then the *pànguān* furtively opened the back door of the earth bureau (*dìfǔ*). I was set free and came back."

After hearing what his wife said, Cai Mo pretended to be lost and asked, "But I didn't send you money, did I?"

Hui Niang pointed to the pile of paper on fire and said, "That is the money you sent to me. In *yáng*-world we use copper for money, whereas in the *yīn*-world, paper is used for money."

Having heard this, Cai Mo ran out and carried two big bundles of grass paper inside. As he proceeded to burn it he cried, "*Pànguān Pànguān,* you let my wife come back, I am so grateful. I'm giving you two more bundles, please treat my parents well in the *yīn*-world; don't let them suffer. When you run out of money, I will send you more." With these words, he carried in two more bundles of grass paper to burn.

The neighbors were fooled by the couple. They thought that burning paper was really feasible. They scrambled to spend their money to buy paper from Cai Mo. Then they went to their ancestors' tombs to burn paper. In no less than two days, the piles of paper in Cai Mo's house were sold out. Ever since that time, the custom of going to the tombs to burn paper has continued.

This story plays on the stereotyped roles of the older brother and his wife, which are indicated in their names, Cai Mo (Cai nobody) and Hui Niang (capable woman).[7] Contrary to the ideal expectations (but in keeping with widely understood mundane realities), the younger brother becomes the originator and teacher to his older brother, who lacks his little brother's skill and is only saved from ruin by his clever wife. In many versions of what I shall dub the "ruse motif," a wife or daughter is the instigator of the ruse and the one who acts out the charade of dying and coming back to life after a sojourn through purgatory, variously called "earth prison" (*dìyù*) or "earth bureau" (*dìfǔ*). The subterfuge is a charade in which someone discovers how burning paper can restore life to the dead. The other part of the charade is the act of mourning, which falls to the less crafty of the two partners in deception—in this case, to Cai Mo. He must first convince his neighbors (and would-be customers) of the depth of his sorrow in ways that Chinese recognize, one of which is the sounds and body language of wailing. This may be augmented by other demonstrations, such as burning something to ash in order to vent one's remorse (*huǐhèn*). The act of burning a thing to ash to vent one's remorse is a common, expiatory act in Chinese, a bit of folk psychology that dovetails perfectly with these stories. Therefore, the charade is not entirely fortuitous, since Chinese believe that burning something helps to purge deep-seated feelings of regret.[8] In other words, the charade that establishes the custom depends on a notion implicit in the folk psychology, that burning paper for the dead is therapeutic. It also gives leeway to explain other features of the paper money custom—why, for example, paper money is made from cheaper, coarser grades of paper.

In another version of the story (Zhang and Zhang 2002:343–344), Hui Niang fakes her death by hanging, which complicates the story somewhat, since a woman's death by suicide was always a potential scandal that her natal family was compelled to look into and sometimes to initiate legal action over. A woman's unexpected death always called attention to itself as a likely suicide, so much so that a woman's death by suicide is a common literary motif. This added burden of a potential scandal, however, helps Cai Mo accomplish his trick. For in order to convince people, especially his in-laws (Hui Niang's natal family), that her death was caused by an acute illness (to avoid the serious scandal that a suicide entails), Cai Mo enlists his neighbors (and would-be customers) in supporting his claim that she died of an acute illness. The issue becomes the *cause* of Hui Niang's death, which averts the question over whether or not she actually died. Any such doubts are erased when the in-laws see how deeply Cai Mo mourns his loss.

> Cai Mo wailed over Hui Niang's coffin, almost beside himself. His in-laws heard that Hui Niang died of an acute illness, and they also saw that Cai Mo was grieving, so they did not ask him any more. . . . He started burning paper at one end of the coffin mumbling: "I am incompetent. All I made was waste paper and nobody wants it. I made you so angry. What is the paper for, I would rather burn it to repent." He cried while he was burning paper, and he burned paper while he was crying.

The thing that makes the suicide motif so effective is that the neighbors think the ruse they are involved in is aimed at helping Cai Mo prevent a family scandal, when in fact the deception is aimed at themselves and intends a deception of historic proportion—the paper money custom. In other words, the people become complicit in their own deception, and every story points out how they go forth to communicate what they have seen, thus turning a self-deception into the widespread custom that we can see to this day.

Some of the stories end by making the obvious point that people soon realized that burning paper did not literally bring the recipients back from the dead (a prospect that would meet with profound ambivalence in any case). But this obvious realization did not (and does not now) dissuade people from the practice of burning paper, which soon became a custom of indemnifying spent lives, which, like spent money, go on circulating in unending flows of cosmic penetration and vitality. The coming and going of lives is like the circulation of money—both circulate in mysterious ways beyond the confines of the immediate, visible world. Other folktales use paper money to rescue this mystery from skeptics and cynics who would question it, and in the process such tales promote the idea that the true source of monetary value (and all forms of wealth) is beyond worldly appearances; it circulates on a cosmic scale, and it is, after all, under the control not of living humans, but rather of a ghostly world.

In a tale collected by Wang Changjing from Xunxi, Hubei (Wen 1991:651–652), a shopkeeper's skepticism about ghosts is based on the fact that no one can say what they look like and therefore the shopkeeper feels no obligation to burn money for ghosts, including his own deceased parents.

> Once upon a time, there was a middle aged man who sold vegetables and food in a small town. On the whole, he did not believe that there are such things as ghosts (*guǐ*). Other people burned paper on Seven Fifteen [the Ghost Festival of the seventh lunar month, fifteenth day], but he had never done so. He would ask people, "are there ghosts?" And then say, "No one knows what ghosts look like." His words were overheard by a ghost who was picking up money. This ghost promptly returned to the *yīn*-world to report what he had just heard to Yama, the King of Purgatory (*Yánwáng*).
>
> On hearing about this shopkeeper, Yama said angrily, "Where are his parents?" The ghost minister quickly replied, "His parents have been in the *yīn*-world for four or five years; he has never burned paper for them." Hearing this, Yama told the ghost general, "Go and teach this guy a lesson. Let him know what ghosts can do."
>
> The ghost general followed Yama's order and he came up with an idea.
>
> In the evening, the ghost general, accompanied by two little ghosts, came to the shopkeeper's place of business and changed into three old men. They entered the shop. The ghost general used night money (*yèqián*) to buy a full table of dishes. [At night the money used by ghosts looks like the money used in the *yáng*-world.] Then he started eating with the two little ghosts. They ate and ate till the roosters were about to crow; then they left. The shopkeeper had

suffered a lot [because the ghosts had stayed in his shop the whole night].

On the morning of the next day, the shopkeeper opened the drawer and was startled: the money paid by that old man was the ash of burnt paper! He remembered that other people had told him that ghosts always buy stuff with money at night, and that money changes into paper ash with the onset of daylight. Then he suddenly found a slip of paper in the drawer with words on it: "You have been wondering what ghosts look like, haven't you? Now you will see them." It was signed, "ghost."

The shopkeeper became flustered. He asked his wife to buy paper to burn. When they were burning paper, he knelt down at the gate and said again and again, "My lord, ghost, please forgive me, I dare not do this again." Ever after that time, he went to the graves and burned paper money (*zhǐqián*) and also when it came to festivals, the middle of the seventh month and at the Qingming festival.

Proof of netherworld beings is in the way money circulates. That which appears to be real money in the dark of night, "night money," becomes ash in the daylight. It reverses the usual flow of burning paper money to send to the netherworld. Money, persons' lives, and other vessels of value flow in interconnected circles that connect the temporal with the eternal. The flow of money transcends questions of what is real and what is unreal. In another story a ghost named Zhu asks his friend Zhao to burn paper for him. Zhao is reluctant and asks, "Paper money is just paper. How can it be used in the *yīn*-world?" Somewhat perturbed, Zhu answers: "Your question totally misses the point! In the *yáng*-world, the real money is nothing but copper. You cannot eat it when you are hungry, and you cannot wear it when you are cold, it too is useless. It is just the custom that makes a thing [like money] what it is. Whatever money is made from, humans and ghosts naturally desire it" (Xu Hualong 1998:396).

Such reversals offer evidence for the other world, even at the level of ghost stories such as one from Lanzhou in 1995. This story is a personal story told to me by a friend who heard it from another friend who claimed that it happened to himself.[9] It sounds like a nightmare to me, but it has the makings of a folktale if honed in transmission over time; for as Anthony Wallace (1956:268) is tempted to suggest, "myths . . . read like dreams because they *were* dreams when they were first told."

It happened in the city of Lanzhou, Gansu Province, to one of my friends who was a cab driver. One night he was working late. It was about two in the morning. He was going to go home. There were few people on the street. Then there was a woman standing by the road waving toward him. So he drove toward her. She got into the car and said she would like to go to such-and-such a place. My friend thought that was the place of the Martyrs Memorial Cemetery (*lièshì língyuán*). There were people living in the vicinity, but that place was an out-of-the-way place. But uh he thought that since this was a woman, it's no big deal. So he let her in and drove her to a residential area close to the Martyrs Memorial Cemetery. The woman got out of the car and gave him a ¥100 note. The fare was ¥20. So my friend gave her ¥80 back. Then he drove back home. Since he went to bed very late, the next morning he got up very late. His wife got up first. After getting up she searched his wallet and found there was a [netherworld] bank note. She was very surprised. Immediately she hit him to awaken him and asked him why there was a [netherworld] banknote (*zhǐbì*) sandwiched between the other [real] money (*chāopiào*). So he thought and thought and suddenly remembered the last passenger who went to a place near by the Martyrs Memorial Cemetery. So he immediately put on clothes, drove his car, went to that Martyrs Memorial Cemetery. There was a crematory nearby. He immediately thought of taking a look at the crematory. He got to the crematory, asked if last night a woman had come here—had been brought here. So the worker at the crematory said yes, there was a woman. There was a young woman who died last night, was hit by a car and was sent over here very late. So my friend said he would like to take a look at this person. Then, in the corpse room [they] pulled her out. She had not been cremated yet. He searched her purse and found she had ¥80 of real money, the change my friend had given her. This thing, although not experienced by myself, it was told to me by my friend, I believe it was probably real.

Here, as in the folktale about the shopkeeper, the main motif is that money used by ghosts at night looks like real money. In the daytime this "night money" turns to ash, or to paper money which is destined to become ash.

The stories above are based on two distinct motifs of the paper money custom. One, the widespread and popular "ruse motif," tells how the paper money custom is based on an original deception to sell useless paper. The other, the "night money" or money-turned-to-ash motif, tells how things of value circulate as materialized (visible) and etherealized (invisible) sublimations of each other.[10] In these tales, there is a strong suggestion that the impetus of the money flow is from the netherworld, since ghosts can spend their money in both the netherworld and the real world. The underlying message: in the end, all money is ghost money. There are in fact temple rituals in which worldly money is recycled to the congregation in a way that it becomes "spirit money," that is, money handed out by the attending spirits and gods. I discuss an instance of this in the concluding chapter. The point that all money and forms of wealth ultimately belong to the spirits and gods is a point made by Marcel Mauss that I take up in the remarks that conclude this book.

The two motifs that I sketched out above can be thought of as having two different social constituencies. The ruse motif plays on the rational and mendacious (profit) motive of the small business types in relation to the gullibility of the (peasant) masses. This scenario strikes the kind of fancy that a literatus from the dynastic period and even a member of the modern intelligentsia might find amusing, though some also take it as a serious historical insight. But no matter how amenable to the educated or official China, stories that the paper money custom started as a ruse by tradespersons to drum up business do not diminish their widespread appeal among the ordinary people they purport to tell about; these folks own the narrative, after all. They are not (and never have been) strangers or anathema to official views of themselves. They not only live with but author the very dissonances that evoke their sense of humor, self-deprecation, skepticism, and sometimes cynicism, while hardly missing a beat in caring for the deceased by sending money and valuables to them.

If the scenario that paper money is a ruse to sell more paper resonates with official China, the other scenario that paper money is simply part of a larger cosmic circulation and eternal replication of valued things—valued things include money and persons' lives—and that it is controlled by ghosts, finds its pillar of support more locally, in the occult of shamans, fortune-tellers, spirit mediums, Taoist priests, and masters of geomancy; for their livelihoods are devoted to getting command over the ghostly world in order to facilitate the circulation of valued things in liturgical ways that many ordinary people more or less accept. Unlike the official strata, that of shamans, priests, and geomancers is in time-and-space closer to the everyday concerns of ordinary people, but its stock of occult knowledge is as remote to ordinary people as the erudition of more distant officials. In the end, the folktales simply speak for the collective intellect of the people.

History

History is often thought to be the actual succession of past events. But it is also the current narrative of past events. This second or narrative sense is based on datable written records of the literati, which, in the case of common customs like paper money, makes grasping the lived realities of its principal users difficult. This is a problem that vexes anthropologists. On the other hand, it is important to keep in mind that, contrary to recent academic trends in my profession to dismiss everything that smacks of "elitism" (e.g., literati productions) and to read peasant customs as forms of "resistance" to the "hegemonic" state, the common folk, for better or for worse, were enthralled by imperial order (though, admittedly, not always by its agents), and many of the common customs, such as paper money and footbinding, entailed this enthrallment.

With these caveats in mind, my approach to the history of the paper money custom is to entertain five hypotheses that purport to explain the advent and/or popularization of the custom. These are that (1) the custom derived from the Confucian tradition, especially as it was articulated in the classic books on rites; (2) the custom became popular with the advent of printing on paper, which was spurred by the spread of Buddhist texts and talismans; (3) the custom developed as the ideological counterpart to the development of fiduciary papers with the increased velocity and distancing of commercial transactions; (4) the custom became popular as a way for common folks to economize on their offerings; and (5) the custom became popular as a way common folks could participate in the reproduction of cosmic and imperial order yet at the same time mock (in both senses of the word) the sumptuary rules by which imperial order maintained itself. This last explanation is one that I have added to the list of more conventional explanations, so it is the one I favor, although I realize that each explanation has its strengths and weaknesses and no one excludes the other four.

I begin the history of paper money where many Chinese historians begin, by citing the Confucian *Book of Rites* (*Liji*). For it is here that the "ultimate sacred postulates" (to borrow a term from Rappaport 1999:288) for paper money are established even though the *Book of Rites* predates the official "invention of paper" by hundreds of years. The first of these postulates is that the "dead" are disembodied souls and spirits, and as such they are sentient beings. On this point, the text from the *Book of Rites*, even in English translation, is compelling and eloquent: "Confucius said, in dealing with the dead, if we treat them as if they were entirely dead, that would show a want of affection, and should not be done; or, if we treat them as if they were entirely alive, that would show a want of wisdom, and should not be done" (quoted in Chai and Chai 1967:148). The *Book of Rites* makes it clear that disembodied beings belong to a different order of sentience from the living, therefore their needs are different. That is to say, each mode of sentience (living bodies, deceased souls at the point of burial, and departed or disembodied spirits) has its own sentient needs and therefore requires a different manner of things offered. Things of value or vessels (*qi*) that accompany the souls of dead bodies or that are offered to departed spirits don't operate the same way as vessels that foster the needs of the living. The *Book of Rites* seems to sanction two kinds of grave goods. One category comprises vessels originally used by the living but now in a state of disrepair: "The vessels of bamboo . . . are not fit for actual use; those of earthenware cannot be used to wash in; . . . the lutes are strung, but not evenly" (Chai and Chai 1967:148). The other comprises replicas made from materials that would not be useful to the living: "the carriages of clay and the figures of straw" (Chai and Chai 1967:172–173). Despite the fact that the *Book of Rites* makes no mention of vessels made from paper (although it does mention straw, from which coarse paper for paper money—and paper figures of servants, mistresses, and movie stars—would eventually be made), its insistence on keeping vessels separated according to the modes of sentience became axiomatic to the paper money custom that took shape hundreds of years after Confucius allegedly authored the *Book of Rites* and remains in force to this day.

A clear and dramatic expression of the *Book of Rites* in today's world is the Winter Sacrifice of Yu County peasants in northwestern Hebei. These folks farm plateaus of loess earth that are punctuated by earthen mounds of deceased family members and ancestral spirits in the shadow of larger mounds belonging to the Han dynasty. I felt this ancient presence one cold November morning in 2007 when I accompanied the extended members of my host family to their tombs for the Winter Sacrifice. The Winter Sacrifice centers around offerings of cold-weather clothes to the new and old tombs. Women sew fine dark cotton or silk cloth into doll-sized (about 45 cm tall) finished tunics, pants, and shoes for occupants of the "new tombs," that is, for those who have died within the past three years. After three years, however, the tombs become "old tombs," the occupants of which receive clothes of the same size and color but now made from paper. As the old tombs recede in time and memory, the winter clothes offered to whatever remains of a bodily and spiritual presence are made by rolling a wad of cotton in a sheet of dark blue paper. Of course, the reader must understand that Yu County peasants do not point to the *Book of Rites* for the exegesis of their offerings; rather, for them it is a rule of thumb, the actual practice of which is endlessly modulated by circumstance.

Parallel with the Confucian admonitions was the other side of the history, the protracted technical development of paper. The first historical indications of people using paper to meet mortuary obligations come from the Chronicles of the Later Han, which tells how paper was placed in tombs as a substitute for metallic coins. This took place during the reign of Emperor He Di (89–106), the same period during which paper was supposedly invented. There is a scatter of textual fragments over the course of the next five hundred years noting how paper is interred in tombs in lieu of metallic and fabric (silk) monies (Hunter 1937:28; Wang Li 2004). It is not clear whether the paper substitute was itself a monetary value or simply a cheaper replica of the more highly valued metals and silks, although there is evidence that even the metallic coins were specifically made for the purpose of entombment, which would comport with Confucian postulates and proprieties.[11]

During the same period from the late Han through the Tang when the technical and practical uses of paper were developed, two other critical ingredients for the formation of paper money came into play: the rise of Buddhism and printing. The rise of Buddhism is credited by many scholars with the advent of woodblock printing, perhaps as far back as the Sui dynasty (581–618).[12] Printed paper enabled Buddhists to promulgate their message among ordinary folks by scripture and talisman. This was a major impetus for the advent of paper money. One of the first literary references to "paper money" is found in a seventh-century Buddhist text: *The Forest of Pearls in the Garden of the Dharma* (*Fa yuan zhu lin*) relates a ghost story in which a man with considerable knowledge of the spirit world tells how "everything of which spirits avail themselves differs from the things that are used by the living. Gold and silks alone can be generally current among them, but are of special utility to them if counterfeited. Hence we must make gold by daubing large sheets of tin with yellow paint, and manufacture pieces of silk stuff out of paper, such articles being more appreciated by them than anything else" (Groot 1969: 2:714). This first description of paper money is completely compatible with what we see today. There are other literary versions of this oft-told story (Hou 1975; F. Wang 1998:368), the principal one being the *Ming bao ji*.[13] By the ninth century, paper money in its most generic form, the perforated sheets of course paper, was manufactured and marketed in ways that are familiar to us today. The literatus Duan Chengshi (803–863) mentions the use of perforated paper in a ghost story he collected and published (Duan 1975:115): during the Tang Xian Zong reign (806–820) in the western part of Chang'an city a man named Hezi tried to add some years to his life by purchasing "clothes and perforated paper [*záo chǔ*]" to burn in an offering to the ghostly agents that had summoned him to answer charges brought by the 460 cats and dogs he had eaten (presumably a violation of Buddhist precepts). Even if there is a strong link between Buddhism and the advent of paper money, the paper money custom developed independently of Buddhism and became more closely associated with the occult and with liturgies of indigenous ritual practitioners, as it is today.

The question remains, what were the original impetuses for the advent of the custom, apart from its association with a religion or the occult? Some will note that paper money became a popular custom around the same time that paper began to be used for fiduciary notes (or real money). It was all part of the Tang-Song commercial revolution, which was partly spurred in 621, when Emperor Tang Gaozu established a new standard of value for the commodity currency of strung cash (*mínqián*) by replacing the ancient standard based on the sheer weight of the cash with one based on the number of uniformly weighted cash per string. The new cash were embossed with the words "inaugural circulating treasure."[14] Their round shape and square hole for stringing was a design that traced back to pre-Han forms of metallic currency and that lasted into the twentieth century. But the standardization helped spur a commercial revolution over the next several hundred years and a rise in the use of paper to convey monetary wealth. By the ninth century, these new standardized strings of cash were being simulated by perforating sheets of coarse papers for transmitting replicas of metallic wealth to the spirit world, and paper was being used for fiduciary or promissory notes, resulting from a complex of practical problems having to do with the supply of copper and the inconvenience of moving large payments of metallic or other commodity currencies (silver, silks, other fabrics, salt, etc.) with increased volumes of trade and commerce (Peng 1994). Merchants began to use printed papers as trading receipts from deposit shops in local systems. In 995, merchants in Chengdu, Sichuan, began to use "exchange notes" as a private medium of exchange. By 1024 the Yizhou government issued its first term of official exchange notes in denominations of one to ten strings of cash. As production of these notes shifted toward the central government, with its interest in regulating commerce, the strings of cash were woodblock printed in simulated images, along with a warning that counterfeiting these notes was a capital crime.

By the twelfth century, the total of fiduciary notes issued each year amounted to 26 million strings of cash (Gernet 1962:80; Ebrey 1999:156). The succeeding Yuan dynasty (1271–1368) increased this momentum: "From beginning to end, the Yuan Dynasty's monetary system was mainly based on paper" (Peng 1994:2:525). And it is in this milieu that Hou (1975:127) mentions the advent of "imitations of fiduciary money," a form of paper money that we know little of until their mutation into simulated national banknotes in the twentieth century. While the use of fiduciary notes in real-world commerce of the Song and Yuan dynasties solved one set of problems, they also encountered constant practical problems, as they were prone to inflation, counterfeiting, wear and tear, and competing monetary jurisdictions. They found less favor on the part of imperial officials in the following Ming and especially Qing dynasties, although throughout these periods, they continued to be circulated on limited geographical bases by private merchants.[15] Thus while paper for real money found less favor among imperial officials of the Ming-Qing period, paper money for the spirits was geographically ubiquitous and historically continuous from the Song dynasty to today—it was, after all, an economy of the imagination.

A fourth and widely accepted theory among scholars holds that the popularization of paper money was a way that common folks economized on their mortuary expenses. This process took advantage of the canonical axiom that valuables offered to the dead (i.e., grave goods) should be degraded or well-worn originals, or scaled-down replicas made from cheaper materials of clay, straw, and so on, and otherwise useless to the living. As Groot points out (1969: 2:708–710), these practices accord with the Confucian doctrine that advocated moderation and economy in mortuary rites to avoid overly appropriating the living's limited resources.[16] (This doctrine was also in accord with sumptuary rules that limited expressions of status distinctions.) Apart from its prescriptions based on sumptuary rank, Confucian economy explicitly allowed poorer families to reduce the size and cost of offerings prescribed by its canonical texts. With the Song dynasty attempt to revitalize and disseminate Confucian teaching among common people with the use of

ritual guidebooks such as the twelfth-century *Family Ritual* (*Jiali*) by Zhu
Xi (1130–1200), there are repeated admonitions that ritual prescriptions be
adjusted to the material means at a family's disposal. For instance:

> The presiding mourner presents gifts. He gives six pieces of black
> cloth and four of crimson, each eighteen feet long. The presid-
> ing mourner carries them to the side of the coffin, bows twice, and
> hits his forehead to the ground. Those in their places all wail to the
> full extent of their grief. If the family is poor and cannot manage
> all of this, then one piece each of black and crimson cloth will do.
> Other things like precious objects of gold or jade should not be put
> into the grave pit for they will be a burden to the deceased. (Ebrey
> 1991:121–122)

Despite apparent allowances for economizing on ritual offerings, there is no
room for paper money in Zhu Xi's *Family Ritual,* even though ordinary people
had been using paper money for four hundred years. Zhu Xi and his literati
predecessors, colleagues, and followers expressed mixed feelings concerning
paper money. While most held that paper money burning is vulgar and an
improper expression of liturgical order (*lǐ*), a few held that it is acceptable as
a sacrament to the ancestors. Notable among these was the philosopher Kang
Jie (1011–1077), who lived in the century before Zhu Xi and burned mul-
berry-bark paper money (*chǔqián*) as part of the spring and autumn sacrifices
to his ancestors. A contemporary, Cheng Yichuan (1033–1107), was amazed
and asked the older Kang why he did this. Kang replied, Since grave goods
(*míngqì*) are proper, why should offerings of paper money not give vent to filial sons and compassionate grandsons? (Groot 1969: 2:716, n.1). The Southern Song emperor Xiaozong (1162–1189), who reigned at the time of Zhu
Xi's influence, reportedly burned paper money for his ancestors. When members of the literati remonstrated that paper money was a common custom (*sú*)
and not proper for his sacred highness, the emperor pointed to the precedent
set by Kang Jie in the previous century. It was Kang Jie's philosophy that
was helping to shape the official state teaching under the orthodox Confucian scholar-official Zhu Xi. And besides, the emperor allegedly remarked,
Kang Jie had expended no real money in making his ancestral offerings. But
Kang Jie's defense of paper money never found favor among the literati and
official classes. More typical was another famous scholar-official, Sima Guang
(1019–1086), a contemporary of Kang Jie: Sima noted the popularity of

paper money by commenting that in sending gifts of condolence to relatives and friends in mourning, everyone sends paper money to be burned; but then he added that such a practice is useless to the family in mourning and that they would be better served by receiving things they need (Ebrey 1991:98n). In *Family Ritual*, Zhu Xi echoes this sensibility where he states that for contributions (to those in mourning) one should use (real) money or silk. He expands: "There should be a list. Only relatives or close friends should do this" (Ebrey 1991:98). Over seven hundred years later, in late-nineteenth-century Amoy funerals, friends and kin of the deceased brought tokens of condolence in the form of silver paper to be burned as "coffin paper" (*guān tóu zhǐ*) (Groot 1969: 1:25, 1:31–32). The usual list of gift expenditures was meticulously kept. Thus, Zhu Xi's admonition was heeded, but the "money" was still bracketed as "paper."

Two other objections to the paper money custom were perhaps more crucial to the rising rule of Confucian sensibilities: the alleged link to Buddhism and the wasted labor in producing it. These are related to the extent that the concern of those in charge of state revenues was to ensure that labor power was concentrated in agriculture and that the product of that labor be used to support state interests. Many among the literati promoters of a state-based Confucianism identified paper money with Buddhism, which many still thought of as a foreign religion ensconced among the masses and absorbing wealth that the state would make better use of (see Ebrey 1991:xix, 80). Besides, paper money facilitated spectacles of the *yīn*-world that were easily manipulated by countervailing occult forces of shamans, priests, geomancers, and monks who were closer in time and space to the everyday inclinations and concerns of ordinary people and anathema to the Confucian sense of order. These same layers of occultic sensibilities as told in common folks' stories about fantastic happenings were nonetheless collected by literati and transposed into literary productions such as *Yijian zhi* (1161) by Hong Mai (1123–1202). Such collections contained many references to paper money, which in these contexts were considered innocuous. The use of paper money as a literary prop continued through every subsequent era and its literary genre—Yuan dynasty operatic dramas, Ming and Qing dynasty novels such as *Jin ping mei* and *Dream of the Red Chamber*, Republican era stories and poems, and even Hollywood productions, such as the 1960 film *The World of Suzie Wong*.

Outside the use of paper money as a literary prop, it also became a topic of historical record from dynastic histories to county gazetteers. From the time of the Northern Song, we find references to Kaifeng workshops making paper monies, specialty shops selling it, and ordinary people using it in their offering services. As the production of paper money became a significant enterprise in local and regional economies (Wei 2006:153–155), officials expressed concern about the labor power wasted on making it. I don't think this point can be overemphasized. And it is here that the alleged "economy" of the paper money custom is weakest, that is, viewed from the airy purview of the genteel and credentialed classes, especially those with official rank.

For example, in 1139, scholar-official Liao Gang (1070–1143) wrote a memorial (*dázi*) to Emperor Gaozong (1127–1162) expressing alarm at how peasants, mostly in the southeastern provinces, were abandoning agriculture to make and burn paper money. This area was the agricultural and tax base for Gaozong's Hangzhou regime, which had imposed heavy tax burdens on the producers of food to pay for Hangzhou's internecine struggles with the Jurchen, which in turn resulted in widespread rebellions and suppression, with a great loss of life and labor and cultivated fields. Liao Gang wrote:

> I have heard that there are things in this world that give satisfaction to people's emotional needs and that cannot be abolished simply by force, because if you try, and it doesn't succeed, then it's better to let those things alone. Then there are those long engrained customs that do harm to the people even though the people do not realize it. These should be prohibited, for if you abolish these, then the common people will benefit, indeed. In this case you have to determine to abolish them. If you do so, it shows that you use your wisdom to release the common people from their obfuscation and to gain a new view on things. I have been surprised at how people perforate [with metal punch] paper to replicate strung cash (*mínqián*) and then they burn it to receive fortune from spirits (*guǐshén*). There is no rationality behind it. It is based on nothing but the preposterous talk and hearsay of ignorant people. Suppose that the spirits have a fully formed human consciousness, then they know that people are cheating them. Even worse is that this custom has been handed down for such a long time, for the purpose of burying, caring for, and memorializing the dead; the people do this to fulfill their filial piety and to show their sincerity in order to receive a blessing. Accordingly, the result is that four or five out of ten southern people have changed their occupation to become paper workers. This custom is particularly popular among

people in Southeast China. It is due to the lucrative benefits and the peasants' laziness. Of course, it is the lazy tillers who go about this business. They expend their energy by day and night to accumulate huge stores of paper money, only to be incinerated in a matter of moments. Such a waste. How much labor power is this? Will it be completely exhausted? I feel pained by the fact that nowadays more than half the peasants in this realm have died in wars, while, in the Southeast, countless fields are left uncultivated for lack of labor because recently quite a lot of people are going about this business of making paper money. These ignorant people just cannot realize that making paper money cannot help their situation. I don't know when this malady can be ended; my main concern is that it is an impediment to agricultural production, even if there could be something useful in burning paper money; but if we think about how it uses up all that labor power for the sake of the ghosts (*guǐ*), the expenditure of all that money and property might as well be given to a wildfire. I hope your majesty resolves to promulgate a ban on paper money, and make clear that it is because [producing paper money] is an impediment to agricultural production and it does not facilitate the [Confucian] Teaching (*jiào*); this will make ignorant people realize the defects of this long engrained custom. Is this not the benevolent thing to do? This is what I mentioned earlier—if by abolishing it, the people benefit, then it should be abolished; some will say that common people do it for the spirits and filial children do it for their ancestors in order to show their sincerity, respect; so then do as the Buddhists, burn scripture papers in limited amounts and also consider limitations as between superiors and inferiors; if people have certain kinds of emotional needs [to show their filial piety] that can be satisfied without doing harm, then let it be. . . . I hope your majesty will make a judicious decision in this matter. (Liao 1934–1935)

The memorial ends with a sense of grudging resignation to the popularity of paper money. Short of being able to ban it, Liao hopes that the use of paper could be modeled after *actual* Buddhist practices. With some exceptions, there seems to have been little appreciation among the credentialed classes for the notion that the paper money custom was an economical means of offering to the spirits. Other than a few examples of a high official or, in the one reported case, a Song emperor using paper money, the custom was

generally insinuated with the taint of Buddhism, or the occult, or otherwise
dismissed as innocuous, quite apart from which the custom gained in popularity and became an integral part of the common offering service, which I
describe in the next chapter.

Though plausible in a complicated sort of way, the economizing thesis does not square a couple of important facts: first, ordinary Chinese have
always sacrificed real things of value at funerals and memorials (e.g., Groot
1969: 2:718; Lin 1996) and have some claim to fame for the expense and debt
they are willing to bear to bury and memorialize their dead, especially under
historical conditions of increasing social mobility and commercialization,
where the sumptuary order loosens or loses its grip on the lifeworld. Second,
and more important, the use of paper to replicate worldly values and money
did not obviate expressions of extravagance. When we couple this second fact
with the fact that popular manuals prescribing orthodox rituals remained
sensitive to sumptuary distinctions, we come to the fifth explanation for the
popularity of paper money: paper money developed a spirit of extravagance
that allowed donors a limitless horizon of things they could burn to signify
themselves in the act of sacrifice. To put it another way, paper money allowed
ordinary folks to mock the ritual practices imposed by sumptuary rules.
From ancient times into modern times, sumptuary rules distinguished persons' social position and official ranks by the qualitative value of things they
were allowed to display (wear, live and ride inside, be buried in, buried with,
and memorialized by, etc.), especially on ceremonial and ritual occasions and
even more especially in mortuary rituals and architectonics (Ch'ü 1965). The
books on ritual, including Zhu Xi's, were sensitive to these distinctions. The
Book of Rites states, "An unrestrained sacrifice brings no blessing" (Sun 1989:
1:152–153). "Unrestrained sacrifice" (*yín sì*) generally refers to an offering
that is "excessive, wanton, vulgar, lewd," and in this context it refers to a sacrifice to a spirit to which one's office does not entitle him, the "punishment"
for which is simply the ineffectiveness of the sacrifice. More ominously, the
authority for enforcing the sumptuary distinctions was included in the legal
code of every dynasty, although how such rules were actually enforced and
with what discretion seems to have become increasingly complicated with
the expansion of "social ladders" such as the examination system (He 1962;
Ebrey 1993:4) and the rise of commercial classes, against whom such rules
offered the greatest challenge. The point here is that to the extent a sumptuary sensibility was engrained in the Chinese lifeworld, it was obviated by
the paper money custom, which is why the custom was seen as vulgar (*sú*)

from the perspective of those whose position or ranks were privileged by sumptuary rules and was so popular among the common people who held no rank but nonetheless were enthralled by the mysteries of rank, of gaining rank, and the possibilities of having some say in how it controlled their lives. In a sense, the paper money custom mocked, in both meanings of the word, the sumptuary rules. For among common folks, paper offerings were and still are offered with the appearance and often the conspicuousness and spirit of extravagance that sacrifice entails. Moreover, these appearances could incur considerable real-world expenditures. The real-world cost of the paper offerings is one of the perennial objections to the paper-burning custom—as paper is a commodity, using paper as money for burning is, after all, "burning money" any way you want to look at it. The theory that paper money became a popular custom as a way of mocking the sumptuary rules of the ruling ranks is made more plausible by the fact that sumptuary rules lost some of their social salience in the wake of rising tides of commerce and resurgence of a new, popularized Confucianism in the ferment of the Tang-Song transition. Paper money was a way that ordinary folks, granted an increasing stake in the imperial order, played with the *distinctions* that separated the various strata of ruling groups and ordinary people from their rulers.

Around the eleventh and twelfth centuries the paper money burning was recognized as a common custom: the genteel classes increasingly insinuated the original impetus for its advent in the laboring classes, who had long habituated themselves to it. By this time, it was so embedded in the ritual fabric of the Chinese lifeworld that it had become a literary trope in countless poems, dramas, and novels: the Northern Song poet Su Shi (1037–1101), resigning himself to political exile on Hainan Island, found the people in this remote place using paper money for their memorial services during the season of Qingming: "Old crows holding meat in their beaks and paper ashes fluttering all around; [now my] hometown is in these immense mountains wherein I settle."

Conclusion

My search for the origins of paper money employs three different ways to tell the story. Ethnology theorizes the paper money custom by comparing it with offering rites of other human groups. This way of telling the story reveals that what is eminently Chinese is the use of replicas, especially replicas made from paper. The other two ways of telling the story are history, generally the purview of the literati, and folklore, the compass of common folk. Each tells one part of the story, and in some larger sense, each is constrained by the other—folklore has a history, and history has some of the attributes of folklore. These constraints require a level of theorization that is absent from the current chapter but is more fully developed in chapter 5.

One of the persistent threads of the historical purview in the current chapter is that the paper money custom was developed by common people in order to economize on mortuary expenses. While this theory is compelling at a general level, it does not account for all the facts. I posed a slightly more complicated theory of historical origins, one that implicates ruling ranks of literati and officials bent on realizing their sumptuary privileges. The fragments of history evince the proposition that with the "invention" of paper, the grave goods of the ruling ranks were increasingly replicated in paper, and this must have entered the discretions of ranked individuals in realizing their sumptuary privileges and limitations vis-à-vis their mortuary practices. As paper and printing became more common, spurred on by the emergence of a Buddhist infrastructure, and Confucian teaching reasserted itself through centralized state formations that sought to enthrall the peasant base with imperial projects, the paper money custom became the way ordinary folks participated and in one sense, a simulated sense, were enabled to outdo the sumptuary privileges of those that otherwise ruled their lives. Paper money burning was a vulgarization of the sumptuary privilege that gave the ruling ranks their appearance of privilege and power. Although the vulgar practice of sumptuary distinctions was a discretionary expense on the part of those who enjoyed no rank, it will always be an open question whether the "mock" was a self-enthrallment illustrating the old peasant saw that "underlings follow higher-ups in matters of behavior" (shàngxíngxiàxiào), or was a kind of allegory that tended toward a disenthrallment, or, more complicatedly, was what I will later refer to as a kind of mystification that ordinary folks are fully capable of recognizing, and do in fact "see through."

The ability of ordinary folks to see through their own mystifications is evinced in the folktales about the origins of paper money. To the degree that folktales take historical happenings into account, they also trace the origin of paper money to the inventive ploys of ancient paper makers (in the later Han dynasty). But these are narratives collectively honed over time that tell people more about what motivates the custom than how it actually began— and people know this! Embedded in these ongoing democratic narratives is the *ludic spirit* and *folk psychology* that are absent from other accounts. This people's history tells two basic story lines: one is the just-mentioned line that the invention of paper money began as a ruse to sell more paper; the other is that paper money is for disembodied beings or ghosts whose sentient needs are the inverse of embodied beings. If there is a hereafter of sentient beings, which there assuredly is in some sense—even Confucius says as much—then it is only human(e) to include the disembodied beings in the circulation of valuable things. We detect in these ghost stories a sophisticated design that actually augments the ruse motif. For if people deceive themselves in making payments to ghosts, people also deceive ghosts by making cheap gifts appear extravagant. Ghosts in turn deceive people by buying the products of real labor in the night with money that must be returned to them in the day. The circles of deception cancel out because most people understand that every reality at some level entails a deception or partial truth to the extent that it is taken as the whole truth—this applies especially to money. Every reality generates an opposing reality, and neither reality exists without the other. This makes the world a tissue of shifting appearances. It is only the shift (the chiasm) that is real (see Sapir and Hsu 1923:33–34), and it is the chiasm or coincidence of different realities where the balance becomes manifest, with its cosmic and moral overtones. This is the purpose of the ritual service in which money takes on an important liturgical function as a sacrificial gift.

CHAPTER 4

Liturgy

Of all the objects in the world that invoke reverie, a flame calls forth images more readily than any other. It compels us to imagine; when one dreams before a flame, what is perceived is nothing compared to what is imagined.
—Gaston Bachelard, *The Flame of a Candle*

Asked why they burn paper money, people say it's what they've learned to do from the old folks; it's an obligation; they desire a blessing of good fortune; they are afraid not to; it's just a gesture of respect; it's superstition; and so on. These individual reflections may be studied as social facts, but they do not explain the custom. Explanations require a structure of relevance that transcends the reflections of individual participants, that frames the custom as a social, psychological, cultural, historical, biological, or existential phenomenon, or some combination of these. Emile Durkheim (1938), for example, focused on how customs maintain the sense of social order. In the case of the paper money custom, the relevant question would be, how does burning paper money for ancestors and other spirits mirror the structure of social relations among groups of the living? The answer, in this case, requires no great leap of analytical insight. As Edward Tylor pointed out in 1871, the principles of "manes-worship . . . are not difficult to understand, for they plainly keep up the social relations of the living world" ([1871] 1958: 2:199). In China, "keeping up the social relations of the living world" entails communicating with and sharing the provisions with which a family sustains its members in perpetuity. Tylor and Durkheim were both interested in elementary structures of religion; for Durkheim (1915) the elementary structure was the

societal formation of a collective conscience. For Tylor it was an evolutionary expression of the human psyche. Over the next half century, the idea of a
structure that transcends individual consciousnesses was refined in theories
of structuralism, which answers the question "Why burn paper money?" by
telling us "how the custom thinks."

"How the custom thinks" is the peculiar way that structuralism (especially its most ardent pioneer, Claude Lévi-Strauss 1970) phrases the absence
of individual agency from its analysis of a system of signs.[1] The system of
signs codifies cultural order that is manifest in particular domains of culture (e.g., kinship, myth, fashion) or, at the highest level of abstraction, the
human intellect itself (Lévi-Strauss 1966). In this chapter, I am interested in
a particular domain of cultural order in a particular culture, namely the liturgical order of the common ritual service familiar to most Chinese. The system
of signs that underlies this liturgical order constitutes what I take to be its
canonical order. I am using Roy Rappaport's concept of canon (1999:224):
"the punctiliously recurring and therefore apparently unchanging spine of
liturgical order." It follows that the canonical "spine" of a liturgical order is
synonymous with its system of signs. Both canonical order and the system
of signs that underlies a liturgical order exhibits that which gives the performance, in its variations (including all the varieties of paper money), the
necessary sense of stability and tradition. Paper money is one of the integral
signs in the system of signs that underlies the common ritual service. I think
it can be shown that the canonical order of the common ritual service provides
a cosmology that is comparable in its sophistication to, though different in
content from, the Genesiac canon of Judeo-Christian and Islamic religions.

The common ritual service (*yíshì*) enables people in the real world to communicate with spirits in the netherworld (*yīnjiān*) or *yīn*-world. There are
different kinds of ritual services. Foremost is the funeral (*zànglǐ*), which is
aimed at helping the deceased pass through a hellish purgatory (an earth
prison [*dìyù*] or earth bureau [*dìfǔ*]) where the carnal body is rived and the
soul etherealized so that it can take up its abode in the *yīn*-world. The process
of riving the body is graphically moralized in popular Buddhism and Taoism, not to mention Hellenism. Second is the memorial service and sacrifice
(*jìlǐ*), which seeks to communicate with the departed souls and increasingly
etherealized spirits that reside in the *yīn*-world.

In general the ritual service creates a sacred space that is architectonically
mobile and independent of geography. It can be created in a temple, at a
grave site, on a street corner, under a flyover, in a wheelbarrow at a construc-

tion site, in the rubble of a collapsed building, or on a foreign seashore.[2] The ostensible purpose is to consecrate a piece of ground, a sacred space, where the curtain is raised between the hustle-and-bustle of this world (*yángjiān*) and the caliginous realm of the *yīn*-world. Here, the embodied beings of this world and the disembodied beings of the *yīn*-world congregate. Paper money is an integral part of this service; it is one of the material means by which the embodied communicate with the disembodied. The other two are food and incense.[3] The three offerings constitute a basic triad to which may be added candles and firecrackers, which are not offerings per se. They establish the boundaries of the sacred space-time. The five moments of the service thus include lighting candles and incense, offering food, and lighting paper money and firecrackers.

The order of service proceeds quite consciously from the lighting of candles to mark the opening, to the lighting of incense to establish connection, to the presentation of food to enact communion, and then the gift of paper money, followed by a finale of firecrackers to mark the end of the ceremony and to effect the complete separation of the supplicants from any lingering demonic residues of their communion with the disembodied. Each of these phases is a microcosm (and metonym) of the whole ritual service (candles + incense + food + paper + firecrackers). The actual performance of a service can, depending on circumstance or whim, dispense with one or another of these parts, just as one part (usually incense or less often the food or the paper money) may be employed as a metonym for the whole.

Although the ritual service may in practice dispense with one or another of the five phases, their sequence is invariant. The Confucian classic *Book of Rites* states the importance of sequence and invariance in the conduct of ancestral rites (Chai and Chai 1967:217). Invariance is a definitive feature of all ritual forms, according to Rappaport (1999:41): "A ritual displays or even flaunts its invariance, for in its very invariance it manifests or represents a *specific* order."[4] Perhaps no aspect of the common offering service is more invariant than its sequence of offerings. The meaning of paper money is entailed in the sequence of offerings because it is here, in the syntax, the prosody of offerings, and the *aesthetics of the senses* that structure or order is manifest; and as we will see, this is not a structure of static elements but a flow of elemental sensibilities that is both its aesthetic appeal and its efficaciousness. The common ritual service in which offering paper is one of the sequential aspects proceeds incrementally from a sedate mood in lighting candles and incense to a crescendo of punctiliousness in offerings of food, then to an increasingly jocund mood and playfulness (*rènao*) in firing paper and crackers. This *yīnyáng* of opposing moods is idiomatic in Chinese rituals and festive gatherings: gravity and jest become one another (*yìzhuāngyìxié*).[5]

Here, as with liturgical orders elsewhere, the ritual service is a discourse that does not depend on verbalization to communicate its meanings. As Radcliffe-Brown (1958:106) wrote, "There is a sense in which people always know the meaning of their own symbols, but they do so intuitively and can rarely express their understanding in words."[6] But why? In my experience, most participants for whom the ritual service is customary can voice a meaning for what they are doing, but many persons hesitate to do so. One reason for the hesitation, especially in responding to an observer's query, is that if one fails to come up with a commonsense or a utilitarian purpose, the verbalized meaning sounds corny or naive, and if the verbalized meaning sounds corny or naive, the metaphysical meaning is robbed of its mystery, its majesty, its ineffability, and therefore its affect, and thus its effect. In my view one of the powers of ritual is to communicate in a language that is material, emotive, multivocalic, and multichanneled, that is, in ways that the ordinary spoken word does not communicate. In the Chinese ritual service, the "talking" or perhaps communicating is done by five kinds of materials—candles, incense, food, money, and firecrackers. It is a language of the senses, of the five senses to be exact, in which the tongue is occupied with more sensual tasks than making words. This is to say not that spoken words are eliminated, but that when employed, they are shaped for their liturgical effects.[7]

Anthropologists Lévi-Strauss (1970), Rappaport (1999), Victor Turner (1967a), Mary Douglas (1973), and Göran Aijmer (1987), to mention a few, have pointed out how materials used in rituals are richly endowed with tangible qualities (physical numbers, textures, colors, sizes, shapes, etc.). These qualities can be manipulated into binary signs (odd/even, coarse/fine, hard/soft, light/dark, whole/part, sedate/boisterous, etc.). These signs are like a grammar in the way they can be combined and permutated to code messages.[8] But liturgical order is not language, as Rappaport (1999:252) hastens to point out, for once coded by canonical order, the liturgical order does not exhibit the flexibility of a true grammar. Rather, it becomes formal and invariant, which is its definitive nature and strength as ritual.

For instance, many people notice that a Chinese food offering may be a whole animal carcass, or it may be the cut pieces of the carcass. At the Qingming gathering in Honolulu, my student asked her grandmother why some of the meat offerings were cut into pieces while others included the whole animal. The grandmother explained that "the cut up pieces of meat were for the ancestral spirits, whereas the whole chicken was for the *púsà* (here referring to Guanyin, goddess of mercy) who has spiritual servants to cut up her food for her" (T. L. Tan 2003:3). Then my student asked her grandmother why she put down three bowls of steamed rice—why three? The grandmother answered: "That way more people can eat." Why, I asked a friend, do you burn the paper money after offering the food? He quipped: "To say bye-bye." Anthropologists see a code that communicates a rather sophisticated message (about social structure) that does not sound so mundane and naive as when persons are forced to verbalize meanings. The difference between cut pieces and whole animals, for example, communicates a sense of social distance and hierarchy. The more prepared the food offering, the closer or more familiar the relationship between supplicants and their spiritual patrons (Ahern 1973). This sociological explanation can be augmented by other kinds of explanations, which go back to the ancient *Book of Rites* (see the Yu County Winter Sacrifice in chapter 3). For the degree of preparation (e.g., dishes and paper clothing) there is also the sense that the more familiar tend to be the more embodied souls of the recent dead, while the less familiar belong to the disembodied, departed, more ethereal spirits, who are closer to caprice in the cosmic flow, so to speak; once it is either etherialized or absorbed into the cosmic flow, the departed spirit does not require things be cooked or finished. However it comes out of peoples' mouths, this rule is always clear and self-evident. As for the number of bowls, whether three (or five), it is an odd number, which is salient in Chinese mortuary rites because it represents a series that has no closure, no end to it, or, in this case, an endless flow of cooked rice—so "more people can eat."

Finally, the question I asked my friend—why the paper money comes after the food offering—was addressed in a provocative article by John McCreery (1990). McCreery began his inquiry with what I believe is a futile question: Why do Taiwanese use real food but unreal money? His Taiwanese informants answered that the spirits ingest the essence of the food, while the money that is unreal in this world, after it is burned, becomes real in the spirit world. (Had they been a bit more provocative, they might have replied that all money is unreal!) Be that as it may, the answer they did proffer was consistent with traditional rationales of paper money (found in folklore and historical texts) and with the different anthropological modes of transmitting valuables to the spirit world (as we saw in the last chapter), although outside these contexts, it may come across as naive or a fiat of reasoning.[9] Unable to elicit a more compelling explanation, McCreery inferred a structural explanation by locating the distinction between food and money, real and unreal, in a third binomial, "before and after." That is to say, the ritual service has a fixed order: real food is always presented before unreal money is burned. McCreery noted that this food-then-money sequence is rooted in the social nature of feasting versus the social nature of paying for things with money. Feasting, which Chinese have refined to the nth degree, is an integrating event—it re-creates communion and thus reduces social distance.[10] Money, on the other hand, signifies an immediate exchange without further obligation, according to McCreery, and thus signifies a restoration of social distance at the end of the ritual service.[11] This adds yet a fourth binomial (reunion/separation) to McCreery's codification of the food-then-money segment of the ritual service. McCreery undergirds this analysis by describing how the code is enacted in a repertoire of exorcist rites conducted by vernacular Taoist priests (*făshī*). He shows, for example, how lowly demons are invited to depart with an emphasis on monetary payments, while more exalted spirits are encouraged to commune, and food offerings are emphasized. McCreery's empirical descriptions of the performance aspect (i.e., how food and money are offered to different kinds of spirits) is ethnographically interesting, but what this has to do with the "unreality" of paper money escapes me.

Although the "reality" of paper money is an important question under other structures of relevance, it is not relevant to the structural analysis of paper money. McCreery began his inquiry on the right track by focusing on the sequence of offerings, but rather than bracketing (i.e., suspending the epistemological reality of) paper money (not to mention its discursive symbolism) in order to keep the focus on the sequence—the all-important syntax, the cosmic concern with timing and temporality—he pointedly dismissed the importance of the incense offering and in effect suspended further consideration of the sequencing and hence, the integrity of the ritual service as a whole. We need to reinstate the rest of the ritual service (candles, incense, firecrackers), which McCreery suspended so that he could question the epistemological status of the food/money distinction. A return to the whole ritual service will obviate the question "Why use unreal money?" and further elucidate the native (and formal liturgical) reasoning that paper money becomes "real" in the spirit world.

Completing the Semiotics of Paper Money: Cosmic Renewal

We return to the proposition that the semiotic function of paper money is best explained by the way it structures the common ritual service taken as a system of signs. To accomplish this explanatory analysis, I will employ two templates, one indigenous, the other exogenous. The indigenous template is the system of cosmic phases known to all Chinese as *yīnyángwǔxíng*. In traditional Chinese thinking, it is the process of continuous cosmic renewal. It is an ultimate sacred postulate insofar as it is a fiat of discursive reasoning behind which there is no higher logical category; and it is sacred in the sense that it is essentially unquestionable (Rappaport 1999:263, 286). Joseph Needham (1954) characterized it as an irreducible mode of cognition, namely "correlative thinking," the assumption that all things are constituted in their *mutual relationship* rather than in their individual substances.

The exogenous template is the ritual process known to anthropologists through the intellectual lineage of Arnold van Gennep (1960), Victor Turner (1967b, 1969, 1974), and Terence Turner (1977). This is a three-phase process that serves as a homeostatic mechanism in the flux of social orders. Here, my focus is more on its symbolic iconicity—that is, the mechanism as a model—than on its social function, although the two are mutually insinuated in one another. The two templates, the *yīnyángwǔxíng* and the ritual process, working in tandem produce the common ritual service, or more precisely its canonical order, the purpose of which is to open the door to the *yīn*-world to facilitate contact between living persons and spirits, a connection fraught with potential disorder, ambiguity, and anxiety. The integral role that paper money plays in this process of creating an orderly connection explains its meaning as a liturgical phenomenon.

Paper money offering is one of three offering phases in the overall five-phase ritual service (see figure 4.1). The three and five phases of ritual service (candle, [incense, food, paper], firecracker) harmonize the three and five phases of *yīnyángwǔxíng*.[12] *Yīnyáng* is the ebb and flow of cosmic renewal. The shift from ebb to flow and back again implies an intervallic phase, a third moment, the moment of renewal, the transcendent moment—transcendent because the shift entails *a moment of transition or reversal* from one phase back to the other. Here again is the chiasm or "flesh of the world," as Maurice Merleau-Ponty called it. The three phases of *yīnyáng* parallel the central or inner triad of the offering service, incense-food-paper—these are the offerings proper. *Wŭxíng* (five phases) is the elaboration of *yīnyáng* into a set of five cosmic phases: water-metal-earth-wood-fire. The ritual service (candles-incense-food-paper-firecrackers) is the analogue of the five cosmic phases. The five materials that make up the ritual service are *materials that change their forms by releasing heat,* a process of sublimation. The sublimation of each material quickens each of the five senses (sight, smell, taste, touch, and hearing), which becomes the experiential and liturgical foundation for communication with the *yīn*-world and cosmic renewal. Each sublimation is an embodied phase of *yīnyáng.*

The Chinese ritual service is also a version (perhaps an inversion) of the well-nigh universal rites of extinguishing fires, fasting, and lighting new fires to signify critical passages.[13] The Chinese ritual service is organized around a three-phase protocol that is centered on a feast rather than a fast: lighting, feasting, relighting. (As will become apparent, we can also say "external fire, internal fire, external fire.") The three phases are signified by bowing or by more elaborate purification ceremonies between the lighting and offering phases. This protocol not only harmonizes the three phases of *yīnyáng* but also dovetails with the three-phase "ritual process" as theorized by Victor Turner: disaggregation, liminality, and reaggregation. The first phase, the

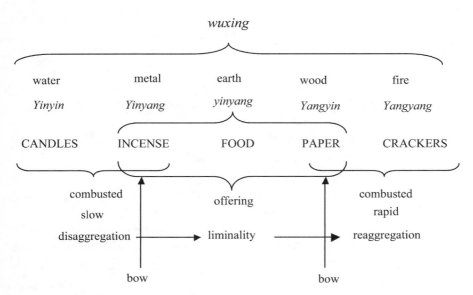

Figure 4.1 The ritual service

disaggregation of the everyday world, is accomplished by lighting candles
and incense. The second or liminal phase is the communion with spirits, in
which offerings of incense, food, and paper are presented; the food service
is the focal point of transition and transcendence. In the context of family
relationships, such as a memorial to deceased members, it connects the living
with the dead across a boundary that is impossible to cross under normal,
everyday circumstances. The third phase, the reaggregation of everyday life
is accomplished by lighting (in effect relighting) paper and firecrackers. All
departures augur a reunion (see Stafford 2000): departure from the mundane world augurs reunion with the spirits; departure from the spirits augurs
reunion with the mundane world—this is what the *yīnyáng* of five phases in
this ritual process makes possible.

In the following pages, I weave the insights of the anthropological ritual
process with the Chinese cosmology of *yīnyángwǔxíng* to comprehend the
meaning of paper money in the structure of China's common ritual service.

The first phase of the ritual process, lighting candles and lighting incense
(analogically under the greater and lesser phases of *yīn*), separates the participants from the mundane order of things by dissolving the cognitive mode of
time and space into psychagogic luminousness and fragrance. "Contemplat-
ing the candle flame," writes Bachelard, "perpetuates a primordial reverie.
It separates us from the world and enlarges our world as dreamers" (1988:2).
Social anthropologists look at this part of the ritual process as a disaggregation of structure, both social and cognitive, resulting in a pervasive fellow-
feeling or "communitas" among the participants (V. Turner 1967b, 1969,
1974), a "transcendental ground" theorized as "higher-level transformational principles" (T. Turner 1977). To put it in other words, the language-
based discourse is suspended, and the primordial discourse of tangible, sense
materials takes over. These materials sublimate into the five senses, evoking
feelings and emotions that communicate on a level beyond words. Here,
the participants are the "embodied" and "disembodied" communicants
gathering around the food offerings. The food creates the transcendental
ground. Commonsense assumptions about the physicality and separateness
of things are suspended. Suspending such assumptions is not a problem for
most Chinese, since the liturgical service is only the formal intensification
of the ultimate sacred postulate (*yīnyáng*), which, as Needham suggested, is
pervasive in Chinese ways of thinking. In other words, if the gathering of
commensals are the living and their deceased predecessors, there is already
the sense that each member becomes complete only in relation to his or

her predecessors and descendants. Thus, feeling and pain may be communicated in metaphysical ways that do not depend on words—I explain this as a "piety of the flesh." Now in the liminal moment or on the transcendental ground of the ritual service, the quickened senses of sight-smell-taste around the medium of food flow into feelings and emotions that know no temporal boundaries; there is a sense of the primordial, of the eternal, of a vast oneness (*tàijí*)—a "time out of time," as Rappaport (1999:216–235) called it, and chiasm or "flesh of the world," as Merleau-Ponty called it. The food offering is the transcending moment of the liminal phase for reasons we shall explore below.

The liminal phase of food offering, having been paved by the fragrance of smoke and ash, gives way to the third or reaggregation phase (under the lesser and greater *yáng*), which brings the whole process back to a renewed order of things in mundane space-time. This is accomplished first by burning paper, often in the form of a bonfire, and finally by burning firecrackers.[14] The holocaust of paper reverses the liminal process by formally separating the embodied from the disembodied, separating the *yáng*-world from the *yīn*-world, dissolving communitas, and, as we shall come to appreciate, separating otherworldly value from worldly values. On the worldly side, the holocaust of paper leaves residues of smoke and ash (as does its counterpart, the incense). In substance and significata, smoke and ash, which is the reduction of worldly substance to its elemental form, is a source of renewal (in agriculture) and restoration (in elixirs), and the material analogue of conviviality, of memory and nostalgia. We sense this in the "paper ashes fluttering all around" Su Shi (1037–1101) as he settled into his permanent exile (chapter 3). The holocaust of paper manifests fire in its purifying function; the crackling of firecrackers dispels any lingering effects of having communed with the disembodied. The combustion of paper and firecrackers is the point of consummation, both in the ritual process and in the aesthetics of the experience.[15]

While Chinese ritual protocol divides the five rites into the three phases of the ritual process, with the food offering as the liminal or transcendental phase, the food offering is itself subdivided into a series of three or five offerings. The three or five basic food offerings then constitute a microcosm within a microcosm: candles, incense, [three/five dishes], paper, firecrackers. Suffice it to say that the three or five dishes are the flesh of sacrificial animals. I will not dwell further on the semiotics of these dishes, since my primary purpose is the semiotic meaning of the paper money offering.

Alchemy and the Process of Sublimation
in the Ebb and Flow of Cosmic Fire

The three phases of five rites not only dovetail with the ritual process of anthropology, but also are in tune with Chinese alchemy. Chinese alchemy, one of the practical applications of cosmology (*yīnyángwǔxíng*), attempted to discover in the continuous transmutation of material forms the twin secret of purification (making gold) and extending life (longevity). The ritual service employs the alchemist line of reasoning: each phase of the ritual service employs a material form that is sublimated by a process of more or less rapid oxidation into a physical sensation that, in the context of liturgical order, signifies a gathering of sentient beings that include the embodied with the disembodied, the psyche with the numinous, in re-creating vitality, life, and longevity.[16]

Each material form takes its turn in contributing its sensory property to the flow of life: the candles bring forth a flickering glow that makes the cosmos luminous; incense provides a smoldering fragrance that permeates the cosmos with desire for the numinous, the presence of spirits; food provides flavorful sustenance, which by comestion (i.e., eating, and the devouring action of fire) and metabolism produces caloric heat and sustains life; paper money shifts the active mode of sentience from tongue to hands, from the touch of food (taste) to the touch of paper (tactility), in making and circulating things of value.[17] Moving from sight to smell to taste to touch, the conveyance of meaning becomes increasingly volitional, volatile, active, and in some sense human. Touching first with tongue, then with hands, is volitional and entails work in the sense of making things and giving things shape. The paper is touched with the hands (see chapter 7) and shaped into a gift, a treasure, a hands-on sacrifice across the cosmic threshold by a comestion of flames. And finally, popping firecrackers dispel the residues of solemnity with playfulness (*rènao*), jocund sounds back through the "blooming, buzzing confusion" of a purified, pristine here and now. Thus, each ritual phase gives off its vital treasure in the form of heat by a sublimation of its material form through oxidation. Each phase of transmutation replicates part of the cosmic design that makes life sensuous and humanity possible. The structure of reasoning is rooted in alchemy, an aesthetic of natural forces, the cosmological crossover between magic and science.

If we can appreciate the ritual service as a liturgical ordering of cosmic circulation through a series of sublimations, releasing heat, then we can begin to discuss the structural articulation of each of its phases. We begin with the food phase because it is not only the centering or earth phase in the opening between the *yīn*-world and *yáng*-world but is also unique in the mode of its transmutation. In whatever ways the participants actually perform the sharing of the commensal between the embodied and the disembodied, between the psyche and the numinous: whatever part of the commensal is left for the spirits and the ants or is ingested by the supplicants represents nutritive value.[18] The ingestion of nutritive value in its "substance" and its "essence" begins a metabolic process of caloric exchange that releases heat, just like each of the other phases. But the release of commensal heat is metabolic and is neither visible nor perceptible. The other four phases, by contrast, are combusted by a visible man-made flame.

Metabolic change is not perceptible because it is an organic process. According to Rappaport (1999:224), following the cybernetics of Herbert Simon, organic change belongs to a region of high-frequency change that exceeds the perceptual capacity of mundane human experience. The other region of change that is beyond mundane perception is cosmic because its frequency is too low. Rappaport holds that in the liminal period of liturgical orders, the temporal region of mundane social time dissolves simultaneously into both the high- and low-frequency regions of human experience. This is what he means by "time out of time." The congregation "moves out of social time toward both the organic and the cosmic, toward both the quick and the changeless" (1999:224). In effect, the cosmic becomes organic, or, in the case of the food offering, metabolic. "The numinous and the holy are thus rooted in the organic depths of human being" (1999:223). Here is perhaps another expression of the chiasm or "flesh of the world" (Merleau-Ponty 1968) or, again, what Chinese refer to as *tàijí* (cosmic oneness).

As already indicated, the liminality of the food phase is marked by specific gestures that separate the food from the offerings on either side. In other words, the ritual service codifies the distinction between an imperceptible natural metabolic process of decay and regeneration and the very visible external modes of combustion. The external modes of combustion signify disaggregation and reaggregation of the lifeworld in relation to the ebb and flow of cosmic fire. In structural terms, this distinction in modes of transmutation between the sign of food and the other four signs is the distinction between visible and not visible, or, more generally, perceptible versus not perceptible (see figure 4.2). Thus, the liminal phase of liturgical order, which is characterized as a period of seclusion from mundane observation (in order

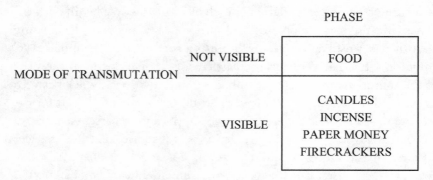

Figure 4.2 Invisible and visible modes of transmutation in the ritual service

for change to occur), takes place at the metabolic level in the Chinese ritual service.

The four other phases are in turn distinguished by differences in their visible modes of combustion (see figure 4.3). The first two (disaggregation) phases (candles and incense) burn slow, steady, and quietly, while the latter two (reaggregation) phases (paper and firecrackers) burn rapidly, flaringly, and noisily. The departure from mundane time and entrance into sacred time is accomplished by a slowing down, increasing quietude, entering a dream-time—signified by the way a candle glows and flickers and incense smolders; conversely, passage back into quotidian time is a speeding up, increasing volatility of molecules, as in a flare-up verging on an out-of-control conflagration of paper and then explosion of firecrackers. But the beginning candles and ending firecrackers also comprise a set in so far as each in its basic principle is antinomical to the food offering. The candles contrast with the food because the sublimation of candles into luminosity makes the world visible, while the transmutation of food by metabolic processes into life's sustenance followed by decay and regeneration is invisible, indeed, imperceptible. The firecrackers also contrast with the food because firecrackers make the world noisy and lively, while the transmutation of food is noiseless (except perhaps for growling stomachs and flatulence). Food signifies neither light nor noise. Candles and firecrackers thus take turns, first by illuminating the cosmic dark and finally by breaking the cosmic silence and reestablishing the temporal order of things. Acoustics (as manifest in the blasting of firecrackers) is

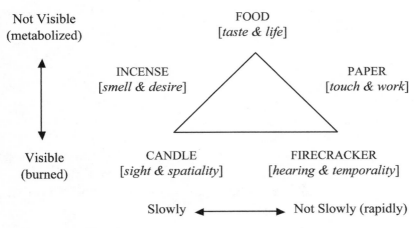

Figure 4.3 Modes of transmutation in the five phases of the ritual service

an immediate temporal phenomenon; it is good for signifying the temporal order, the booming and buzzing segmentation of time in a here-and-now materiality. The electromagnetism of light, by contrast, is a cosmic phenomenon, one that is good for signifying primordial beginnings, as we find in many canonical orders (e.g., Genesis 1:3: "And God said, Let there be light"), or let there be space, for light gives the sense of spatial existence. How, then, are the signs of liminal form connected with the signs of cosmic light (space) and worldly noise (time)? How do they communicate with each other in structural terms?

Candles and firecrackers communicate with food through the two signs of transforming the visible into the invisible, incense and paper, which between them form a binary set of slow versus rapid oxidation. The incense is between candles and food because it burns slowly, along with candles, but rather than illuminating the dark, it gives off smoke and ash, material significata of the most primitive human/humanizing instinct for conviviality.[19] The fragrant vapor of incense is ingested in a way that is reminiscent of the comestion of comestibles—food and drink. Here we might borrow a term from Lévi-Strauss (1973:20), who refers to tobacco as a sign of the "meta-culinary" because it occupies a structural position that transcends the difference between the raw and the cooked.[20] In the Chinese ritual service, incense [smoke] is not only "meta-culinary" but also transcends the visible/invisible aspects of the cosmic process. It evokes dreamlike qualities, divinities that are experientially real yet positively unreal. It raises the curtain between *yīn*-world and *yáng*-world, which compares to the widely reported use of tobacco to attract the attention of spirits among native Americans (Lévi-Strauss 1973:60; Radin 1972:115; J. E. Brown 1971:21). Of course, aromatic weeds, woods, and resins are in many cultures the medium of metaphysical connection and communion. Thus does incense connect and unite incompatible elements—candles with food, and, more obviously, embodied supplicants with disembodied spirits, both of whom, the psychic and the numinous, imbibe the fragrance of life.[21] People often say that "incense is the food of the spirits." And, as already remarked, ash—in this case, incense ash—is widely ingested as a restorative and regenerative ingredient.

While incense mediates candles and food by creating a dreamlike period for commensality, paper money mediates the incompatible processes of sacred food offerings and exploding firecrackers. Paper money shares an essential quality with each: Paper money and firecrackers are similar (although not the same) in the rapidity and commotion of their combustion. But they are opposite in the way the paper expends itself in the hereafter, while the firecrackers expend themselves in the here and now. The significata of paper money is otherworldly; that of firecrackers is worldly. The paper money conveys a store of value that is not visible to the world of light (see the "night money" motif of folktales, chapter 3). The flammable form that the paper money shares with the firecrackers is not shared with the food. One of several common denominators of paper money and food is the unseen value that each form contains before it is sublimated. Food stores nutritive value in the form of tasteful dishes; paper stores otherworldly value in the guise of worldly goods. Both stores of value are social, and both are released in a process of decomposition and regeneration. Both also leave worldly remainders that have lasting utility beyond the conduct of the ritual service.[22] The utility of remainders is something that food and paper share with incense. Thus the three inner phases are unlike the outer two phases, which only offer direct tangible values (light and noise) in framing the immediacy of the ritual service.

Modes of Signification

The transmutations in the ritual service (flickering, smoldering, metabolizing, flaring, and exploding) use different modes of signification. The signification of firecrackers stems from the popping effect: the physical transmutation of firecrackers into "crackers" is part and parcel of their meaning. The relationship between the means of conveying the message and the message itself is so immediate, self-evident, and penetrating to the ear that its signifying function is that of a signal—it signals, "Wake up!" "The end!" "Separate!" "Get back to the temporal order of things!" "Shoo the ghosts away!" "Time-out is over!" "The clock is ticking!" The staccato sounds of crackers popping break up the eternity of the liminal period, in which cosmic change is measured, if at all, by a heartbeat or a breath or a change in the orbit of a star.

The reverse can be said for the candles that open the service, although their luminescent force against the optic nerve is a soft flickering glow, unlike other forms of light (such as Shakespeare's "garish sun" and Dickinson's "sunrise yellow noise"); the flickering glow of candles (a medium of the lesser *yīn*) breaks up the noise and garishness of daylight or the pitch of dark. The candle's glow is a low-intensity continuous flicker, opposite to the firecrackers' high-intensity popping. Firecrackers' popping puts emphasis on the popping, the sharpness between the onset and cessation of the "pop," while the flickering glow of candles puts emphasis on the lingering radiance or flow between flickers that gives the candle flame its glow.[23] The flickering glow exudes a sense of being that is beyond or between the structure of things; a sense of the primordial flow that, like the glow, endures. In the liturgy of the common ritual service, the candle flame signifies an opening to primordial forms of spatiality and existence.

The incense signals by enveloping olfactory nerves with sweet fragrance, a powerful attractor in the natural order. Human olfaction has been underrated by ethologists (see Stoller 1997, 2002). No other sense is quite so acutely attuned to evoking memory-based emotions like nostalgia. In the liturgical order, it invites a gathering, a presence beyond the pale of living human sentience—one that includes the sentience of other beings, now disembodied beings, numinous beings. As we move along the continuum of indices, the significations become increasingly complex and metonymic: food adds nutritional sustenance to the sweet fragrance by adding the sensation of taste. This entails an intentional act of touching the thing with the tongue—food is the only object that releases its heat (in this case, life-giving heat) internally, imperceptibly, after comestion. Food signifies the gift of life for the commensals.

Moving from the act of tasting the food by eating it to the act of touching the paper by handling it, working it, and shaping it, we move increasingly toward what is arguably the most intentional, creative, self-referential, self-producing, and uniquely human phase in the chain of transmutations—making and circulating things of value on a cosmic scale. Because of its flammability and its light weight, it has long been the medium for circulating value in the spirit world and in the real world. Paper is the sign of circulating value. Thus, while food and paper money achieve semiosis through metonymy (food is life-giving sustenance; paper is circulating value), the candles and firecrackers achieve semiosis through signals. Incense, both a signal (attractor) and a sign (desire/commensal), mediates the difference between the other two sets of indices. Although the five transmutations of the ritual service employ different semiotic modes of transmission, the different tonalities actually deepen the harmony between cosmic and organic renewal that is the ultimate effect of the ritual service. The semiotic function of paper money (i.e., in terms of its structural meaning) can only be discerned in the overall system of analogues that makes up the ritual service as a whole.

Here is the liturgical order, a canonical microcosm of the ebb and flow of cosmic matter:[24] the advent of heat (vitality) and sentience (optical, olfactory, tactility of tongue and hands, and auditory) and the transmutation by decay and regeneration of life and value. This places paper money in an aesthetic context.

Conclusion

A structural account of meaning depends on the internal symmetry and consistency of sign-values—differences that generally lie outside the purview of everyday discourse. It's how a custom thinks rather than how its individual participants think or converse or perform. This is doubly true of a liturgical service, in which the canon or "spine" of the service is defined as immutable. Although the surface reality, the actual performance, leaves room for certain levels of individual variation, truncation, and self-referencing, there is no room for individual encoding or changing the deeper structure, which is what this chapter has focused on with regard to the integral role of paper money in the common ritual service of Chinese. In this service, all the material forms are sublimated (by means of oxidation) into the five experiential, sensorial effects (sight, smell, taste, touch, sound), which trigger and signify a higher order of sentient being that melds the cosmic with the organic. The ritual sublimates mundane things into sensorial effects that have cosmic significata, that is to say, the elevation of significata from the material world of sensation to cosmic mysteries of sentience, sustenance, and value.

The three main offerings plus the two auxiliary materials, their sublimations and significata, entail in their uniqueness and in their various permutations different modes of semiosis and an integrated message about the nature of being human. The bang of firecrackers, glow of candle flame, and fragrance of incense smoke all combine a signal with a metonymical sign. The flavor of food sustenance and the tactility (materiality) of paper money are mainly signs, not signals. Both are metonymical, but the significata of burning paper are more apparent than the significata of metabolizing food. At yet another level, only the three central sublimations (incense ash, metabolized food, paper ash) leave decomposed remainders that have powers of regeneration beyond the ritual service—they, after all, are the offerings proper. In terms of semiotic modalities, incense is the most comprehensive. It shares semiotic modalities with each of the other signifiers. Thus, incense may be thought to be the principal signifier in the ritual service.

This system of sublimations, aimed at revitalizing the cosmos to serve human purposes, could very well be taken as the canon of the liturgical order, in which paper money adds the quality of domesticity or "human value" to that purpose. The paper phase is the last formal offering and the penultimate phase of the overall service. It marks the passage from cosmic metabolism back to the social metabolism of the temporal world and mundane time—that is, the separation from and departure of disembodied spirits and (re)union with embodied persons. The paper-burning passage signifies the uniquely human capacity of making things valuable through the touch of the hands, which in conjunction with the controlled use of fire—each phase of sublimation is about a controlled use of fire—is the essence of domesticity and humanity.

If the liturgical service is thought of as a celebratory recapitulation of a being that is human, then the burning paper suggests that human being is disclosed in the world of things that humans make with the touch of their hands and restore to eternal return with their control of fire. Thus, from metabolic communion in which spirits ingest the life of the food offering while the living metabolize its flesh comes the artifice of the human touch, producing the things humans value, ringed with the aura of original value, of spiritual value, and thus things that, for better or worse, become our humanity.

CHAPTER 5

Ideology

Everything goes just as you wish, a favorable year and a
bumper crop:
>   Ignite incense inviting emolument horse general from every
>   direction [so] then everything [comes] as you will—progeny
>   and wealth both come in [as] emolument horse assists and
>   protects the whole family of the disciple [to have] security and
>   [a] good business making enormous profit with meager capital
>   throughout the year.
>   —Forever Protecting Security, Longevity, Riches,
>   and Honor Charm

The charm cited above is one of countless wallet-size pieces of grainy paper,
dyed green in this case, and printed with the image of a horse next to those
auspicious words. The whole edifice is a bricolage of "feudal" and "capitalist" expression: the horse is the ancient message bearer and sign of strength
and swiftness; the inscription uses words like "emolument" (lù), the store of
cosmic fortune with which one enters this world and which one exhausts in
death (Hou 1975:99; Seidel 1978:423), plus the guaranteed income derived
from official position and patronage, to refer to the ultimate desire for a huge
profit from a small investment (yìběnwànlì). To many modernists, this combination of signs, not to mention the charm itself, seems inchoate. But it is the
genius—or might we say the charm—of Chinese civilization to have fused
into a prototype two things that we moderns take to be entirely separate.
The prototype that mutually insinuates cosmic and official patronage with
entrepreneurial profit is the primary point of reference for the argument I set

out below, which begins by asking whether the paper money custom constitutes an ideology. My answer, in short, is that ideology is a modern discourse to which the paper money custom answers *nowadays,* but that in the *longue durée* of late medieval and early modern dynastic history, the money-burning custom answered to a very different way of beating the drum of production and reproduction: ritual.

The proposition that paper money is an "ideology" was first posed by Hill Gates (1987, 1996). Gates pointed out how the popular religious beliefs underlying paper money idealize the social relations of the material world, in which "money is an untarnished and absolute good." This is not an overly exuberant statement on the face of things, especially if we suspend the everyday misgivings about money that find expression in Chinese apothegms and folk idioms (see note 8 in chapter 2). But just as the paper money custom uses "money" to stand for all kinds of tangible wealth, so also the most popular spirit in the pantheon of gods, the Spirit of Wealth (*cáishén*)—also known as the Money Spirit (*qiánshén*) and Gold Master (*jīnzhǔ*) and identified as the Star of Emolument, from which one's allotted store of affluence flows—signifies the dispensation of wealth in all its forms. From early times the Money Spirit has been recognized in people's dreams by the physiognomy of his round face and square mouth (i.e., the shape of ancient cash). One legendary dream-encounter is told about Jia Sidao (1213–1275), who allegedly usurped control of military and economic policies as the Hangzhou regime was losing its war against the invading Mongols. Jia promulgated the Public Field Law to increase state revenues from agriculture by converting portions of private holdings based on official rank to government-controlled public lands. This incurred the wrath of landed interests, and since the voice of landed interests was that of the Confucian literati, we have come to know the legend of how the round-faced, square-mouthed apparition warned Jia: "I am the Gold Master. I take care of all worldly affairs; you do not." After the augury of the apparition proved true, Jia realized, so the story goes, that he had come face-to-face with the Money Spirit. The distinct pattern of ancient coins is not only personified in the physiognomy of human faces, but also appears in charms and public icons, including the architecture of imperial temples, which, as we noted in a previous chapter, models the cosmic flow between heaven and earth that makes human life possible. It is reasonable to conclude, thus, that for Chinese, the lifeworld is a "cash nexus."

I use the term "cash nexus" guardedly, that is, simply in its iconic monetary sense, and thus in a distinctly different way from its original European reference to a market-driven system that transforms social relations into eco-nomic things (Carlyle 1840). I rather think of the European process that Car-lyle and Marx pointed to as commoditization, economization, or reification, a historical process that depends on a monetary system but is not the same as the simple ubiquity of coins or cash to facilitate the flow of goods. To under-stand the cash nexus of the Chinese lifeworld, we need to separate the omni-presence of "money" in all of its historical forms and uses from the historical process of commoditization, which prior to modern times was sporadic and partial. China's cash nexus is cosmic, ancient, and imperial, and precedes and transcends the kinds of ties that envelope the modern system of commod-ity relations.[1] The Chinese lifeworld, until very recently, was monetized, *but not commoditized.* Indeed, the whole of Chinese history could be viewed as an attempt on the part of dynasties to maintain a monetary system (a cash nexus) and control of trade with a noncommoditized system of production, that is, in effect, keeping those who circulated goods for profit from getting control over the system of production, a task that was facilitated by upholding the system of production based on agriculture coupled to the system of sumptu-ary ranks.

Professor Gates describes a seamless succession of Chinese customary practices that uses money to exchange goods, to endow religious establish-ments, to reciprocate, sustain, indemnify, obligate every kind of social rela-tionship (with both the living and the deceased), to charm the fates and ward off evil, to replicate lives and purchase longevity. The book by Yan Yunxiang (1996) on the "flow of gifts" in a Heilongjiang village spells it out in mag-nificent ethnographic detail. Here the *gift of money* is the lubricant and the measure of a person's life. Here, giving and receiving monetary gifts is talked about as being alive, while reneging or opting out of the flow is tantamount to being dead (1996:103–104). This is not only metonymical, for at times (e.g., the famine of 1961) the vitality of the social network—that is, "the flow of gifts"—becomes a matter of physical survival. Gifts for all occasions routinely take the form of money. Careful records of the amounts of money given and received are routine practices, such that "any changes in personal relationships will be reflected in the gift list" (1996:50–51).[2] The gift list is used as an index of remembrances, personal feelings, favors, and material assistance between givers and receivers. Conversely, "market transactions are mingled with gift exchanges and monetary gifts are offered both as payment and as tokens of gratitude" (1996:102).

It only remains to show how this "social metabolism," in its various mixtures of patronage, reciprocity, and exchange, much of it in the form of money in kind, in cash, and in replica, becomes a vital force in the cosmic succession of lives and deaths, births and rebirths, all of which are matters of monetary debts and credits. Paper money extends this metabolic process to lives that have been dimmed by death, that have receded from the light of the world, that are no longer tangible in the here and now, that belong to the memorial and imaginary and invisible realms of reality. The feeling that life incurs a sense of cosmic indebtedness, that money is life, that life, like a string of cash, is a string of years or incarnations, bleeds into the notion that both money and lives circulate in mysterious ways, through various incarnations, and a person's troubles in the present incarnation (*jīnshēng*) may be the consequence of debts and obligations, even unknown debts and obligations, piled up in previous incarnations (*qiánshēng*), or may be put off on his posterity or on his own incarnation in following incarnations (*láishēng*). This scenario of beliefs about the *yīn*-world is a concentrated reflection, counterpart, or mystification of the experienced social world. It requires very little in the way of religious belief or faith to imagine it. Still, to what extent people hold on to any of these beliefs or the whole scenario, or add details to it, is an individual matter and thus an empirical question, since the Chinese lifeworld remains an open door on such matters—people are free to imagine or interpret the *yīn*-world any way they see fit. Apart from how people construe their beliefs, the liturgical services entailing paper money, for untold millions of people, is integral to making a world workable and coherent.

The Material Base of a Monetized Lifeworld

Folk scenarios such as the ones that narrate the paper money custom invite ethnologists to describe them in the spirit of a collective conscious and explain their function. Gates thus shows how the paper money custom is the material expression of popular religious beliefs. More precisely, these beliefs amount to a "folk ideology" that serves the historical formation of material forces. The folk ideology of paper money serves a particular late medieval, "historically conditioned form of capitalism," which Gates labels a petty capitalist mode of production and endows with the acronym PCMP. This petty capitalism is further embedded in another, more ancient mode of production based on the extraction of labor power by means of tributary payments to the imperial state: the tributary mode of production (TMP). The TMP also engenders an ideology, a patriarchy clothed in the virtue of filial piety. The ideology of patriarchy somehow works in tandem with the ideology of the

PCMP founded on petty, household-based production of commodities for market exchange. The PCMP is the material base for the belief that lives and money circulate in a cosmic market where individual fates are dickered and borrowed from banks managed by gods.

At this point I need to square my concept of a cash nexus with Gates' dual modes of production, since the cash nexus is a material form that transcends the PCMP and TMP; or, in other words, the cash nexus does not separate production from exchange. The problem with the PCMP is that it is defined more by the way goods are *exchanged* than by the exploitative way in which they are produced. The PCMP tends to separate the direct trade of peasant labor power in a market from the system of patronage and tributary payments and to reflect that separation at the level of ideology. I hold to the view, perhaps a stricter reading of Marxian terms, that the direct trade of peasant labor power in the market does not warrant conceptualization as a mode of production, and even less that such trade generates its own ideology or has some historical force of its own (see T. Turner 1986). For me, the Chinese TMP infused its spirit into almost every level of the social relations of production and reproduction, and the paper money custom reflected this if it reflected anything. This particular formation found unparalleled historical success and ended only recently, with the expansion of the European capitalist formation based on the modern capitalist modes of production, which in its turn infuses its *spirit of reification* into almost every nook and cranny of modern social relationships (Lukács 1971). The problem with the dual modes of production scenario, in my view, is the problem of articulation at the level of production, coupled with a neglect of centrifugal tendencies which Chinese formations clearly manifest and to which the symbolism of a cash nexus points. It would be helpful to have a holistic term that goes beyond a particular cultural history ("the Chinese") and theorizes (i.e., explains) the overall formation, even if having such a term runs contrary to current neoliberal and postmodernist conventions. This term should comport with the peasants' actual mode of production and its idealizations; at the same time, it should be ethnologically useful for generalizing and comparative purposes. The term should also complement a *ritual form of discourse* rather than an "ideology," which I reserve for the discursive practice of modern capital (see note 13 on my definition of ideology).

The historical-materialist tradition of Marx and Engels appropriated the term "feudal" to signify a historical mode of production centering around the exploitative relationship between lord and peasant. Granted, there are many problems with this term, not the least of which is its triteness. Even with their broad concept of "feudal," Marx and Engels hesitated to extend the term to the Chinese social formation, for they viewed the Chinese formations (in Hegelian terms) as lacking the dialectic of historical development. They did not appreciate the capacity of a feudal formation to develop around a different dialectic (*yīnyáng*). Thus they tentatively pushed the Chinese formation to the side with a geographic label, "Asiatic," which correctly recognized the centripetal (and despotic) tendencies of the historical formation. But the concept failed in other ways, quite apart from its unfortunate geographic reference. Extending the term "feudal" to cover the Chinese formation provides a broad theoretical construct (E. Brown 1974).[3] For openers, the feudal construct applied to China needs to emphasize what I call the Carolingian or centripetal tendencies in feudal development over the manorialism or centrifugal tendencies. Second, the mode of production is keyed to a dialectic of social relations around forces of production, which in China took the form of a *highly structured agrarian-based* "community of goods" differentiated by "regimes of value."[4] The domestic household produced the labor power that was appropriated in various regimes of value by nonproducers, a labyrinth of traders, merchants, local landowners (gentry), state agents, and officials on up to the Son of Heaven, in order to support agrarian infrastructures (dikes, canals, bridges, temples, granaries), stored for emergencies (such as flood, drought, pestilence, famine) and otherwise expended on the consumption, sumptuary, and prestation practices of the nonproducing and ruling ranks.

The product of the labor the vast majority of peasants carried to nearby markets or other centers of appropriation was less a commodity, as the concept of PCMP suggests, and more of a good: "Even in the case of goods destined for the market [as late as the Ming and Qing dynastic periods], production was not divorced from agriculture, and remained for the most part a subsidiary occupation; it was not petty commodity production in the full sense of the term. In short the domestic handicraft industry acted as a brake on the expansion of the independent handicraft industry and the emergence of embryonic capitalism" (Xu and Wu 2000:379). The difference between a commodity and a good is based on the fact that the peasant producers were by and large not wage earners; rather, they were domestic workers in a highly structured (unequal) and imagined (and ritualized) community of goods.[5] Production was focused on agriculture; it was labor-intensive, task-oriented, and organized on the basis of Chinese family and kinship norms. This organization of labor included other regimes of recruitment and compensation, from forms of domestic slavery to the occasional hireling who might be paid a wage of sorts.[6]

I think of the petty production of Chinese peasants as a feudal mode of production that extended the relations of production in the domestic household, the actual site of productive labor, to the imperial household, the ultimate overseer of the production process.[7] The domestic household was a microcosm of the imperial macrocosm. With the onset of the Tang-Song transition period, this became a highly developed, increasingly bureaucratized feudal mode of production. The Son of Heaven was a de facto warlord to the extent that dynastic change was always in the offing (with the constancy of peasant uprisings and challenges from disaffected peripheral kingdoms) and predicated on subduing and playing off competitors for the Mandate of Heaven by appeal to the sword. But once secured on the battlefield, tenure of the Heavenly Mandate was predicated on the Son of Heaven's sheathing the sword in the writing brush and becoming "a parent to the people" (Zito 1997). This move was affirmed by recruiting an army of brush-wielding officials (literati) from the pools of common humanity and its multiple tiers of patronage seekers, ideally from freeholding peasant producers, to the extent they succeeded in passing a series of imperial-sponsored examinations based on prowess with the writing brush. This held out the possibility, no matter how remote in actuality, that men of humble circumstance (generally supported by landed families or descent groups) could obtain stature, perhaps even official rank and lifelong emolument in the flow of imperial patronage. Sumptuary rules further enabled the *appearance* of nobility. *The whole purpose of this hierarchy of milking posts, of benefices, under imperial aegis was to preserve the agrarian infrastructure of the imperial state and its ritual practice of civilization.*[8]

The household farm (with its domestic rituals) was self-consciously a microcosm of the imperial macrocosm in which the Son of Heaven managed (through proclamations and requisitions backed by the force of arms— these were more often mobilized regional militias of peasants than standing armies—and the majesty of rituals like the Grand Sacrifice) the products of labor that were produced and circulated under heaven. The Son of Heaven was the ultimate householder. This system of extracting the labor power (the means of imperial hegemony) was idealized by the neo-Confucian virtues of filial piety (*xiào*) to parents and loyalty (*zhōng*) to the imperial family—filial piety and imperial loyalty were two sides of the coin that harmonized the domestic householder with the imperial householder. To understand how

Chinese civilization worked, we must grasp the alchemy of making domestic piety into imperial loyalty. This Confucian alchemy (of a *ritualized hegemony*) was explicit and written into the law: harm to a parent was *treason* to the imperial parent and punished as such—the sword was unsheathed with the dreaded stroke of the brush to red-check the name of an offender to be cut—but of course the whole ritual apparatus was designed to obviate such draconian applications of law. The hegemony of the state hinged on capturing two kinds of value: first, the power of peasant labor, and second, the meaning of peasant domestic virtue (filial piety).[9] These "domestic values" were implicit in the mode of production, in this case the bureaucratic feudalism of agrarian China, in which two of those "effective forms" were footbinding and the paper money custom. Both were ritual forms, and this highlights the difference between the (modern) wage system and the old system of peasant production. But I will come to this in a bit. For now it is important to grasp the whole lifeworld of Chinese peasants, in all its aspects, bent as it was toward agricultural and demographic fertility in the *yīnyáng* of cosmic renewal actualized in ritual forms, from the domestic level to the imperial level.

The connection from the domestic household to the imperial state was idealized by means of the five relationships (*wǔlún*), which hinged on an elemental reciprocity or sense of equity in which the filial piety between children and parents, the partible system of inheritance among older and younger brothers, the hierarchy and mutuality between husband and wife, and the loyalty between minister and emperor ends with the sense of equity, mutual benefaction, and patronage (not "equality") between friends. Here the concept of "face" facilitates communication that is predicated in social hierarchy (see Zito 1997:48). In fact, the affection between older and younger brothers (structurally and ritually unequal, but materially and jurally equitable) mirrors the whole configuration and resonates in the ever popular motto of the Three Kingdom heroes, "All men are brothers," in which the spirit of Guan Yu (paragon of virtue and loyalty, d. 219) is enshrined by both merchants and warlords, the latter of whom consummate their accession to the Mandate of Heaven upon sheathing their *sword* in the writing *brush*, the *wǔ* (marshal) in the *wén* (civil), the *yīnyáng* of Chinese imperial feudalism.

Different modes of production have different ways to mollify the exploitation inherent in them—this is a key point in my argument. The kind of exploitation that gripped domestic labor was integral to a householder-based feudal mode of production, which became a highly developed form of feudalism. The spirit of the paper money custom was in this householder-based feudal mode, with its tributary offerings and patronage-giving and with little or no dickering with the gods as one might do with shopkeepers and bankers. This point does not downplay the importance of the local markets and commercial centers, not only in the lives of peasant producers but for the overall system of feudal extraction. The appropriation of labor power by exchange of goods, especially agricultural goods, in local markets, was conducted in correspondence with the ethos and material interests of state agencies and agents in the circulation of goods (cf. Mann 1987). The state employed many strategies for controlling this circulation, especially by means of local self-regulation of trade, including what Susan Mann (1987) identifies as "benevolent markets" in the eighteenth century at the apex of Qing influence. Local descent groups whose elite status was based on credentials earned through the examination system and who also had clear commercial connections were held responsible, and thus held themselves responsible, for meeting the state tax quota, while also exercising authority over the operation of local markets. Although physically separated in space and dress and other sumptuary privileges from imperial magistrates behind city walls, tradespersons from rural peddlers to rich urban merchants were linchpins of the feudal cum imperial system. These differences between the credentialed and the commercial were not about "culture" or "cultural identities" (cf. Hansen 1990:5). They were distinctions of a moral order of patronage that actually facilitated a kind of collaboration and mutuality in the appropriation of the labor power. In spatial terms, Perry Anderson's (1974) description of tenth-century feudal Europe went double for China's protracted feudal development: "The rise of these urban enclaves cannot be separated from the agrarian leaven surrounding them," for the urban markets in China not only stimulated increased production, especially in agriculture, but were also siphons for enhancing imperial revenues in all of its forms.

In my view, then, the traditional Chinese formation was imagined as a highly structured community of goods—a feudal commonwealth, a household headed by paterfamilias at the domestic level of production and by the Son of Heaven at the imperial helm. This imagined, idealized, and ritualized community of goods included a social economy of giving and countergiving, which was agonistic and competitive *in extremis* and which in turn easily melded with market modes of buying and selling. Sharing, gifting, and marketing were to some extent embedded in what I am calling a *cash-nexus-based social economy* and geared toward reproducing an impressive hierarchy of sumptuary positions that in holistic terms was a highly developed feudal formation.

In sum, China's feudalisms were much older and protracted over millennia and perfected and, with its bureaucratization dating back to medieval times, far more centripetal and *advanced* than its counterparts in Europe, most of which by comparison were short of the mark (of a so-called pure or manorial feudalism) and short-lived. As Xu and Wu (2000:380) put it, "In Europe the handicraft industry acted like a centrifugal force, disintegrating the feudal economic structure as it grew; in China its function was quite the opposite, and it gave stability to the feudal economic structure." At a higher level of abstraction we could say that the European formations evoked a Hegelian dialectic (of paradox) rather than a *yīnyáng* (of conciliation), and thus were more *progressive* in the sense that out of paradox, contradictions, instabilities, general collapse, and regard for combat rose a distinctly aggressive and expansive European world system that only in our time, indeed, in the last few decades, would finally batter down all Chinese walls (enclosing a well-field mentality) to build its Golden Arches and "happy meals" (cf. Watson 1997). Perry Anderson's characterization of European feudalism, I believe, holds even truer for China's more developed variant: the dynamism in the feudal formation had much to do with the part played by commerce, trade, and markets, even though "neither labor nor the products of labor were commodities" (1974:147).

The Cultural Formation of Paper Money

The paper money custom was part and parcel of this bureaucratic feudal formation. The chrematistic and the ceremonial were indistinguishable in the burning paper; entrepreneurial "capital," along with all other blessings of wealth, good fortune, and longevity, flowed from one's allotted affluence in the firmament, while one contributed to the celestial store of largesse by burning paper money.

With so much effort expended on moving such massive amounts of earthly wealth, albeit simulated wealth (but what else is money but simulated wealth?), to be warehoused on the other side, why is it that so few people imagine "that side" as a paradise (chapter 1) and even fewer seem eager to get there? There are of course insubordinate voices speaking to this matter: one blogger (Murongqiubai 2006) with tongue in cheek (and with more subtlety than I can convey in this brief discursion) questions why government agencies recently proscribed some of the new exotic offerings (chap-

ter 8) while allowing the traditional ones. The authorities imply, according
to this blogger, that the new exotic offerings are merely conspicuous status
markers for the rich and that they must be bothered by the notion that the
communist dream of material equality in this world has been realized in the
yīn-world, what with everyone, rich and poor alike, able to send so much
wealth to the other side: "No wonder the current suicide rate is so high.
Probably while entrusting a dream, some ghostly spirits let out the news that
in the *yīn*-world, paradise is already a reality." Back in the real world, people's
eagerness to get to paradise is likely tempered by two other scenarios. One
is the popular imagination that if there is a paradise over there, the ordeal of
getting to it has to be unpleasant because it requires the death and decay of
the body. This process is scary enough; but Buddhist and Taoist spirit masters, playing on the indigenous notion of a cosmic justice, have for centuries
turned the process of decay and disembodiment into an ordeal of atonement
for worldly corruptions. This ordeal is popularly represented in graphic arts
(murals, scrolls, prints) that show the recently deceased being butchered in
the most gruesome manner imaginable. At this point—that is, after release
from the corrupt body—the second scenario becomes relevant for many folks:
the sentient hereafter is just more of the same as what they have in the here
and now, only in the hereafter, it is all invisible to the light of day, to the
extent that anyone cares to countenance something shadowy rather than
nothing at all. The notion of a paradise (*tiāntáng*) seems ever more remote
from this omnipresent mundanity, even though the implicit exegesis of the
paper monies suggests otherwise.

The exegesis of a paradise is implicit in the hierarchy of metallic monies
replicated in paper: copper cash, silver bullion, gold treasure. The hierarchy
of metallic values is analogous with other hierarchies, such as social relationships. One schema, for instance, compares copper with elder brother, silver
with mother, and gold with father. In the realm of paper monies, copper
cash is synonymous with everyday ghosts (weighed down with worldly corruption), silver bullion belongs to more remote spirits such as ancestors still
suspended between a worldly existence and pure divinity, and golden treasure
exalts spirits that are moving toward a more purified or ethereal detachment
from the world. These levels of separation between worldly and otherworldly,
earthbound and celestial, can also be looked at as degrees of separation of the
embodied materiality of the soul (*pò*) from its spiritual ethereality (*hún*). To
the extent that this is an exegesis of the paper monies, it is more implicit than
explicit in ordinary talk and ritual performance. The point I am coming to

is yet another paradox in the system, a paradox that makes the system work. The "paradise" to which few people endeavor in any realistic way is as elusive as the end of a rainbow, for to the extent it is associated with amassed wealth and golden treasure, it is associated with existence as purified spirit, which has no need of material wealth in any worldly sense. In other words, the gold represents transcendence and transmutation from worldliness to otherworldliness, from mundanity to spirituality, from temporal corruption to everlasting purity. Thus, a paradise that is signified by the pinnacle of material value (gold) becomes the pinnacle of immaterial, intangible, invisible value, that is, pure and enduring spirit, the essence of exalted divinity. This is far from a religious belief or faith in a supernatural; it is more a matter of "gold bearing fortune" or "forever favoring paper gold," and the "authenticity of gold," as the epigraphs inscribed on various paper gold from Quanzhou proclaim. Here "authenticity" may mean that the offering is genuine gold, which it obviously is not, or it may mean something more subtle and "original": that authenticity is looked for in the papery artifice of gold, and it is the *quality of the artifice*—that is, the *aura of human endeavor*—that makes the "gold" effective in creating and communicating with the exaltation of spirits. I elaborate this point in the last two chapters. This point also feeds into the next chapter, which expounds the thesis that the personal work that goes into making an offering is crucial to its authenticity and effectiveness. The authenticity of what is clearly an artifice of human endeavor (making gold) is the material index of the purity of the supplicant's intentions. Making the gold shine is a more reliable or enduring or concrete index of the purity of the supplicant's intentions than the fleeting sound of uttered promises is.

Ritual practice is where the paper money custom comes into its own. The proposition that paper money embodies the ideology of a petty capitalist mode of production, that its ritual offering takes the form of "petty-capitalist" ways of bargaining and haggling, and that this contrasts with official rituals which put "constant stress on the submissiveness of the human participants . . . and on the participants' 'purity' and 'emptiness'" (Gates 1996:168) needs to be reconsidered as a generalization. It is questionable whether this spirit of "haggling" even describes the exchange of paper money in the marketplace: more than a few persons have told me that when purchasing paper money, you are not supposed to dicker over the price. Paper money is set apart from ordinary commodities, although, as a commodity or a good, it is not in any sense "sacred." Even spirit masters whose job is to recruit demonic powers high and low to effect the master's will don't dicker with the spirits but command them, often through the office of a higher divinity, and by means of paper money and talismans that simulate imperial edicts (Groot 1969: 6:1041), with their "bureaucratic efficacy" (Ahern 1981:11). These edicts are printed on countless charms and can be found in ensembles of gold paper offerings burned in the Kaifusi Guanyin temple in Changsha, discussed in chapter 2. With the paper offerings to the gods the "contract," to use Mauss' term, is a moral one conducted according to feudal relationships; it is not usually negotiated according to modern market notions of a utility or a price, which may be why people use paper money.

Space allows me only one example. In the autumn of 1999 I encountered a middle-aged woman dropping her wooden divining blocks on the offering floor before Wong Tai Sin's altar.[10] She was unable to get a positive response from the god that fulfills all desires even though she had laid out in front of her a cornucopia of Big Longevity Gold paper (*dà shòu jīn*). Obviously frustrated, she left her offerings in place and unattended, and hurried off to the paper vendors outside the temple; she came back with more packs of gold paper. After adding the additional gold to her display of largesse, she received her desired response. Obviously this woman was "negotiating" with Wong Tai Sin, but what and how was she negotiating? Did she offer gold in the spirit of haggling over a commodity or even as a quid pro quo, "I'll give you more money if you give me a positive sign"? Or did she offer gold in the spirit of "O Lord, hear my earnest request, for my intention is as pure gold"? Was she haggling, as with a shopkeeper or banker, or was she remonstrating, as with some high feudal lord, to the extent we want to draw such a comparison? For me the answer is obvious. She did not simply offer money or even collateral. Using the phenomenological method of "free variation in the imagination" (Spiegelberg 1975:50), I ask myself, Why not offer a single paper money *banknote* with a face value of $8 billion? Of course, anyone in the vicinity, close enough to hear me murmur the question, could come up with the answer, and it would probably go something like this: Wong Tai Sin would say, "What am I going to do with your money? Eight billion is a finite amount; it means nothing to me. What catches my eye is the purity of your intention, the durability of your obligation, the spiritual value of your offering-request—and it is these transcending qualities that you communicate through the shine of the gold you sacrifice, not the emptiness or weightlessness and potential mendacity of words or finite face value of a modern banknote."[11] Purity of intention matters to Wong Tai Sin; it is explicitly stated that he does not help gamblers with their numbers. At the Wong Tai

Sin Temple, most devotees today offer only incense, and many will say that since Wong Tai Sin is a great divinity, he does not need things like food and money (unless of course it is real money for the upkeep of the temple). In Chinese and other cultures, gold is the sign of eternal purity. It enables true intention to navigate the gulf between the supplicant and the great divinity. This fits with the theory that offerings are often discursive acts, obviating ordinary language more than simple monetary exchanges do.

If we are looking for signs that "the gods are bankers" or that the money burning custom somehow reflects a capitalist ideology, we need look no further than the facsimiles of the modern banknotes (just mentioned and examined more closely in chapter 7) where the paper money makers of our time have recruited the high divinity, the Jade Emperor (*Yùhuáng*), to be bank president and the King of Purgatory (*Yánluó*) to be vice president and the notes have actual face values that you could *potentially* haggle a price over. It is important to note, however, that these mutant forms of paper money—some people call them "ghost bills"—reflect neither a "petty capitalist" nor a feudal mode of production, but rather the modern capitalist formation; and, although by no means universally acclaimed, these notes were available as offerings to ordinary spirits in every place I visited in China and Chinatowns around the world. This is the topic of chapters 7 and 8.

The Ritual Mode of Mystification

If Chinese paper money is the ritual expression of a lifeworld enveloped in a cash nexus, we cannot help but be drawn to the first chapter of *Capital,* where Marx argues that under conditions of capitalist production, money assumes the form of a fetish. For Marx, the term "fetish" evokes the idea of a thing whose identity, value, and power (or animus) derives from the circulating nature of the thing itself rather than from the human labor that produced it. Money and all other things that take the money form (i.e., commodities) are prone to fetishism to the extent they are produced and circulated under the rule of capital, in which the human labor or "the socially necessary labor time" that it takes to produce a useful thing for the sole purpose of exchanging its use value is itself a commodity (a factor of production purchased from its owner-agent, the laborer). This is a system of commodity production in which a commodity (purchased labor time) produces a commodity (exchangeable use value) that is exchanged for a commodity (money) for the singular purpose of accumulating an added commodity (profit). The money form of value supersedes all other forms of value (labor value and use value) and their sensual characteristics.[12] The whole process of production and circulation gives the appearance of "money making more money." Hence, the fetish of money. But the whole point of Marx's analysis is to show how the money fetish hides the fact that "money making more money" is an illusion—that monetary profit comes not from exchange but from "surplus labor." The commodity in its money form disguises its original animus in the "willing" of its human labor to work more hours than is socially necessary to produce useful things. The sacrifice or exploitation of human labor in the form of a commodity is the germ of ideology, which I will expand upon in a moment.

Marx went on to suggest that the fetishism inherent in the system of commodity production and exchange takes on different guises in different historical formations. "The whole mystery of commodities, all the magic and necromancy that surrounds the products of labor as long as they take the form of commodities, vanishes therefore, as soon as we come to *other forms of production*" (Marx 1906:87, my italics). Marx states that "ancient social organisms of production are, as compared with bourgeois society, extremely simple and transparent" (1906:91). Further, "the mode of production in which the product takes the form of a commodity, or is produced directly for exchange, is the most general and most embryonic form of bourgeois production. It therefore makes its appearance at an early date in history, though not in the same predominating and characteristic manner as now-a-days. Hence its Fetish character is comparatively easy to be seen through" (1906:94). These "embryonic" or "precapitalist" formations ostensibly include China's system of petty production. The Chinese formation exemplifies the transparency of a system that is not fully commoditized and therefore *deceives itself in an altogether different direction.* The petty system of production mystifies its exploitations by dramatizing them in plain view, in such sacrificial dramas as footbinding and paper money burning (the phenomenology of which is the focus of the next chapter).

Marx's theory of the fetishism in commodity production thus suggests a distinction between two different ways of disguising the extraction of labor power in the circulation of its products: reification and mystification. Reification, an appeal to the material essence or natural substance of a thing, is the means by which the industrial-based commodity system totally dominates society and penetrates the lifeworld, such that the value of labor power becomes identical with its wages. The discourse that makes this reification seem reasonable and natural, even self-evident, is the work of ideology.[13]

The other way of disguising labor power is, for want of a more distinctive or definitive term, mystification, which mediates the presence or absence of a thing by the ritual and magical ability to make the forms of things visible or invisible. *I use "reification" and "mystification" to refer to different modes of alienation, identification, self-deception, fetishization, and value formation.* I associate mystification with the advent of writing and money and modes of production in which the exploitation is more direct, self-evident, and transparent. These are "precapitalist" modes where commoditization of labor is nil or episodic, neither systematic nor dominant; where the subjugation of labor is more direct (slavery, serfdom, household work); and where capital "circulates" at such a slow pace that it loses its identity as capital, especially in the hands of officials cum merchants.

I associate reification with the advent of capitalism in the sense that economy and society, production and exchange, price and value are phenomenally separated—the original use of "price" for a "priceless treasure" became increasingly anachronistic between the Franco-Prussian War and World War I as "the things that once we deemed of price Consumed in smoke of sacrifice" (Binyon 1917:49). This was also the moment when the world economy began to shift into its *consumerism* mode (Robbins 1999:3) and Georg Simmel wrote *The Philosophy of Money,* with its emphasis on exchange as the source of value, and neoclassical economics became the dominant discourse of the modern lifeworld, all of which I discuss in the concluding chapter on value. And with the separation of price from value, bourgeois or neoclassical and Marxist economic theories went their separate ways. I am suggesting that we follow suit and divide the two concepts of reification and mystification, which, strange to say, Marxists have used interchangeably.[14]

For under mystification, these gestating contradictions between economy and society are miscarried by magic and ritual practice. Marx's dictum helps to explain the rather unique form that the cash nexus takes in China. That is where the cash nexus is expressed in offerings of sensuous objects that resemble money in its manifold forms—gold, silver, copper, silk, cloth, and so on. Here we can glimpse the relationship between the mode of producing value and the way it is mystified as an actual material thing. It follows from what has just been said that the mystification of labor value—the sacrifice— is tangible (ritualized) and comparatively "easy to be seen through" because the labor value is based on (1) skilled peasant and artisan *task-oriented* labor, in (2) a production process that is geared as much to subsistence as to market exchange and patronage and that draws no clear line between the owners and the workers with regard to the means of production, in which (3) the social relations of production include "direct relations of subjection," which are not readily reducible to simple abstract labor but are acted out in ritual forms.

Not only was the Chinese system of production, at best, only partially commoditized; it also functioned under a naive (and refreshingly simple) commonsense form of the labor theory of value. The Chinese labor theory of value held in commonsense with our classical economists that value comes from the work that is put into producing things. But where classical economists reduced the work to a quantity of labor time (in order to count it), the Chinese theory held on to a moral philosophy of the labor and its product relative to the needs of an imperial order. Marx's exposition of two kinds of circulation (in chapters 4 and 5 of *Capital*) helps illuminate this point. The formula C-M-C (money [M] is used to sell one commodity [C] like rice in order to purchase another, like salt) orients exchange to quantifying or equalizing the qualitative differences or use values (utilities). Conversely, M-C-M (money is used to buy a commodity like rice in order to sell it for more money) orients exchange toward quantitative differences in exchange value. Or, as Engels put it, "The ultimate object of C-M-C is use-value, of M-C-M *exchange-value itself*" (1937:56, italics in original).

The petty producers and tradesmen were prompted by different modes of exchanging and circulating goods (or what I take Appadurai's different "regimes of value" to mean): the C-M-C was more of a peasant orientation, while the M-C-M was more of a merchant orientation. The point I am making is that the two modes of exchanging and circulating goods were separate, and as such they did not configure a system of commodity production and exchange. The Chinese were acutely aware of the moral implications of this difference, which was reflected in the stratification of status groups based on the qualitative criteria of production. The C-M-C—we should change the terms to G-M-G (G for "goods" and M for mediating the give-and-take of equivalent "use values" by reciprocity, trade in kind, barter, or cash money)—was morally superior in imperial China and was so recognized and given its due in the imperial order. This labor theory of value was predicated in the moral order of the fourfold ranks of common people, which favored the labor of the "mind" (scholars and officials) over the "body" of the masses, and among those who labored with their bodies, it favored peasant producers over artisans and merchants.[15] These were also sumptuary distinctions. In other words, the true value of things was in the *moral quality of the labor*—that is, the quality of the sacrifice—that produced the value of useful goods, beginning with food. From the beginning to the end of *Capital,* Marx's whole exposition is about the quantitative or abstract nature of labor power measured in units of time. This sensibility is lacking in the petty production of Chinese, which is task oriented rather than time oriented, immediate and concrete rather than abstract, family and collective rather than individual, and so thus is its alienation and exploitation hidden in plain view, in the manifest "fetishisms" or, more accurately, magical rituals of footbinding and burning paper money.

The important thing here is that the production-consumption dialectic achieved a certain equilibrium in which the labor value (the goods of petty producers) circulated through various phases and regimes of value at a low velocity, adapted to seasonal rhythms, encountered numerous barriers in its appropriation by landowners, merchants, and imperial agents. The tributary system was only one among many factors that dampened the velocity of labor value, and it was completely embedded in the enchantments of everyday lives. I believe that along with customs like footbinding, the custom of burning paper money was part of this mystification process, this enchantment of the lifeworld. Despite the use of monetary forms, the custom did not mystify commodity production. The system of domestic production was completely integrated in a social formation that mystifies the sacrifice of labor power *by dramatizing the sacrifice.* In this sense, too, I will argue that to the degree paper money was an agent of mystification, it was clearly a function of the whole social formation (and not the reflex of a petty capitalist mode of production).

Once again, we call on *yīnyáng,* "the primacy of conciliation over paradox" (Ricoeur 1966:341), to help us understand. The state and the market, two different systems of appropriating labor power, are not inherently antagonistic or centrifugal, or if they are, rituals like burning money mystified their complementarity and centripetalism by mystifying the value of labor power. In so many ways attested to thus far, they were as the round cash is to its square hole, or heaven is to earth, or day to night, or *yáng* to *yīn.*[16] Each got its momentary raison d'être from its relation to the other. Insofar as one was morally preferable and politically dominant, it would be the *yáng* of the imperial state, which made the sunlight of civil order possible or the square hole in the round coin possible. The omnipresent *yīn* of the market was not antagonistic to the imperial state; market and state were in dynamic tension and mutually insinuated, each in the other. Here was a dialectic that did not sow the seeds of its own destruction, a point that Hegel and Marx and Weber grasped but without recognizing the historical, *developmental dynamism* of the *yīnyáng* dialectic. And even today, in its encounter with the modern formations of capital on a global scale, the dialectic seems resilient.

Thus, under conditions of peasant production, the production process is task-oriented, more concrete and less abstract, neither commoditized nor reified, more holistic, and this virtually describes how it is mystified in the tradition of paper money offerings, a point I will elaborate in the next chapter. The task-oriented nature of producing things (things, goods, and utensils more than commodities) means that labor is expended without the necessity of counting it—it benefits the whole group, the family or family firm—the household that extends to the imperial household and to cosmic order. The spirits that represent this collective unity, this collective unity to which labor is sacrificed, become the objects of veneration of votive offerings and sacrifices—ancestors, occupational and other deities. The "exploitation" necessary to create material value is thus mystified within the primordial bonds that form the work unit and its external connections to the tributary and market regimes of value or its expression in a highly developed feudal formation.

Modern Times

The main purpose of my book is to describe how the thousand-year-old paper money custom is not only a thing of the past but a thing of resurgent popularity all around China, and of special significance (to me) in those areas that experienced the radical iconoclasm of Mao's revolution. In one important sense, China, at least the China I have always known, *is its past;* even during the Mao years it seemed, paradoxically, to be refreshingly old-fashioned. Only in the recent decade have I sensed some irreparable monstrous crack in that edifice as the brick-walled lanes and alleyways (*hútòng*) of Beijing have been buried under skyscrapers of steel and glass. During the periods when the paper money custom was under official interdiction, even during the Mao years, its vibrancy was only dampened—the interdictions only made its practice furtive; they did not end the custom or even modify the custom. But in recent decades, with the penetration of global capital, the paper money custom has revived and significantly modified its forms (see chapters 8 and 9). Capitalism is far more destructive of sacred traditions and the authenticity of things than is socialism (or what briefly passed for socialism in the twentieth century).

For as it turns out, the Maoist revolution had the unintended consequence of revolutionizing the old feudal mode of production only to prepare the ground for and reconnect with the formation of world capital. Like the sixteenth-century Calvinists in Europe, the Maoists in China served as the "vanishing mediator" (Jameson 1988) between the old and new orders. Where the Calvinists reconstituted the Roman monastic ascetic order in everyman's daily life, the communists reconstituted the old imperial order to quicken the flow of capital by eliminating the nonproductive embodiments of the old patronage system (landlords and old official classes managing merchant capital) and redirecting much of the "surplus" into modern (state-managed) capital and industrial enterprises. As it turns out, Liu Shaoqi's "poisonous weed" *How to Be a Good Communist,* which said that one became a good communist by appreciating the work ethic of the idealized Confucian official, was right on the mark! Here is the vanishing mediator! (The "vanishing" is graphically illustrated in some of the ghost bills in chapter 8.) In this case, Liu became the sacrificial scapegoat. In effect the communists, under the myth of "building socialism," married the feudal mode of production to the capitalist drive to accumulate, invest, and expand, coupled with the attempt to wipe out the system of petty production by elevating petty producers into proletarians (rural and urban) and replacing old officials with cadres who understood how, once released from feudal shackles, indigenous productive forces could ripen those Ming and Qing dynasty "capitalist sprouts." With the disappearance and apotheosis of Mao after 1976, world capital finally flooded into China, mainly in search of cheap unorganized but state-disciplined industrial labor. At the same time, the state (and collective enterprises) increasingly relinquished control over indigenous and collective capital to private entrepreneurship. Entrepreneurs became clients of state officials (Wank 1999:11) in ways that replicated the old order of treading a fine line between patronage and bribery. "Continuities between socialist policies and past practices are indeed striking," observed Mann (1987:210) in reference to the way "socialist marketing, like Confucian marketing, seeks to serve a public good, not merchant profits" (Mann 1987:210). But there is one big difference between this new order and the old: capital now flows into *commodity production* (and not just agrarian) on a petty and a grand scale.

Where direct interdiction of "feudal customs" under Mao's vanishing mediation had only a short-term success, it seems that the new capitalist formation is having a longer-lasting impact insofar as it has prompted the paper money custom to adapt in ways that place the older ritual mystifications in contention with newer ideological reifications. The most obvious manifestation of this synthesis, or mutation—this reified form of modern paper currencies—is in the form of ghost bills (*guǐpiào*). These are facsimiles of modern bank and treasury bills, with their "big face values" and "small face values" that signify the encompassing system of commodity exchange (the subject of chapters 8 and 9).

Conclusion

Anthropologists laboring under neoclassical assumptions (Skinner 1964, 1977), and even some neo-Marxist concepts (Gates 1996), have emphasized a centrifugal peasant world based on a market economy, with its capitalist contraries reflected in ideologies like the paper money custom. This chapter reorients these earlier pathbreaking works toward a process of reproduction that binds a mode of production to its historical formation. I argue that the paper money custom was a mode of reproduction etched deeply in a highly developed and successful feudal mode of production. This mode of reproduction is ritual with its function to mystify the lifeworld of common folks in the cosmology of the imperial project (i.e., civilization). In other words, burning money was the common folks' way of participating in the mysteries and enchantments of the cosmic-based imperial order that ruled their lives.

From its antiquity and down through the dynastic period, China used money, even coins, for purposes of circulating goods; but at the level of production and reproduction those (mostly agrarian) goods were not, in the substantive sense, commodities. They were valued for their good as subsistence, patronage, and trade in local bazaars for other useful goods. The goods of petty production assumed the form of "commodities" in their orbits of commercial circulation only to the extent that they are now seen (i.e., largely in today's economic terms) apart from their moment of production. For their part, Chinese imperial order also separated production from exchange, but on moralistic grounds, completely opposite to the capitalist grounds of utility. Imperial order did this by placing a higher moral value on productive labor, which it defined as growing food, than the work of buying and selling things. From my perspective, I see the whole process, from producing goods for circulation through the local and regional bazaars and up through imperial milking posts and elsewhere, as the "cash nexus" of a social economy in which the chrematistic and the ceremonial were intertwined, even sublated and discursively reproduced in ritual commerce with the world of spirits. But this commerce was less about dickering with spirits and more about obligatory patronage in the form of a potlatch for the spirits.

As such, the paper money custom was the active dramatization of sacrifice that participants were fully capable of "seeing as such." The ritual of burning money helped to enthrall the people in the imperial project and its cosmic design. It was a perfect expression of this order, but it was obligatory ritual, not ideological belief. In other words, the paper money custom is more about a ritual act, a mystification of what is immanently human. It is not a Western-style belief system that poses a reified world at war with itself over a *nature* constituted in positive realities (ideology) versus a *supernature* that requires a leap of faith (religion). Ritual, which is highly self-referential (or self-producing), addresses the mode of exploitation by dramatizing it in material symbols, while ideology reifies or naturalizes the mode of exploitation by making it disappear in the discourse of a quasi-science, economic science: for example, the *fairness* of wages, the *freedom* to sell labor power, the *autonomy* of the individual. Each kind of myth is lived at a different level of conscious activity (ideological versus ritual practice).

In pursuing this thesis, I argue that the technical and social processes of production were realized in a complex and dynamic bureaucratic feudal mode that was not transformational—it was slow to let the forces of production outpace the relations of production. It even seems as if *the social relations of production were so powerful that they held the technical forces of production in check—this is the key to understanding the human-centered, agrarian-based Chinese civilization.* China's feudal mode of production was a complex of differentiated and interdependent labor regimes. The interdependency was the Chinese dialectic of *yīnyáng,* which neither Hegel nor Marx appreciated because it perpetuated (reproduced) form without transforming substance. And this is precisely how devotees imagine the world-relationship between the embodied and the disembodied as it is mediated by the *authenticity* of a human artifice that Chinese call paper money.

Although the historical materialist paradigm, which allows the feudal mode of production a greater share of historical development than is accorded to it by the European experience, provides a compelling explanation, we should not stop here. Paper money not only reflects a dialectical unity in the forces and relations of production; it is a tenacious and widespread cultural formation rooted in the commonsense lifeworld, that is, the natural attitude that takes things just as they appear to be (Husserl 1962). It is in the structure of consciousness that common sense and magic cohere in ways that led Malinowski (1958:90) to wonder how we might discover where one ends and the other begins. My aim in the next chapter is to delve into this chiasm of the lifeworld where common sense coincides with magic by suspending the preconceived suppositions about paper money, the suppositions of observers and devotees alike, in order to see how those suppositions constitute the objective formation of paper money by the way it is handled in acts of consecration. We thus move in a dialectical manner from the macrocosm of history to the microcosm of experience. More specifically, we move from the modes of production and reproduction to a mode of being that replicates value in acts of sacrifice.

CHAPTER 6

Sacrifice

> The essential act possesses a name. Its name is sacrifice. . . . It is the
> gift to the being of which one forms part.
> —Antoine de Saint-Exupéry, *Airman's Odyssey*

When things of worldly value are willfully destroyed—immolated—in ritual fire or by some less dramatic medium, it is widely regarded as a sacrifice. There are other definitive elements of sacrifice, but complete immolation requires the fewest qualifications. Of the three offerings in the common ritual service (incense, food, paper), paper is the only part that is a sacrifice in this unqualified sense, for it is completely immolated. Devotees are acutely conscious of the need for its *complete* immolation. If incense is the overall signifier of the ritual service, and the food offering signifies the purpose, the reunion of the spirits of the living and dead, then paper money signifies the sacrifice. On the face of it, this seems corny. How can we call burning paper replicas a sacrifice? In this chapter I make the case, and in so doing I argue that the sacrifice of paper replicas of valuable things becomes the keystone in the canonical structure (chapter 5) and historical function (chapter 6) by the way it structures the lifeworld in acts of valuation: consecration and consummation.

Ritual burning can be, and often is, conducted in a manner that appears entirely perfunctory—supplicants hunkered down on one knee, or standing around, nonchalantly feeding a fire with handfuls of paper notes, poking around in the burning embers with a stick . . . This, indeed, is one of the connotations of the term "ritual," that is, going through a stereotyped motion with little sense of conviction or meaning. This is not the place to address the anthropology of ritual—I leave the reader to the magisterial work of the late Roy Rappaport (1999), which augments much of my own thinking on these matters.

One of Rappaport's insights is the extent to which ritual is self-referencing because it is a public act that undertakes an obligation; and in Rappaport's anthropology, upholding obligation is the one moral sensibility that finds universal acclaim. Anthropologically, we could say upholding an obligation is The One Commandment. It follows from this that the self-referencing, obligatory nature of ritual action is one form of self-actualization or perhaps, in a stronger materialist sense, self-production (Sangren 2000); it is this material-mediated obligation-driven interaction with others in which people find, experience, and re-create their selves. Here the works of Marcel Mauss take hold and the rhetorical power of Saint-Exupéry resonantly expresses a truth that Chinese can relate to: "It is in your act that you exist, not in your body. . . . It is an everyday fact. It is a commonplace truth. . . . When the body sinks into death, the essence of man is revealed. Man is a knot, a web, a mesh into which relationships are tied. Only those relationships matter" (Saint-Exupéry 1984:387–389); and to the extent that only those relationships matter, they are the stuff of obligation and sacrifice.

On Sacrifice

If we go back to the common ritual service (chapter 4) in which paper money is one of the phases in the ritual process, we can see that it is the part of the offering that undergoes *complete* immolation by fire. This contrasts with the animal, vegetal, and liquid offerings, which in the case of livestock are usually presented as postmortem carcasses and undergo commensal comestion rather than destructive immolation—the spirits get the life of the animal, while the people who raised or paid for it get the leftovers, the flesh. Although attempts to define sacrifice beyond any particular ritual formation are noteworthy for their failure to establish universals, most classicist accounts, East and West, agree that killing and immolating animal or vegetal life for benefits that are not ostensibly utilitarian constitutes a sacrifice (Hubert and Mauss 1964; Hamerton-Kelly 1987). Another attribute is feasting on the body and life of that which is sacrificed in a communion of the embodied and the disembodied participants (Smith 1957; Burkert 1987). Extending this notion of commensal communion, some propose that sacrifice is itself a cuisine (Malamoud 1996)—a cuisine, others add, that is shot through with political significance (Détienne and Vernant 1989), a pointed example of which is the commensal politics of the Chinese festive table, especially when it offers the seat at the head of the table to the member who is to receive the honor of being expelled or otherwise cut off (Girard 1987) (see chapter 4, n. 10). The notion that sacrifice entails giving up a part of oneself for the benefit of another part of oneself, or for the whole of what one is part of, seems basic to me—it's why I use the words of Saint-Exupéry as the epigraph for this chapter. This includes giving up parts of one's body (as in footbinding and other sanguinary acts of self-sacrifice) and beings and things into which one has invested his or her own being. Too little attention has been given to the process of preparing or consecrating the part of oneself that is to be given to the larger body. This is the question I attempted to address in my article on footbinding (Blake 1994) when I shifted the age-old diatribe from footbinding's reputed attributes as sexual exotica (Yao 1941; Levy 1967; Ko 2005) to an underlying process in which a mother prepared her daughter for her fate in a world authored by men. Such forms of human immolation and mortification entail the phenomenology of willing (Pfänder 1967; Ricoeur 1966), which is what makes the act seem so horrifyingly sublime. As we move to infrahuman animal sacrifice and on to the sacrifice of precious things and replicas thereof, the "will" is increasingly imparted by the persons on whose part the sacrifice is made.

The paper money custom, for its part, is an acutely conscious recognition that the quotidian world is an artifice, layers of folded, fragrant papers, that becomes real only when the artifice is transposed to the yīn-world of the unseen. The problem is that the paper is only a replica of treasured things, not itself a treasure in any worldly sense. Added to this is the fact that these replicas are not live beings, and to the extent that they have been machined and exchanged as goods or commodities (i.e., utilities for real cash), they are either deadened to the world of authentic artifice or made to look ridiculous under the modern looking glass. Except for the fact that they are domesticated things, man-made things, which is to say, "an integral part of man's own world, [thus] interchangeable with him" (Heesterman 1993:9), they are a long way from being worthy sacraments. As such, the paper destined for destructive immolation is made ready by a series of consecrations that realize its "use value" by turning its "exchange value" and "sign value" (Baudrillard 1981) into "spiritual value." Here, perhaps, we can appreciate Arjun Appadurai's (1986) conceptualization of things moving from one regime of value to another and changing their nature in the process. Once fit for immolation, the paper monies are restored to cosmic circulation via the fiery mediator of the visible and invisible. Most of the rest of this chapter details various aspects of the consecration process that ends in a true sacrifice, although not one that requires blood.

Chinese on Sacrifice

The idea that the custom of burning paper replicas entails a "sacrifice" must strike most readers as a stretch. I'll try to make it less so. I begin by examining some of the Chinese terms and concepts for sacrifice. Let us first consider a commonplace offering:

> In 1995 I accompanied a friend and his sister to their mother's grave mound in their mother's native village in rural Hebei. My friend's mother's brother's wife had always prepared the bundle (*bāofu*) for her nephew and niece to offer to their mother in the nearby burial ground; she would also add one bundle each for her husband's other departed relatives. The bundle is conventionally a parcel of goods wrapped in cloth to carry on a trip, but here it is a bundle of paper monies wrapped in coarse unbleached, yellowish-brown paper. The word *bāofu* also carries the connotation of "burden" in the sense of an obligation. The unspoken presumption here is that by burning a *bāofu* for one's parent, one may experience the lifting of a weight on the conscience. On the day that we three arrived, the auntie saw her nephew pull a little pack of olive-green notes labeled "Hell Bank Note" from his knapsack. He had brought them from Honolulu— like coals to Newcastle, I thought to myself; never mind that the notes were manufactured in Hong Kong—they bore a canny resemblance to American treasury notes and are in fact referred to as *Měijīn* (American money). The auntie recognized the notes but didn't say anything that I was aware of. She sent her daughter to a nearby shop to purchase big rolls of coarse, yellowish-brown paper, then herself folded and cut this paper to resemble old-fashioned strings of cash. When we finally located the mother's mound (it was unmarked), my friend got down on one knee and, with his cigarette lighter, kindled a little fire of Hell Bank Notes inside the circle that his auntie told him to scratch in the earth. Handing the notes, a few at a time to kindle the fire, he called upon his mother in a quiet rhythmic monotone. Afterward the auntie added the heap of cut yellow papers in a great bonfire.

Since the notes are facsimiles with face values of modern paper currency and therefore are definitely countable, my friend peeled them off with a cadence that resembled counting, although he was conspicuously not counting, for he peeled a few at a time to kindle the flame, and his cadence was realized in calling his mother over and over in a quiet rhythmic monotone. Each utterance was given a tangible value that could be burned to the other side. His manner reminded me more of how Iroquois chiefs used wampum to give tangible weight to the spoken word. Also called "words," the belts of wampum would often be laid down one after the other "as the material embodiment of their arguments" (Graeber 2001:125). Obviously not a purchase or a payment, peeling off the notes was more like the sort of act conveyed by words such as *gòngyǎng* or *shànggòng* (to make offerings, to provide for one's elders). His offering was a simple gesture, but it was conducted in the spirit of the uncounted or uncountable largesse that most offerings evoke, and just to put an exclamation point on it in the form of a bonfire, the auntie added the big pile of authentic paper money that she had prepared on behalf of her side of the family.

Burning an uncountable largesse to the other side, especially when it is done in the context of the whole nine yards of ritual service, smacks of sacrifice. Here the word *jì* is considered appropriate. The graph for *jì* compounds the three graphs for animal flesh, hand, and altar: the flesh of an animal is laid by the hand upon the altar. The animal flesh is thus displayed to the spirits that they may partake of its life force.[1] The signification of the hand seems significant because it plays such an important part in the animal sacrifices of other peoples. Although the hand in the Chinese graph lays upon the altar already-killed flesh, it nonetheless reminds us of ancient Hebraic rites that included placing a hand on the victim before its immolation, that is, "the laying on of hands" by which ancient Hebrews, along with other ancient people and certain Nilotic people of recent times, consecrated their blood offerings.[2] Perhaps the parallel for this in the Chinese Grand Sacrifice is the special ritual of "viewing the victim," in which the emperor and other ritual specialists inspected the livestock and witnessed its slaughter (Zito 1997:158).[3]

For the common service, however, "the laying on of hands" seems relevant to the way Chinese handle the papers before offering them. I have become ever more aware of this phenomenon while watching countless persons, mostly women working with their hands to maximize the display of their paper treasures. For example, at the Wong Tai Sin temple in Hong Kong women constantly fidget, adjust, and reassemble their ensembles of paper, up to the point of final presentation. Here, for example, one woman gently jiggles and tugs a corner of the red-colored Noble Benefactor Charm to give it more visibility around the edge of the glittering Big Longevity Gold papers folded into First Treasures. This continuous finessing of the papers was to maximize the communicative effect of this feast of light on the great spirit and also on those standing by. But I think fingering the papers accomplished an even more implicit purpose: to impart something of the devotee's self into that chiasm of red-framed golden light.

Once a foreigner who worked in Taipei asked me why her neighbors felt it was so important to touch the paper money before offering it: as she put it, they take several sheaves and bend them back and forth and flutter them, letting each leaf touch the hand. Of course we can see bank clerks doing similar behaviors in order to count the bills. But similar behaviors may have different, even opposite meanings. People fluttering paper money before offering it do not count the leaves. When pressed to explain what they are doing, they usually respond quite rationally, "Well, of course, separating the bundle of leaves so they will burn easier."

This explains the fluttering but not the touching. For those who might reflect on the touching, there is the rational, often explicit concern with imparting the identity of the sender. In other words, there are explicit rationales and conveniences to the ritual of touching the paper with eyes and hands—of laying hands on the paper—before immolating it. This concern with efficiency and identity is affirmed in the occasional practice of including with the paper bundles personal body parts (nail or hair clippings) or, more often, written inscriptions (names and addresses of senders) on the offering bundle. But this only reinforces the inference that touching or rubbing the paper offerings intends such an identification. In any case, what it means to impart a personal identity by touching the paper is more than meets the eye, for in many instances there is a certain exuberance in the handling of paper money pending its immolation.

Before entering the Chaozhou section of a rural Hong Kong cemetery during the Double Nine Festival,[4] a portly middle-aged man with all the phenotypical and sartorial marks of a prosperous lifestyle burned an impressive array of paper materials in the furnace of the tutelary spirit. The array included facsimiles of paper notes or ghost bills, the largest and most colorful banknotes available at the time. What was so striking was how absorbed the man was in the business at hand (while the other four members of his entourage, three young men wielding sickles and an adolescent, sat waiting).

After removing the cellophane wrapper, the man fluttered the pack of notes a few times; then holding the pack in his left palm, he pressed the fist of his right hand onto the center of the pack and, with several quick and audible motions, twisted his fist clockwise, thus fanning the paper notes into a pet-alled disk before casting it into the furnace. At the time, I was struck with how audible, protracted, and determined his handling of the papers seemed. From the notes I made later that day:

> He was absorbed in what he was doing. He never straightened from a stoop, which made his concentration more obvious. He took a stick and poked around in the furnace to make sure every last scrap was burned. Immediately after this, still slightly bent in concentration, he walked over to where the adolescent boy handed him an armload of bright red packages and boxes with lots of gold shining through cellophane windows. Back at the furnace, he tore open the packages and boxes to deposit their contents into the furnace, after "caressing" each deposit with his fingers.

In preparing papers for the flames, there is often more handling of the paper than is necessary just to cast them on the flame or to ensure their com-plete immolation. Once again, if asked to explain their practices, people fre-quently offer a perfectly utilitarian explanation: that they are merely making sure the papers will burn completely. But my impression is that the handling often exceeds the utility of ensuring a complete oxidation, which in any case can be accomplished by a stick to stir the embers, although some devotees will point out that using a stick to stir the embers is not propitious—it actu-ally destroys the identity of the sender! This reasoning is based on a rule of the common liturgy that is also conveyed in folktales.[5] Not all devotees are aware of this rule; the man burning paper at the Chaozhou tutelary shrine had no qualms about using a stick to stir the burning embers after making such a to-do of pressing and fanning the paper notes. And the work he put into pressing and fanning the papers seemed more than merely utilitarian, more than was needed to work air molecules in between the surfaces of the leaves. I think it is fair to infer that he was preparing the papers, presenting the papers, exhibiting the papers, identifying the papers' sender, perhaps we could say *consecrating* the papers before immolating them.

Under the pressure of this man's hands, the papers, having lost their exchange value in the act of purchase were, in effect, recovering their "use value" (albeit a nonutilitarian use value) by intensifying their sensual value in the form of a sacrament. The process of consecration, which included restoring and intensifying the sensual value of the papers by handling and exhibiting them before the flames, aimed at an even more elementary kind of transition: with a restoration of sensual value, they were changing from a visible purchased good to an otherworldly, invisible treasure with spiritual value, or, in other words, from a good to a sacrament to eternal value. In some sense, consecration involves *restoring* the paper to its essential (i.e., sensual) nature so that it can become the vehicle for transmitting a more original, essential, transcendental value (in Platonic and Husserlian terms, a monetary *eidos*): touching the paper in determined ways reinvests the paper with the sensualness of its materiality. This in turn invests the paper with its combustibility (a critical concern of most devotees), with its capacity to communicate value by the process of dematerialization, a process comparable to the abstraction entailed in the exchange value of goods, but in this case, a "changing value" in its most literal sense—changing the mode of valuation—in the sheer dematerialization and seeming disappearance and transmutation of the good. By touching, pressing, twisting the papers, in effect by laying hands on the papers, the man beatifying the shrine of the tutelary spirit worked something of himself into the offering. That "something" that goes behind, suspends, or exceeds "cultural meanings" becomes more apparent in the work of folding, which I take up presently.

Mindful-Body Work

This direct apprehension of the materials generally escapes consideration of conventional materialist and structuralist explanations (as per the two preceding chapters). The direct apprehension of the materials perceives and experiences the sensual qualities of the materials in shaping them and preparing them for their departure from the visible world. This is the moment when the papers lose their commodity or exchange value as mere things or utilities and become a sensual, transcendent value in the donor's hands. Here sensual value is more than sheer positive sensation or nervous stimulation that is passively received by "the sense organs" when handling the papers. It is this, to be sure, but more. Handling is part of a holistic configuration of visual, tactile, olfactory, and acoustical experience that is made acutely manifest in the ritual service. In his last work, *The Visible and the Invisible,* Merleau-Ponty (1968) moved away from the phenomenological conventions of perceiving the intended object in the solipsism of individual experience toward an ontology, or chiasm, of the flesh, a concept that I believe befits the material spirit of a traditional Chinese lifeworld. In chapter 1 of the present work, I mused on how the chiasm of flesh might help us to grasp the nature of the papery partition that in traditional Chinese thinking divides and joins (crisscrosses) the world in its two (*yīnyáng*) cosmological phases. One of the ways Merleau-Ponty (1968:139) conveyed this notion of the chiasm of the flesh was by assimilating it to the ancient (Greek) concept of the "elements." In my view, the flesh is even more assimilable to the (Chinese) cosmology of five phases (*wǔxíng*). In chapter 4, I invoked the five-phase cosmology as an analogue of the five-phase ritual service, where each phase sublimates an element of human experience or psyche that makes the world sensible and visible.

Now we are at the point in the process where one of those phases, the paper phase, is being consecrated for the ultimate sacrifice by the folding of the paper into vessels of ultimate or spiritual value. Here again, Merleau-Ponty's ontology of the flesh helps us to appreciate this experience because this is where the tedious work of folding the paper into round objects, into complete vessels, into whole worlds, comes closest to some level of experiencing the ontology of the world in its intertwining, its flesh, its material spirit—the crisscrossing of the paper in its sheer materiality with that of the sensate body. Or, to paraphrase George Eliot (1913:69), like all objects to which a woman devotes herself, they fashion her into correspondence with themselves: the natural vegetal colors against the shine of silver stannous or glittering gold or radiant red dye that light the eyes in spectrums of festive colors, the supple coarseness, the soft resistance against the vibrating skin of flexing fingers, the woody resins that inspire with each inhalation a new lease on life, the internal cadence of a murmured or whispered or imagined sutra or other *rhythmic* sound-sign that gives the outer tedium "a world of cheerful work" (*Die Welt der fröhlichen Arbeit*), as Karl Bücher proposed in *Arbeit und Rhythmus* (1919:475). Folding paper vessels turns the tedium of work into a sensuousness of sheer materiality, of combustibility, of transmutability, of transcendence, that corresponds with the vessel (the mindful body) of the folder herself. The work of folding is a way of being-in-the-world, of being-beyond-the-world, and of being-of-the-world. The question of how it does this takes us back to the anthropology of ritual work and the work of ritual.

This immeasurable value in relation to bodily exertion or work is captured in the Chinese term *huó,* which refers to life, living, livelihood, and work. The semantic network evoked in the term *huó* suggests that life is work. In

this sense, the exertions and strivings of the mindful body are aimed at sustaining and reproducing a lifeworld. Mindful-body work produces value that
is different from "surplus value," measured more in quality than in quantity,
and tends to be creative, self-actualizing, and self-producing. Mindful-body
work includes many kinds of *quality work:* the work of childbearing (literally,
the "production of life"); in an earlier period, the work of binding feet; always
the work of wrapping New Year's dumplings; or wrapping a bundle (*bāofu*) to
take on a journey, which in paper connotes the burden undertaken to support
and provide for family spirits, work that is contiguous with the work of folding paper treasures (*dié yuánbǎo*). I choose these forms of mindful-body work
because each shapes an important vessel of the Chinese lifeworld. The work
of birthing and binding feet belongs completely to women. Phenomenologically, birthing and binding mirror each other as they entail the unwrapping
and wrapping of living human flesh. The flesh that is unwrapped (the organ
of reproductive labor, the gestating womb) separates from itself and makes
visible to the world the child, who upon surrender to the masculine world
of names becomes the means of male immortality, in the Chinese scheme of
things. The flesh that was wrapped, the organ of tractable labor (the foot),
was confined and secreted and thus separated from the visible world, where
it became the mysterious object of male desire and female control under a
matriarchy of the muted. The matriarchy of the muted was the binder's inner
mode of being-in/beyond/of-the-world, constituted in a mother-daughter
pedagogy (Blake 1994). The phallus in the organ of tractable labor (the principle of masculine control) was the great mystery, forever hidden, implicit,
and unreal, obviously an artifice of feminine, aesthetic, ritual practice, and
social reproduction. As each mode of work progresses to the point of consummation, to the final product, it is never quite finished. The consciousness of
striving is protracted as it suffuses the pain and suffering in a discipline.

Wrapping dumplings and folding *yuánbǎo* works on extrasomatic objects
but still belongs primarily, although now not exclusively, to women. Wrapping dumplings shares with wrapping feet the confinement of a piece of
once-sensuous flesh, which in the customary dumplings is dead pig flesh and
in the foot is withering human flesh. This connection can be appreciated in
the simile of pig flesh as female fertility.[6] But the work of wrapping human
flesh and pig flesh is altogether different insofar as wrapping human flesh
is the *hidden* uterine practice by which a mother and daughter forge a transcendent relationship inside, and hidden from, the visible patriarchal order
it reproduces; while wrapping dumplings is the essence of social conviviality

and commensality (Watson 1987:398 n. 18; Stafford 2000:101). If wrapping feet and wrapping dumplings confines tangible material substances, then wrapping or folding paper vessels confines pockets of intangible stuff. What that stuff is, is the principal mystery of this chapter. What it is, is comparable to the stuff that is bound under the small shoe. Feet bound in cloth and ingots of folded paper are comparable in the sense that both produce vessels that have no utility—one holds atrophied flesh, and the other holds *nothing* but dead air, yet both signify *by virtue of their outer wrap* that which is immanent (*there* but can't be seen), arbitrary (whatever anyone cares to imagine it as), and generative: like the root of the water lily in the muck and mire of pond bottoms, it brings forth a living thing of beauty and even of immortality; hence the euphemism of the golden lilies for bound feet, and in a similar sense, the folded treasures of gold (*yuánbǎo*) encloses that which brings forth fire, the element of transformation from impurities to purities and thus immortality.

When asked, "Why fold?" many persons fall back on the utility of facilitating combustion of the paper and thus imply that what they are wrapping is, in fact, air. Some express discomfort with any other explanation. The perfunctory, sometimes annoyed tone of the speaker's voice could just as easily be in response to the question "Why wrap dumplings?"—obviously it is to facilitate retention of the juices. Of course a moment's reflection tells us that the wrapped dumpling must be completely sealed, while the seal on the folded paper is hardly airtight, although a really well folded *yuánbǎo* seems airtight, and such perfection in appearances is considered necessary by many devotees, because what is concealed inside is more than molecules of air—even more than the breath of life. When we look closely at the work of folding the paper, we realize that there must be more to the explanation than utility, for the whole point (of the consecration) is to dispel utility to manifest a transcendent meaning. We discussed in a previous chapter how an apparent rationalization on the part of devotees may index the structural meaning of offerings. In this chapter, I continue this line of reasoning to show how a simple rationalization based on utility may express the deeper or implicit material spirit of experienced reality. Here, for example, the reference to combustibility covers more than the sheer physicality of increasing air molecules. Combustibility includes the notion of revaluation, transmutation, and transcendence.

Having written this, I don't want to leave the impression that persons who fold these papers are oblivious to deeper, implicit meanings or unable to reflect on their own experience, much less to actually experience a deeper sense of meaning. When pressed a bit, persons doing the folding do find words, however inadequate the words may seem to them, to express their work as an act of devotion. They may not use fancy words like "consecrate" or "consummate" to describe their act of folding, but they often make the point by making it concrete—or capricious to the point of ludicrousness, which is still another level of understanding the seriousness of things. I got a taste of this one morning upon entering the Guiyuansi (Buddhist) Temple in Hanyang, Hubei. In a side chamber of the front gate, housing the Maitreya of Buddhist eschatology, I encountered four women folding yellow ceremonial paper (*huángbiǎozhǐ*) into "monks' hats" or "holy hats" (*sēngmào*) and depositing them into two giant wicker baskets (figure 6.1). They were folding the monks' hats to use in a ceremony to redeem their friend's soul from Purgatory (*chāodù*). One of the women iterated that each hat was worth "one hundred million yuan!" I took this to mean that the "price" of each hat was, for all intents and purposes, uncountable, invaluable, beyond anyone's imagination. I frankly can't remember what prompted the woman to say this, but how and

Figure 6.1 Women folding monks' hats in Hanyang Buddhist Temple

what she said invokes the mystery of folding, which occupies the rest of this chapter.

In a working-class neighborhood in Shanghai I asked a group of women who gathered (on my behalf) to discuss the paper money custom whether the paper is worth more when folded. Several women chimed in unison with a resounding "yes!" "How much more?" I queried, "I mean, compared to that unfolded piece, how much more is this folded *yuánbǎo* worth?" The women responded again in near unison, "This is hard to tell." Another echoed, "It is hard to tell the value (*jiàzhí*)," as the cacophony of voices resumed the give-and-take on techniques of folding the various kinds of *yuánbǎo,* a topic that was easier to find words for.

The notion that work is the source of value is echoed across China. One of the most explicit expressions of this as it pertains to paper money was when I asked my friend from Zunyi (Guizhou) whether the perforations made to simulate strung cash in sheets of money paper were done by machine. He adamantly replied, "No, no machine is used. . . . the people say if a machine is used, then there is no labor, and if no labor is expended, there is no respect for the divine [*shén*]. They use a mallet and punch to perforate stacks of sheets." He overstated the fact that "no machine is used," since much of the paper money that people use in his hometown is machined, but his point that paper money made by hand labor is thought to have true value (i.e., in the eyes of the spirits) is probably accurate; at least, it supports the thesis I am pursuing in this chapter. Another support comes from a less likely source at the opposite end of the socioeconomic spectrum. The big online store Taobaowang has a department selling "sacrificial paper goods." Right above the Web page display of these goods is the statement "With a little time out from everyday life, one can make these things by oneself without the need to spend a lot of money to purchase the finished product and what is more, self-made things affirm one's regard for the deceased" (Taobaowang 2010).

Social Organization of Folding

Before continuing with the connection between the work of the body and the original value that is enfolded in the paper—that is, the concrete meaning of that emptiness—let us consider the social relations in the work of folding. The vignettes cited above make us aware that practices of folding paper money entail social relations among the living. The work of folding may be done at any point before burning. From my experience I would say that the ideal conditions for folding paper money is in a cohort of devotees folding their papers in a local temple. Folding in a temple, especially when scriptures are chanted, increases the *líng* (magical efficacy or soulfulness) of the paper and augments the consecration process.

The four women folding monks' hats at the Guiyuansi [Buddhist] Temple in Hanyang worked quickly but used different routines to mark the rhythm and dispel the monotony. Three of them completed the whole hat with each leaf of yellow paper they picked up, flicking the completed hat into the basket in front of them, while the other, seated at the second basket, folded her hats in two stages. She made the initial folds on a leaf of paper, put it aside until she had a bunch of partially folded leaves, then came back to each to complete its folding.

At the Wenshuyuan (Buddhist) temple in Chengdu (Sichuan), four friends labored in common on each ensemble of folded papers. The four women were sitting at a square table amid persons sitting at other tables drinking mid-morning tea, talking, socializing. One woman separated yellow "boundary sheets" (*jièdān*)—this is a golden charm with an incantation printed on it— and handed each sheet directly across the table to the second woman. The second woman took several leaves of unbleached "white paper money" (*bái zhǐqián*)—the silver money—to place between the leaves of the gold charm, upon which she wrote, in the indicated spaces in the text, the name of the deceased and the address and name of the wife who was doing the rite of transition out of purgatory (*chāodù*). The third woman was sitting next to the second and pulling pieces of the white paper money apart and handing them to her friend directly across the table. This fourth woman folded several sheets of the silver money into the gold charm as we do when we fold a letter to fit an envelope. When I asked what she called these folded packets, she merely replied that the fold must have the red seal of the gold charm (*jièdān*) on the top so it is visible to the receiver. The folded packets were flat like envelopes (not puffy and full of air), and after about ten were made, the fourth women stacked them in a pile. The logic of this ensemble is clear: the golden envelope was the means by which the living sent the enclosed silver to the deceased via the office of the Buddha.

The little cohort of women in the old working-class village enveloped by the city of Shanghai provided evidence for how the knowledge of folding and paper money custom in general is distributed and exchanged. Seven matronly women assembled for my benefit to discuss the paper money custom. The youngest of them was the no-nonsense local party secretary and her assistant.[7] We repaired to the cottage of the oldest woman, whom the others addressed as Auntie (mother's sister) and looked to as the font of knowledge. Although deference was paid to what Auntie said and her paper folds were verbally admired for their aesthetic qualities, all of the women engaged with more or less equal fervor the topic of folding. The cacophony of voices, enveloped in indexical expressions of local vernacular and knowhow, flowed over me and beyond my immediate grasp as every member of the cohort tried to learn, query, or tell the others something of what they knew, never learned, or had forgotten about folding. Most of their discussion was around the techniques of folding different styles of vessels, referred to as First Treasure (*yuánbǎo*) or ingot (*dìngzi*). The treasures these women seemed most attuned to were the relics of Buddhism: the immortal lotus, the hats of the Bodhisattvas, and the "canonical treasure" (*zhèngzōng yuánbǎo*). The last, with its gold-tinted top and solid-looking center, is for placing in front of the Bodhisattva, whereas the others, of "silver," are burned for the deceased (figure 6.2).

That was in 2000. In 2009 I was surfing Liba.com,[8] which proclaims itself to be the biggest virtual community in China, posting about twenty thousand messages per day, when I came upon an individual (*Linsiting* 2008) identified by a picture of a pet dog and tagged as a "foreigner," who asked, "Does anyone know how to fold tin laminated paper, in particular, the 'silver trunk' (*yínxiāng*), which is square shaped and uses 21 pieces of tinfoiled paper?" The question received 240 responses, including an early correction that the silver trunk is really the square pavilion (*fāngtíng*). As I read this,

Figure 6.2 Folded stannous papers from Shanghai

I wondered whether this was the same object that the cohort of working women nine years ago referred to as square ingots (*fāngdìng*) that are fastened together to form the immortal lotus. The traffic on this virtual community gave me a feeing of déjà vu in the way its participants brought a potpourri of memories, of certitudes, of quips, some with a comic air, some regretful that granny was no longer around to impart her knowhow on the matter of folding and maximizing the value of the treasures thus made. One participant added a point I have not heard elsewhere: that the folded papers made by children are worth more than ones made by adults.[9]

Back with the cohort of working women in 2000, Auntie took meticulous care to hide the corner folds of her *yuánbǎo* so it would be perfect, a sign of purity, for otherwise, she warned, it is worth nothing. Then there were the simple gold bars (*jīntiáo*): soft yellow paper rolled into a tube with ends indented to keep the shape. These are burned for the dead and are popular among rural folks—"a very useful method of folding," declared one woman. As the discussion turned to charms that repel evil, someone noted that the leaf of red paper that tops the pile of a hundred stannous laminated papers (*xībó*) is thrown into the offering fire of silver *yuánbǎo*. But why? the party secretary wondered: "When I buy *xībó*, there is always a red paper on top; my grandma just lights the fire and throws it into the fire. I do not know what it means." "Oh! to drive away demons!" said the others: it prevents other ghosts from snatching the money you intend for your own family members. The business of assuring good fortune, which is the same as keeping the family productive and prosperous, and which always includes its deceased members, depends on keeping demonic forces, personified as thieves or something worse, at bay. Implicit here is the importance of *yáng* (the lighted side, the shining side, the sunny side, the mirrored reflections of metallic surfaces, lamplight, and candle flames), which always dispels the darkness and lurking evil. This is also accomplished by incanting paper monies with spoken or printed words (scriptures) that manifest the light. The women talk about the pay-for-passage scripture (*jiào guān jīng*) that shines a lamp in the dark and the seven stars scripture (*qīxīng jīng*) that is chanted into lamp (wick) grass (*dēngcǎo*) that can be got from the temple and kept in a clean bag. It can also enchant the ghost bills by means of physical contact—Shanghai people often use the term for real banknotes (*chāopiào*) to talk about ghost bills. An old woman I encountered at an upscale suburban cemetery a few days earlier tried to sell me some simulated "banknotes" (*chāopiào*), and when I hesitated, she assured me that they had all been enchanted with scripture at the temple. (I have more to say on this encounter in chapter 8.) Suffice it to say that the cohort of working women, all of whom dismissed the facsimiles of modern banknotes as "outside" their custom, would certainly assume that for such paper facsimiles to be effective they would need the infusion of chanted scripture. In Shanghai, the paper monies are often talked about using terms for real money; but there is also an emphasis here on the necessity of having all paper monies enchanted with Buddhist scripture. Other well-heeled Shanghai persons who identified themselves as "Buddhists" were adamant that Buddhism has no necessary connection with the paper money custom. Quite true; still, it is plain to many people that the two are deeply complicit, at least to the extent that the paper money custom, especially in the Shanghai region, envelops itself in the panoply of Buddhist icons and ecclesiastical blessings.

The blessings can be gotten by visiting a Buddhist temple such as the Jade Buddha Temple in Shanghai, to which I walked one day in 2000 with a summer storm brewing. The temple was alive and vital with a service for salvation of deceased family members. Those who wanted special attention for a particular family member joined the throng in a side building, where they could fill out the proper identity forms and pay a fee of real money. In the main hall a large coterie of temple monks and their lay followers, mostly women dressed in black, chanted scripture. A host of other persons, mostly women not formally participating in the service, sat in surrounding corridors and in a smaller hall behind the main hall folding *xībó*. They were young, middle-aged, and older women sitting on folding metal chairs. There were a few males among them—a couple of young men who seemed to be dozing or small-talking, and one or two smaller boys with their mothers. All of the males were in the company of a woman or group of women who were folding silver. One young boy of five or six years was running around while his mother folded the silver, and later the kid went to sleep on two folding chairs. His mother just went on folding and folding while the monks and laypersons chanted their scripture. There was cadence and rhythm and resonance and synchrony in the chanting that somehow carried over to the individuals' folding, but how the chanting echoed through the *separate reveries* of folding bodies remained a mystery to me.

Behind the main hall was an altar for bodhisattva Guanyin where a small group of monks sat in a circle reciting scripture. Around them the women folding silver *yuánbǎo* sat in clusters of twos, threes, and fours, but the persons in each cluster seemed oblivious to the presence of others (including me) as they worked away at their task. Some placed their yet-to-be folded stacks of *xībó* on the altar to receive the benefit of whatever mystical forces flowed along that lofty place. Beyond the great hall, along the covered walkways and in every nook, there were people folding silver. Here I saw more men, middle-aged men with wives, although again it was the women who did the lion's share of the folding and kept to it without breaking their stride. Much of this folded silver, along with incense, was burned in a line of incinerators behind the main hall. The burning continued throughout the day.

Outside a temple, the cohort may work in one of its members' homes, although this is not the occasion of a typical social gathering. Less ideally, but from my experience quite common, is the person folding at home alone. Most of these devotees are women, most older women. Often a cohort of women work on their own time to accumulate boxes or baskets or bags of folded papers as a collective. These may be part of their contribution as patrons of a particular temple; the temple converts the folded papers to an exchange value when they sell it to visitors for the purpose of reconverting to an offering. Or the store of folded papers made by a cohort of devotees may be drawn on when a member of the cohort is suddenly met with a mortuary obligation, or they may work in anticipation of a festival like Qingming.

I have also encountered women, mostly, folding the paper at the point of offering in a temple, at a wake, and at a grave site (figure 6.3). Here, the work itself is most apparent to the intended recipients (and of course to others in the vicinity)—and the perennial but unanswerable question is which of the two, the otherworldly recipient or the live audience, the dramatic action is meant to impress. (Durkheimians would say the one and the other are basically the same as far as the function of the custom is concerned.) Whatever else it is, the action (according to Rappaport) is essentially self-referencing. It tells the actor who she is in terms of the obligations she willfully undertakes. In a slightly stronger sense, the action is "self-producing" (following Sangren 2000), since in the case at hand, the folder (devotee) and the folded (vessel) are mutually insinuated. A dramatic example is recorded in a note I made while visiting Wong Tai Sin temple in Hong Kong (October 30, 1999): In the crowded court fronting the main altar, one young woman kneeling very upright was folding Big Longevity Gold paper (*dà shòu jīn*), and she folded each one in the most conspicuous manner possible, holding it out in front of her to make sure the divinity could "see" and appreciate each fold that was aimed at attracting his attention. Her motions were conspicuous, labored, deliberate, concentrated, slightly exaggerated, and steadfast, and not done, as

Figure 6.3 Woman folding *yuanbao* at Wong Tai Sin Temple,
Hong Kong

I have seen in other cases, with rapid, lithesome flicks of the fingers. It was
in performing her work that her offering manifested itself to the divinity and
anyone who cared to watch, because upon completing each *yuánbǎo*, she let
it drop from her outstretched hands into a basket with such a nonchalance
that it evoked total detachment and depth of emptiness and purity, at least in
me—I can't speak for her, and I was not about to ask.

The Shape of the Object

There are numerous kinds and styles of folded paper treasures, in shapes ranging from ingots to envelopes. Folded papers give visible shape (depth and

volume) and outward expressive meaning to whatever inestimable treasure they conceal. The outer expressions are themselves signs of great value, from Buddhist relics to bars of bullion: some are widespread variations on a theme, others are more original to a region or a locale, and each to some extent is idiosyncratic to a personal style or finesse. Let me mention just two examples from different parts of Hebei.

Yu County peasants are renowned for their decorative paper cuttings (*jiǎnzhǐ*) for pasting on paper windows. They also have a unique way of folding the silver (i.e., "white") paper for ghosts (figure 6.4) and gold (i.e., "yellow") paper for divinities alluded to in chapter 2. To make a "white paper" offering, cut two pieces of rectangular white paper (about 19 by 8 cm); lay one across the other at about 45 degrees; place two pieces of silver-colored paper or foil (about 2 by 2 cm) and then another two of gold in the center; fold the outer or bottom paper in half on its long axis so the opposite corners of the inside or top paper holding the treasure form two triangular projections off the base. Then fold the base in half again on its long axis to further enfold the interior pocket that holds the treasure. Then crease or crumple the center where the two triangles come together so the fold stays together; the overall shape is a base topped by two intersecting pyramid-shaped mounds, or a hull topped by two sails—in any case, a treasure trove. The Yu County "yellow paper" for higher divines looks more like a regular envelope; but it contains the same silver and gold chips of treasure as the "white paper," only here three of each instead of two. In practice, there are people who pay scant attention to these numbers. For them the difference between the two offer-

Figure 6.4 "White paper" or "silver" from Yu County, Hebei

ings, one for ghosts and one for divinities is the color of the folded papers and the style of folds, as noted in chapter 2.

There is a lot of room for individual styles and innovations, variations on a theme. For example, while visiting a village in central Hebei, I saw a mom with her two preadolescent daughters bring a basket of tiny blue paper First Treasures (*yuánbǎo*) to the grave of her husband, their father. Each little blue ingot was hardly bigger than a joint in my finger. I'd never seen such tiny folded papers; I imagined it took some delicacy to fold them. They were indeed the handiwork and offering of the two little girls, for as the little blue treasures were ignited, a cue from the mother provoked a torrent of wailing from the two little girls, while the mother stood by; and as the fire passed its zenith, a second cue ended the wailing as abruptly as it had begun. Then the mother packed up and left with her two youngsters in tow.

We have seen that whether or not different regions prefer different kinds of treasures and papers, the knowledge of how to fold the ensembles of paper treasures seems to be readily sharable and, in fact, widely disseminated, if for no other reason than that devotees are eager to pick up the knowledge and skills to an extent that probably exceeds their interest in the paper money custom per se.

The thematic shape of much of the folded paper is the First Treasure, or *yuánbǎo*. Its generic upside-down trapezoidal shape signifies a multiplicity of vessels—the hull of a ship, a laden vessel that moves through space like a boat delivering a fortune in cargo;[10] or a shoe (especially in China), carrying the good fortune of fertility; or a crown, haloing the power to make visible, to disclose, to signify, to command. The augury of good fortune carried in *yuánbǎo* is almost as ubiquitous as the square-holed cash; often the two are collaged together in popular charms, thus combining plebian copper (money) with patrician gold (purity). Like the cash, *yuánbǎo* is a popular charm that lends its vesselled shape to every kind of kitsch, from candy to baubles hanging off rearview mirrors. Ostensibly it is derived from the Yuan dynasty silver ingot or sycee, a type of real-world money. But the term *yuán* includes the meaning of being "first," or "original," which has special relevance to how value is created in the experience of folding the paper *bǎo*. In the practice of handling and folding, the *longue durée* of the historical gives way to the intersubjective moment of the phenomenological: the "empty" space created by folding the paper into a *bǎo* changes the good or commodity of exchange value into a vessel of sensual, material (combustible), and ultimately invisible, pure, eidetic, original, or spiritual value.

Value Is the Work

Coming back to the main point of my argument, the value contained in each such object is the work of a mindful body losing itself in the work of folding. The work of folding brings into oneness the mindful subject (folder) and the object of her work (that which is folded), and the work in its unity of subject-object takes the form of a "treasure vessel." The mindful body is a "treasure vessel," as is that into which it objectifies itself, the folded paper. This is the work of mystification, mystifying the mindful vessel of body and First Treasure (*yuánbǎo*) as a spiritual treasure with all the attributes that a spiritual treasure entails, such as being emptied of worldly corruptions as it burns.

I come now to the crux of my argument, the nature of the lifeworld work and why it makes a thing of original or first value. The folded paper contains an empty space (or a volume of air molecules, which everyone comprehends as that which facilitates burning, hence transforming). But at the experiential level, the folded paper contains the work that is put into it. Except for the utility of enhancing combustibility, the work is not intended to create worldly use value, much less exchange value, and yet it is very determined: it is utterly tedious, in some sense lonely work, but also "a world of cheerful work." It is not timed work but task-oriented work—that is, the measure of the work is usually by volume (as in filling up baskets or bags); the hours or number of pieces are rarely counted. Or to put it another way, the timing is in the rhythm. In this sense, it is sensual work, pure work, the work of devotion, of sacrifice, of self-sacrifice. This is the work of a mindful body objectifying itself and subjecting itself in the shape of folded papers destined for immolation and often referred to as "First Treasure." This means a thing of inestimable value that springs from the origin of all value, *the creative power to transform, a creative power that is located in the vitality of the body (life itself) that is mindful of its moral obligations to others.* Phenomenologically, the point of the work is the work of self-sacrifice. This brings us back to our starting place, where we wondered whether paper money can be construed as a means of sacrifice in the ethnological sense of the term.

In some ways the *yuánbǎo* are a more sophisticated and truer sacrifice than what the usual blood sacrifice entails, insofar as the blood sacrifice, according to Evans-Pritchard (1967:279) and others, is ultimately a sacrifice of oneself—of one's life—by means of a substitute:[11] "What they [the Nuer] surrender are living creatures, gifts more expressive of the self and with a closer resemblance to it than inanimate things, and these living creatures are the most precious of their possessions, so much so that they can be said to participate in them to the point of identification." The Christian Eucharist follows exactly the same logic, although on a grander historical or theological scale, in which the communicants recall/embody their original human sacrifice by eating (symbols of) the sacrificed body. The Eucharist is a blood sacrifice of an unblemished victim/substitute, which in this case is not a domesticated animal, an ox or goat, but God, who has been domesticated by making himself human (in the body of Jesus). Compared to an ox or a man, the *yuánbǎo* is an inanimate vessel. But it is more than a homology of a bleeding body. It is the objectified human body in its mindful working mode. Folding paper objectifies the body not through the spilling of blood, especially the blood of a substitute, but through work—work in its purest form, work in its most original, unalienated form,[12] work that signifies humanness (*rén*) and objectifies itself in ceremony (*lǐ*).[13] According to the Potters (1990:189),

> When the Chinese wish to affirm and symbolize relationships, they must utilize symbolic forms that do not draw on emotional expressiveness, but on other means of social action. The critical symbolic dimension for the affirmation of relationships is work, and the related and subordinate concept of suffering, which is thought of as an intrinsic aspect of work. Both work and suffering are understood, not in terms of inner experience, but in terms of outward results, especially measurable ones.

Although the Potters' pronouncement on the role of inner experience and emotions in Chinese culture has been fairly critiqued (Kipnis 1997:105–108), I think their point on the signifying and objectifying nature of work in Chinese relationships describes exactly the kind of sensibility that goes into folding papers.

This is not worldly labor that produces use values for exchange with others; this is, rather, the perfection of human life in the Chinese idiom of humaneness (*rén*) and ceremonial obligation in the form of giving (*lǐ*), or what we would say is a work of devotion and sacrifice to that which one is part of. In other words, folding these gold and silver papers reflects not only the sacrifice entailed in the feudal mode of production but also the sacrifice (of the self) that is necessary for civil order to exist, the highest ideal of Confucian learning.

I think it is at this point that the phenomenological can be remarried to
the historical, the experiential, and the ritual—and thus the feudal relations
of production with the forces of production. But now we see some of the
tensions in these unions. It has to do with the way the body objectifies itself
in self-sacrifice. I think the Chinese historical formation, which is of course
in flux, facilitates certain cultural formations—that is, forms of body-objec-
tification through self-sacrifice. These have a certain aesthetic value in the
way one avows the sacrifice by hiding it in plain sight, in the form of folded
paper monies. Paper money, like footbinding, is a dramatization of the true
cost of Chinese notions of civil order. And if these dramatizations somehow
undermine the naturalness of that order, they do so in ways that also uphold
that order. That is why they are sacrifices.

Conclusion

This chapter has attempted to combine anthropology with phenomenology,
a philosophy that is not easy to reconcile with anthropology to the extent
that anthropology uses positive methods to describe a web of symbols, while
phenomenology uses an intuitive method to describe the way the phenomena thus symbolized are experienced. "To the things themselves" is how the
radical empiricism of descriptive phenomenology discloses the experiential ground of the lifeworld, a ground that is difficult for anthropology to
access. I have in mind an anthropology that theorizes how history and culture
and experience and being are sublated in a higher dialectic of explanation,
rather than, for example, merely conflated into a text that rests on its literary
merit or a practice theory that, for all its insights, models itself on the very
phenomenon that it seeks to explain.

Although still wading in the shallows of an anthropology founded on a
phenomenologically informed historical materialism, I have tried to show
how the paper money custom *allows* persons, mainly women, to make a true
sacrifice, not of paper per se, or of blood per se, but of toil per se. The element
of sacrifice in the paper money custom may be realized in the act of folding
replicas of precious metals, which I take to be a mystification of labor power
under an advanced feudal mode of production. This is different from the
modern system. In Marx's theory of modern capital, the sacrifice involved
in producing the surplus labor value gets inverted and distorted in images
of fair compensation. The sacrifice, so to speak, is hidden in the ideology of
wages. This conforms with the kind of total abstraction that a fixation on
exchange value represents, and this is reflected in a reified lifeworld of a self-

interested human nature. Exchange becomes the ideological basis of moral order and cognition. Having wedded the world of exchange value to Darwinian utility and divorced it from Platonic eros and its biblical admonitions to "lay up for yourselves treasures in heaven . . . For where your treasure is, there will your heart be also" (Matthew 6:24–25), Americans, up until now the vanguard of modernity, live in a profoundly alienated—some say schizophrenic—lifeworld, in that they inscribe their professed "trust in God" in the most mundane sign of Mammon—money. Both the commodity and the trusted *supernatural* God, whose motives are unfathomable, are abstractions; and every exchange of a commodity reifies the trust Americans profess in God. As Americans act on their ego instincts, the economic system prospers according to economic ideology of "the invisible hand," and until further notice, they assume that God, for reasons known only to him, approves.

In the traditional Chinese lifeworld, exploited labor has *represented itself in* various ritual practices that are more transparent as "sacrifices" for those domestic spirits that rule the lifeworld. I call this mystification. These more transparent forms of sacrifice are most salient and poignant in the mindful-body work of folding silver or gold papers into a First Treasure and, until sixty years ago, bending and binding feet. The work that goes into folding paper or binding feet (vessels of paper and vessels of flesh) creates an inner and outer dimension in both the intentional object and the intending subject. The outer reality of the intentional and intending vessel is given over to the sensual materiality of an aesthetic world. The inner space becomes inaccessible by virtue of the work expended on its outer form. The inner space is the result of the work; it is the result of the sacrifice; it is the sacrifice; it is the mystery. It is this "emptiness" of inaccessible interior space—the dead air of the First Treasure or atrophied flesh of small feet—that *supports* the outer visible *yáng* form, the ostensible order of the world as gold bullion or golden lilies (a euphemism for bound feet). In my mind, the historical materialist and phenomenological analyses are consummated in the way that labor power (expended in work) is the thing that is sacrificed for the sake of the paterfamilias, the foundation of imperial order (civilization) and its cosmic vitality.

CHAPTER 7

Ghost Bills

In God We Trust
  —U.S. Treasury Note

Elliot: He's a man from outer space and we're taking him to his
  spaceship.
Greg: Well, can't he just beam up?
Elliot: This is *reality,* Greg.
  —*E.T., the Extra-Terrestrial*

The adjustment of reality to the masses and of the masses to reality
  is a process of unlimited scope.
  —Walter Benjamin, "The Work of Art in the Age
  of Mechanical Reproduction"

The thing that makes ghost bills stand out from other items in the traditional corpus of paper monies is their likeness to real currencies, a mode of
representing that I refer to as simulation (less exact likeness) and facsimile
(more exact likeness). An important feature of this sameness is the absence of
a shift in medium by which the replication is effected. In the other replications of money, there is an explicit shift signified in the term itself: "paper
money," or *zhǐqián,* a metallic currency (*qián*) cast in paper (*zhǐ*)—that is, a
thin veneer of base metals glued to paper. With ghost bills, the replication is
simple simulation of one paper medium in another paper medium. Another
one of those deep ironies, ghost bills seem to defeat the conceptual power of a
"paper money"—they are a paper simulation of real money made from paper.
Thus, ghost bills appear more real than the other, older forms of paper money.

The realism extends to the terms inscribed on the ghost bills, which never include "ghost bill" (*guǐpiào*) but do commonly include *zhǐbì* (paper note), a term used for real banknotes. The exactness of the simulation thus provokes questions about realism, questions that are new to the custom.

The precision of the simulation forms a continuum from more to less exact. The more exact include facsimiles made by the most modern means of technical reproduction (Xerox machines) as well as ones made by the most primitive means of technical reproduction (contagious magic). Xerox technology and contagious magic both use real currencies to imprint or impress blank sheets of paper. The technique of impressing the image is different, of course, and the grades of paper receiving the impression are different too: Xerox paper uses a fine-grain white paper; contagious magic uses money paper, a coarse yellowish-brownish paper in which the natural straws are still tangible and visible. The Xerox leaves a visible image; the magic leaves no visible image, only an imaginary image, but infuses by hand the numinous and rarefied power of the ¥100 RMB to circulate wealth. Use of Xeroxed bills is rare: it's pricey, it flouts the law, and it requires a machine; money paper impressed by the human hand with the power of the real RMB is cheaper and has a feel for tradition and the aura of authenticity. Images that are less exact because of either technology or creative fancy are made by industrial printing processes, while the least exact images, technically and creatively, are made for local markets or social networks by simple hand-carved woodblock or soap-block prints (figure 7.1). Each way of making ghost bills has its attraction. The most colorful and widespread are the commercially manufactured ghost bills, which make up the bulk of specimens that I describe and analyze in this chapter. Rarer are carved soap or woodblocks made and used within a local or domestic social network, such as one based on kinship.

From a distance the manufactured ghost bills are hardly distinguishable from the shape, size, and formats of real-world currencies. Even up close, some ghost bills bear a remarkable resemblance to national currencies, especially the Chinese RMB and the U.S. dollar. There are instances where the real-world currencies and ghost bills are confused, switched, or mistakenly or deliberately substituted. These instances will be taken up in the next chapter. In this chapter, I describe the semiotics and use of ghost bills. At issue is the extent to which the ghost bills represent a paradigm shift in the paper money tradition. My thesis is that by adapting the paper money tradition to the forms of the modern monetary system, the ghost bills function to maintain a vestige of a charmed world in a system that is laying siege to it. Whether this

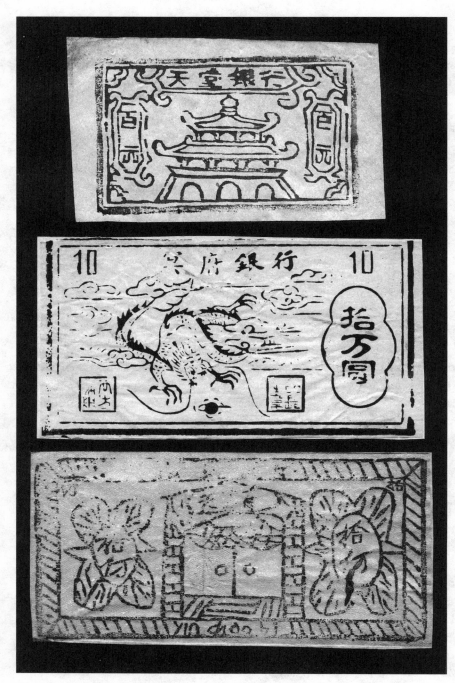

Figure 7.1 Woodblock-printed ghost bills from Hebei

adaptation, a form of cultural involution, with all of its irony and paradox, is workable in the long run or represents the last hurrah of the paper money tradition remains an open question for me.[1]

In one sense these ghost bills verge on violating a fundamental tenant of the paper money custom, which I have mentioned several times: the notion that real-world money is no good in the *yīn*-world. It is precisely this likeness to real currencies that some people find unsettling and others find humorous. Although many people, including devotees, express misgivings about the simulations of real-world paper currencies in the paper money tradition, these simulations have become popular in recent decades.

History and Diffusion of Ghost Bills

Since the paper money tradition is based on replicating every conceivable form of material wealth, I surmise that whenever that form has been represented in paper currencies, the paper money tradition has imitated it. Hou (1975:127) mentions that imitations of fiduciary money appeared in the twelfth to thirteenth centuries, although based on the evidence it is hard to say to what extent they became a permanent component of the paper money tradition. After the Yuan dynasty (1271–1368), official paper currencies were used only intermittently and therefore offered only intermittent templates to imitate. We might also note that many of the official paper currencies that were printed by the various dynasties included on the face of each note a warning that counterfeiting is a capital crime, plus a promise to reward anyone who reported a counterfeiter. Since paper was the medium for counterfeiting as well as for simulating, and to the extent that simulations effected a fair likeness of the original, the line between money meant to deceive worldly beings (a capital crime) and money meant to affirm spiritual beings (a capital virtue) was too taut with the whimsy of official interpretation to risk losing one's life over. That is also a surmise based on placing myself in the shoes of a would-be simulator. Be that as it may, the earliest report of paper money (ghost bills) simulating Western notes appears in the early nineteenth century (Hou 1975:16–17), and the first artifactual evidence for such a ghost bill is an original specimen (Hunter 1937) that was issued, according to the Chinese epigraphs on its obverse side, in May 1923 by the Official Money Bureau of the Beiping Municipal Government Ministry of Wealth. The print quality outdoes all of its successors; and if one were unable to interpret the epigrams, the bill could easily pass as either the real McCoy or a counterfeit. The reverse side is marked with English: "Ten Copper Coins."[2] Still, in one sense the real paper currencies are already "paper money," and during times of great inflation they could be used to meet obligations in the yīn-world, as apparently happened during the great inflation of the 1930s. And then again, where the production quality of real paper currencies is low, the real note could be confused with the facsimile produced for the yīn-world, as may have been the case for some "ghost bills" that have survived from the Yan'an period. Finally, a facsimile produced in 1950s Hong Kong established a pattern that is still much in use—this is the familiar "Hell Bank Note" that now lends its name to almost half of all paper facsimiles in the current corpus of ghost bills. "Hell Bank Note" is also the most common English gloss for ghost bills.

Although we do not yet know for certain to what extent the paper money tradition simulated premodern paper currencies, which were only intermittently issued by the state after the Yuan dynasty, the Chinese paper money tradition has likely simulated the modern banknotes and official treasury notes continuously since their advent in the nineteenth century. Accordingly, as the real currencies circulated in widening orbits of commercial centers, the ghost bills followed in their wake, although this process was not smooth and is still incomplete. Some places have been slow to incorporate these "Occidental" forms into the local traditions;[3] many individuals show disdain for the realism, while others take it in stride. One retired worker in Hebei, when asked why he doesn't burn ghost bills—whether they are too real—laughed and said, "None of it is real. . . . I just burn the clothes paper and copper cash out of habit. I don't believe it actually gets to the spirits." Nonetheless, as we shall see in the next chapter, the ghost bills and their countless commutations, permutations, and transmutations help scoffers make a laughingstock of the whole paper money tradition.

Ghost bills have achieved a certain notoriety in many local traditions, on the other hand, even where they might be least expected, in rural villages of central and northern China. Here people keep the old ways of making their paper offerings, either from paper made in neighborhood workshops or now increasingly from store-bought paper imported from other regions. They also make their own paper notes or ghost bills, and have been doing so for as long as people we talked to could remember (i.e., the 1950s). The process is simple: you press a real-world paper note against sheets of plain paper in a way that transfers the numinosity of the real note's exchange value to the plain paper. The reasoning behind this method is based on the logic that physical contact transfers essences. This is contagious magic (Frazer 1920:

1:174–214). This sympathetic mode of reasoning is similar to the way the same persons simulate the strings of cash by folding and cutting large rolls of paper with a scissors or punching them with a special iron tool. This practice is based on the logic that things that look alike are the same, hence, imitative magic (Frazer 1920: 1:55–174).

While many villagers make their own paper money, including ghost bills, the last ten or twenty years have seen an explosion in the volume of output and diversification in styles of manufactured paper notes. In addition to proliferation and diversification, the notes have undergone a rapid inflation in face values (as of this writing we have an $8 billion note; see figure 7.5), making what was once a sign of realism into something between surreal and hyperreal. Somewhere I read that in Taiwan, a highly inflated note was dubbed an "environmental protection paper money" because its face value obviated the need to burn so much paper. However, the inflation of face values has not checked the volume of paper consigned to the ash heap. The irony is that while these paper notes simulate the instruments of a rational economic system, they are still bound to a world enchanted in ritual commerce with spirits. The rationalist assumption had been that paper money was a simple representation of real-world money, that the object (mistaken or silly as it may be) is simply to transfer real-world wealth into the spirit world or something of eternal value. As previous chapters have shown, this does not adequately comprehend the act of offering paper money.

The Semiotics of Ghost Bills

The degree to which persons using ghost bills pay attention to the messages printed on them is difficult to generalize. Few users, at least in my experience, pay attention to the semiotic messages printed on the notes. Users seem to pay as much or as little attention to what is printed on the ghost bills as they do to what is on the official currencies. Obviously, the exchange value printed on the face of official banknotes is of practical use. When it comes to ghost bills, the attention paid to the exchange value printed on the face has less practical relevance, perhaps, but it does have a certain discursive salience in the distinction between "big face values" and "small face values," a distinction that possesses no specific numerical value. It simply expresses a widespread concern that the recipients are able to use the bills in daily expenditures, so the "small face values" are often the more desirable because they are more realistic. For example, I often ask devotees, "Why don't you just offer one ¥50,000 banknote, like this one here?"—I hand them an inconspicuous little note (T-888) to inspect; I could hand them an ¥8 billion note, but it is hard even to count the number of zeros on such a bill, much less to fully grasp the amount—"Isn't ¥50,000 a sufficient amount for one offering?" The response of an elderly woman in Hong Kong was memorable: she seemed chagrined to have pointed out to her that the little note she had been using for years was worth so much, because she had never bothered to notice, but this revelation did not seem to change her attitude. Nor that of anyone else I asked, for the object is to burn a lot of paper—the exchange value is relevant only to the extent that one does not want to simply offer big face values.

Some don't even pay attention to the overall patterns or gestalt of signs that distinguish ghost bills from real-world paper currencies, which, as we shall see in the next chapter, can have grievous consequences in the real world. It is safe to say that the semiotic patterns remain in the background until there is a reason for bringing them to someone's attention. The only time that a person brought the content of a note to my attention was when a vendor in Chengdu, trying to justify the outrageous price she was charging for the notes, pointed to "all the things" (i.e., pictures of commodities) that were printed on the notes. But this was a singular incident. All other times it was I who brought the semiotic content of the notes to people's attention. Suffice it to say that the rich patterns of pictures, epigrams, and designs are manufactured and consumed by countless Chinese, and whoever it is that pays attention to the semiotics, the signs tell a story. Now I want to describe some of these semiotic elements that go into the construction of those stories.

Method of Analysis

I have collected different notes from wherever I found them on trips around China (and trips to Chinatowns overseas). The aggregate is remarkable for its volume and variety as a result of the proliferation since the 1980s. At the aggregate level, the differences represent all kinds of variations. For the purpose of presentation here I winnowed the aggregate of specimens down to one hundred species.[4] What is a species? I employ two criteria to decide which specimens represent a species of ghost bill. First is the interesting fact that most ghost bills have a serial number. These numbers do not specify a particular bill, as on real currencies; they generally specify the particular species of bill printed by a particular commercial firm. This of course fits my purpose. Of our sample of a hundred species, eighty-nine have serial numbers. But simple reliance on serial numbers is not adequate, since a few specimens that are otherwise quite different from one another have the same serial number, while a few specimens of the same species have different serial numbers. The second and more telling criteria for deciding a species type is my intuitive judgment of significant semiotic difference. In making these judgments, I ruled out mere differences in physical dimensions with or without accompanying differences in denomination or face value. For example, I disregarded the differences in two versions of E-66888 issued by the Bank of Paradise (*tiāntáng yínháng*) and featuring a profile of the Shakyamuni (Buddha) with hands folded in the gesture of supreme enlightenment (*uttarabodhi mudra*), one in a larger format (288 cm^2) with a face value of ¥500 million and the other in a smaller format (179 cm^2) with a face value of ¥100 million (figure 7.2).

The same note was later printed with bright red, yellow, and blue colors instead of the original, more subdued single reddish-brown color scheme, and some folks in Zunyi (Guizhou) interpreted the image on the front as the venerable King of Purgatory (*Yánwángyé*). For my purposes, the differences in the forms of E-66888 do not warrant designation as different species. Thus a variation due to a shift in color scheme or misprint, of which there are countless instances, do not warrant designation as a separate species. Stating the criteria in more positive terms is difficult because significant variations often fail to manifest an overall gestalt. Often there is a simple shift in one part of the iconography or epigraphy within the same overall gestalt that in my view warrants designation as a species type. Let me give one of many

Figure 7.2 Bank of Paradise ghost bill E-66888 obtained in Beijing

examples. Here I have two notes that appear to be facsimiles of the popular ¥100 RMB bill which depicts China's "Four Great Leaders" shoulder to shoulder. One bill, AC8633863, I obtained from a little shop in Pudong, Shanghai (see figure 7.6); the other, AC68938698, came from a stall in the Shatin New Market, Hong Kong. The obverse sides are the same in every detail except that the Shanghai bill depicts the busts of three emperors, while the Hong Kong bill depicts four emperors (with slight differences in countenance). Both depict an extra bust, noticeably faded and shunted off to the others' right side, presumably representing the one who was deposed in the Cultural Revolution (more on this later). In my view, this slight difference in iconography distinguishes the two bills as different species. The fact that they have different serial numbers adds to my conviction; and when we turn the two bills over to peruse the reverse sides, my decision is confirmed, since the Hong Kong bill is a virtual facsimile of the real RMB, while the Shanghai bill frames a Buddhist sutra, about which I will have more to say later.

In deciding whether two bills are different species, I do not, however, allow the obverse patterns to be decisive. The designs are concentrated on the principal sides of notes rather than on reverse sides. For purposes of quantifying my data, the numbers are calculated on the basis of the principal sides of the notes unless stated otherwise. The principal side of the note is the printed side of a single-sided note or the obverse of a two-sided note. (Nine notes are printed on one side; all of the others are two-sided.) Most reverse sides represent a smaller number of generic patterns. In other words, a number of different species share the same reverse side. This leads to some interesting discrepancies. But discrepancies can also be found on the same side of a note, since certain motifs may be used in different permutations to reconfigure the face of a note. For instance, on the reverse of NO (No.) 482178, an old-style Chinese building atop the city wall is captioned with the English epigram "Ten Thousand Dollars," while the numerical values in the four corners and on the obverse side simply specify that this note is a "20" (figure 7.3).

The permutations of signs by which individual styles are discerned do not lend themselves to sorting the different species of notes into definitive subgroups or varieties. The only exception may be the group of notes that mimic a real-world national currency. This comprises about one-third of the notes. I will discuss these later in the chapter. Among the notes that make no attempt to mock real-world currencies, there are nonetheless some salient images that suggest a shift within the paradigm. Here I am thinking of how the cast of central figures that commonly depicts the bust of an emperor along with epi-

Figure 7.3 Ghost bill (No. 482178) inscribed in pinyin obtained in Quanzhou, Fujian

grams and seals that identify the Jade Emperor as bank president is displaced by a depiction of Buddha. Whether this represents a significant shift in the message is hard to say, especially given that the aura created by an image of Buddha is not reinforced by a corresponding shift in the surrounding signs. Notes that depict an image of Buddha may or may not label the Jade Emperor as bank president, but none label the Buddha as bank president. The semiotics of these paper notes suggest that the *yīn*-world is but little differentiated and that it is an area of the lifeworld that is open to individual imagination, to reinforce a point that I have made in previous chapters.

Hell Bank Notes

The "occidental" appearance of these notes, their shape and format, is amplified by epigrams printed in English. The most ubiquitous English epigram is "Hell Bank Note," which is printed on one-third of the notes. (If I count reverse sides, then over half of them are so inscribed.) Why would an English epigram, especially an epigram that identifies a currency as one that circulates in "hell," be printed on something that belongs so exclusively to a common Chinese custom? Even granting that the destination of the note is "hell," the English "hell" is only a rough conveyor of the nearest Chinese cognate, *dìyù* (earth prison). The communicative function of this English epigram is enigmatic. We can infer that the English has some communicative purpose for persons who can recognize the script as English, or possibly read the English. The evidence indicates that this epigram originated in Hong Kong at least as far back as the 1950s, when Hong Kong was a Crown Colony of Great Britain.

Perhaps the English epigram lent the note a certain credibility, a certain realism where the real currency was English, while also conveying to the colonial authorities that these realistic-looking notes were not intended to counterfeit the real-world paper currencies. But this does not explain why this particular epigram remains popular after the accession of Chinese sovereignty over Hong Kong (1997) and in places where Chinese sovereignty was never at issue. For those who would infer more than the sheer inertia of tradition to explain the continuing popularity of the label "Hell Bank Note," the enigma deepens when we realize that this English label is superfluous, since most notes specify in Chinese the sphere of its circulation, the name of its issuing bank, and the type of paper currency that it represents—this term is usually suffixed to the sphere of circulation, for example, "circulating paper note" (*tōngyòng zhǐbì*). These three logographic domains are found on most of the notes, not only those dubbed Hell Bank Note. Let us discuss each domain in turn.

These hundred notes include nine different designations for the sphere of circulation. The most common designation is *dìfǔ*. This word literally refers to the earth bureau, which administers an underground toll booth (*dìyù*) that popular liturgies of Buddhism and Taoism turn into a bureaucratic state–based purgatory. Here earthly sins and malfeasances are adjudicated by an imperial magistrate and the exact punishment meted out prior to reassignment to heaven or to a new incarnation back in the real world. The common presumption is that these paper notes have some use in paying off the officials of the *dìfǔ* to gain their leniency. After all, punishments meted out by the *dìfǔ* are draconian and are well known in the graphic representations of popular culture. Ordinary people are steeped in the notion that officials, wherever their venue, above or below ground, give leeway to those who make gifts of money. There is a slight hitch in this scenario, however. Popular depictions of Buddhist purgatory have special chambers reserved for officials who take bribes. Even a culture that is driven by patrimonial gift-giving recognizes that bribery is a malfeasance, and in a just world—in the cosmic ebb and flow, where there is recompense and justice—the punishment for bribery, extortion, and embezzlement is harsh. But even before the newly deceased enter their period of disembodiment, when the soul is freed from its worldliness, from its corruption, they are relieved of any money they may have brought with them, at least according to some popular depictions.

None of this gloom and doom is depicted on the paper notes, however. Nor do all notes designate the sphere of circulation as the earth bureau. Others designate the sphere with slightly more ambiguous terms: *yīnmíng* (netherworld), *míngguó* (netherworld kingdom), or *míngfǔ* (netherworld bureau). *Míngfǔ* may appear on the same note with the epigram for *dìfǔ* (earth bureau) or even *tiāntáng* (paradise). And a large number of epigrams combines *tiān* (heaven) with *dì* (earth), while still others mark their sphere of circulation as *tiānfǔ* (office of heaven), which suggests that heaven is also a bureaucracy; or it may lose its worldliness altogether and simply be designated *tiāntáng* (paradise). Each permutation of terms suggests different connotations for different imaginations. It is pointless to generalize more than to say that in the next world there are torture chambers and pleasure gardens and everything in between. The common rationale for the circulation of money in purgatory is to pay for leniency, while the rationale for money in paradise is that the two (i.e., money and paradise) are synonymous—one can hardly imagine a paradise that is not loaded with money, unless of course one is joking. While Chinese has numerous terms for heaven or paradise, the only one found on these notes is *tiāntáng* (halls of heaven). The Buddhist heavens (*xītiān*) that suggest nirvana and extinction rather than a pleasure palace are not in evidence—anyone seeking nirvana (extinction) has no need of paper money.

Most notes also indicate the bank (in a few cases the stock exchange) that issues the note. There are sixteen named Chinese banks (one of these is in Vietnamese) and six named English banks. Most Chinese bank names begin with *míng* (netherworld), and the most common bank name is *míng dū yínháng* (Netherworld Capitol Bank), which is on more than a third (thirty-seven) of the notes. Twenty notes have *míng tōng yínháng* (Netherworld Circulation Bank), and a couple simply inscribe the name as the Bank of Circulation (*tōngyòng yínháng*). Fourteen notes give a variation of *tiāndì yínháng* (Bank of Heaven and Earth), and eight notes indicate that the bank is the Bank of Heaven (*tiāntáng yínháng*) or the Heaven Capitol Bank (*tiān dū yínháng*). Some of the earth-bound banks are suffixed with *yǒuxiàn gōngsī*, which designates a "modern corporation with limited liability." Banks whose names are rendered in English include direct translations (or transliterations) of Chinese names found on other notes (Earth Bureau, Heaven Bureau, Heaven and Earth, and Bank of Ming Mai). The Bank of Ming Mai appears as *míng měi yínháng* on another note that refers to the Netherworld Bank of America. The last two banks in English do not have Chinese cognates: Hell Bank and the Hell Bank Corporation. These last two named banks are on notes that specify the Chinese name as *míng dū yínháng*. Nor do these last two notes specify what kind of currency it represents—neither note is designated as Hell Bank Note, only that Hell has been incorporated with limited liability.

Most notes, however, specify the type of currency they represent. Forty-two notes designate themselves as *zhǐbì* (paper notes), while the next most common designation is eight notes labeled *míngbì* (netherworld note). The other designations include *chāopiào* (paper currency), which is the common term for real-world paper currencies. An unusual designation is *jīnchāo* (gold bill). This uses a current note to represent gold bullion. This in effect substitutes a current note for the traditional gold paper. Here the term *jīnchāo* is prefixed with *shénfó* (spirit of Buddha) and the motif includes the imperious Jade Emperor, the bank president, looking over a sea of gold coins in which immortal beings and beasts are wading and floating. This ¥1 billion note (YS-49085; figure 7.4) is particularly exquisite as notes go, not only in the details of the depictions and quality of print, but in the way it configures ·popular signs, icons, and images that evoke the three teachings (*sānjiào*) of Buddhism, Taoism, and Confucianism.

The reverse side of this note is a mat of alternating First Treasure (*yuánbǎo*) and copper cash, which we find on a few other notes (e.g., the Money Tree) that represent themselves less as ordinary paper notes and more as charms. A related kind of note is the *tōngbǎo* (circulating treasure),[5] which marks the less pretentious denominated notes of ¥100 million and ¥500 million (the smaller and larger versions of E-66888) issued by the Bank of Heaven (*tiāntáng yín-háng*) and featuring a profile of Buddha gesturing supreme enlightenment.

Another kind of paper note is the *gǔpiào* (stock certificate). Examples

Figure 7.4 Spirit of Buddha gold bill (YS-49085) obtained in Beijing

include YH96863 and the two styles of YH96865. This note (YH96865) is an example of two different styles with the same serial number and face value of ¥100 million. In one, the Buddha lets fly his demon-destroying sword while overseeing a parade of immortals holding high their signifying paraphernalia; in the other, the Jade Emperor is flanked by different kinds of fruits.[6] Fruits, like the animals on other notes, are word pictures for treasured things: security, prosperity, progeny, longevity, and so on. The other certificate bears a face value of ¥500 million but is less esoteric in its word pictures: it has the Jade Emperor sandwiched between a new car and a Western-style bungalow.

Identity of Human Figures and Bank Officials

Another remarkable feature of these notes is the pictures of things printed on them. These can be grouped into any number of categories and, again, permutated in a variety of combinations to convey certain messages. The pictured things by my reckoning include humans, animals, plants, atmospherics, buildings, ritual objects, utensils, and goods or commodities. The things that draw the most immediate attention are the humanlike faces, if only for the space they occupy. Only five notes do not feature a humanlike face on the principal side of the note. Of the ninety-five that do, there is a high degree of stylistic variation. Most of the humanlike faces are busts of emperors, recognizable as such by their dress, and particularly their hats. In Chinese hats signify social rank, identity, and reputation. The emperor hats are characteristic of the Qin and Han dynasties, with their mortarboard shape, fringed in front and back by strings of beads. Seventy-seven of the notes are printed with an image of an emperor. Some of these include more than one emperor, a point for discussion when we take up those notes that mimic real-world currencies. Next in frequency of occurrence are images of Buddha in three manifestations: the original Buddha (Shakyamuni), the Bodhisattva Guanyin (goddess of mercy), and the Earth Treasury Bodhisattva, who ministers to deceased souls (*Dìzàng*).

Seventy of the images dressed in imperial garb are associated with seals of office, titles, and/or signatures of a bank president (*hángzhǎng*). These signifiers, particularly the seals and signatures, with few exceptions identify the bank president as the Jade Emperor. The Jade Emperor is the most exalted spirit in the indigenous pantheon. Most notes that signify a bank president also signify a bank vice president (*fù hángzhǎng*), and most of these are identified with the seal and signature of *Yánluó,* the official head of the earth bureau. *Yánluó* is often depicted in popular culture as the presiding magistrate of the Fifth Court of purgatory.

The exceptions to this pattern are some notes that are close replicas of American Federal Reserve notes and have signatures (without the Chinese seals and titles) of Secretaries of the Treasury James A. Baker and Robert E. Rubin. These are on the old and new $100 Franklin notes, respectively. Another note that does not replicate American money or any other national currency but nevertheless has a signature in the place of the American Secretary of the Treasury is a Taiwan note (AL1967710) signed by Mary B. Chun, whoever she is.

Just as James Baker is not Ben Franklin, we cannot be certain what the relationship is between the various forms of entitlement on the standard paper notes and the pictorial images of an imperial or ecclesiastic countenance. The signs of mercantile office do not refer to depictions of Buddha, if for no other reason than that the title of bank president is always next to the seal or signature of the Jade Emperor, and the Jade Emperor is not Buddha. Buddha does not have—perhaps I should say, does not need—a seal of office, much less a signature. Buddha's authority is not exercised through trappings of bureaucracy. Rather, the signs of entitlement point to the visages of imperial authority, which must be the Jade Emperor and not the King of Purgatory. The only direct evidence for this connection is found on two notes (CR71042 and NO [No.] 48178) where a picture of the emperor is captioned as the Jade Emperor (in Chinese characters as *Yùhuángdàdì* and as the "Bank President" here romanized as "Ying Hang," which standardized in pinyin is *yínháng*).

The use of signatures is remarkable. Most signatures are in a romanized longhand; fewer are in Chinese *cǎo* or cursive. Some notes have the signatures under old-fashioned seals; others have only the seals; and still others have only signatures. The imperial signatures written in romanized longhand are the only manifestations of a Chinese vernacular in these notes. The irony manifests at many levels: using Roman script and writing in (English) longhand, an anonymous signatory writes the imperial name according to its local sound. Yuk Wong captures the sound of a southern vernacular, while the same name, Yu Huang, that of a northern vernacular or its derivative in the common language. To be frank, I had the devil of a time trying to read most of these romanized signatures, so I cannot with any certitude offer many examples of vernacular and idiosyncratic styles.

There is a significant number of English inscriptions on these notes. Most of the English-language inscriptions spell out face values in dollar amounts or are transcriptions from modified replications of American treasury notes. Some seem a bit incongruous, such as "In God We Trust" above the depiction of Independence Hall on the reverse side of a simple replication of the new U.S. $100 Franklin treasury note (AL38730332 D). Above the English is Vietnamese "Ngan Hang Dia Dhu" (Earth Bureau Bank). Another note (XYZ-20001663) depicts an imperial countenance with a caption in English, "Yu Wang" (Jade Emperor). The Taiwan note (Al 1967710) labeled The Otherworld Bank of America, which inscribes the name Mary B. Chun in the place of a secretary of the treasury, depicts a cluster of skyscrapers captioned with the word "heaven." The reverse side depicts a jetliner in the clouds, without a caption. The skyscrapers presumably represent real capital investments or possibly urban residences or both. This note seems to convey a different message from the Hell Bank Note.

More significant than notes printed with English inscriptions are the nineteen notes that use pinyin to romanize Chinese epigrams. These include the pinyin for face values, types of notes, spheres of circulation—in other words, romanized epigrams that are usually given in Chinese characters. For example, on note Y-6396, *dìfǔ tōngyòng zhǐbì* transcribes in pinyin the Chinese characters that are inscribed below it (earth bureau circulating paper note). One note (YA97-801188) has all its epigrams in pinyin, none in Chinese characters; and in the spirit of focusing on the anomalous, another note (NO [No.] 482178) obtained in Quanzhou has words printed in pinyin but in reverse syntax, "yongtonfuditangtian" (*sic*) (*tiāntáng dìfǔ tōngyòng*), which tells us that this general purpose currency circulates in heaven by authority of the earth bureau (see figure 7.4). This epigraph is replicated seven times on the obverse face of the note, in different font styles and sizes! Along the upper border, the name of the bank is indicated in reverse syntax as "hang-yintongming" (*sic*) (*míng tōng yínháng*), or the Netherworld Circulation Bank. (The two words are separated by the inscription of the corresponding Chinese characters in their traditional syntax.) This particular note replicates in format and design the $20 U.S. treasury note. The pinyin inscriptions simply replace most of the English inscriptions on the U.S. note; and instead of President Jackson's mug in the center, we have an imperial countenance of the Jade Emperor, the bank president. Here is a good example of the degree to which one of these notes is able to resemble in overall impression or gestalt of a real-world currency while the semiotic content, and its syntax, repeatedly communicate the message that this note is destined for circulation in the netherworld.

More pertinent to the anthropology of the *repetitive message* is that repetition is one of the ways that magic and ritual work their effects on us; but in case one feels less mystified and more amused upon seeing YA97-801188, with the same epigraph written seven times, in reverse syntax, we are informed by Henri Bergson (1914:34) that such repetitive iconicity evokes "mechanism," which finds its natural outlet in laughter. We will encounter this threshold between the gravity that the ritual purpose of these ghost bills inspires and the levity that some of the iconicity provokes with even greater force when we come to the repetition of emperor faces on simulations of RMB. It is apparent that many of the ghost bills take advantage of the wisdom in the popular idiom quoted at the beginning of this book: that the threshold between gravity and levity is as *yīnyáng*, a mutual becoming.

Replicas of National Currencies

These paper notes or ghost bills carry the aura of an occidental-based monetary culture through their sizes, shapes, and formats. While most notes mask these forms by their otherworldly content, over a third mimic real-world national currencies, especially the PRC, American, and Hong Kong British currencies. These can be further grouped according to the precision of their simulation. The degree of precision extends from exact copies to inexact, crude copies, all the way to subtle parodies.

Let's begin with the exact copies, and here I refer to a sheet of three Xeroxed ¥100 RMB notes. This is the note that depicts in profile the Four Great Leaders of the People's Republic of China, from left to right and in order of rank: Mao Zedong, Zhou Enlai, Liu Shaoqi, and Zhu De. The significant thing about this sheet of Xeroxed notes is how I obtained it and what this tells us about the ingenuity of the tradition and the persons who peddle it. On a midsummer day in 1993, I was riding my bike along the dusty, little-traveled road to Babaoshan People's Cemetery in a western suburb of Beijing when I came upon a family sitting by the side of the road selling paper notes. The notes were concealed in a cloth bag, but I knew from experience that persons sitting alongside a road to a cemetery with a bag are likely vending paper monies, so I stopped to inquire. The lady vendor, next to whom sat her husband and two daughters, pulled little packets of paper notes from her cloth bag to show me. The little packets looked as if they had been put together by the vendor herself because they consisted of fewer notes than I was used to seeing and they were stapled together. After seeing her small lot of notes, I asked if that was all, and after hesitating, she pulled the sheet of Xeroxed RMB from her bag. I was struck with frissons of ingeniousness, pathos, and incongruity, and, on reflection, my part in making it so. Suffice it for now to say that the ¥100 RMB notes are a popular fetish in China.

These flirtations with the counterfeit have become more sophisticated; in a news report from Yinzhou District of Ningbo, Zhejiang, dated 2006, we have large-face-value counterfeit bills added to the paper money corpus. This particular specimen is not in my hand, so I can only report what I read: "This reporter found that almost every stand was selling a kind of otherworld note (*míngbì*) which exactly resembles the RMB. . . . [T]he otherworld note is almost completely the same as RMB in terms of the color, form, calligraphy, patterns, face values, flower patterns, also the brail numbers" (Zu 2006). The reporter consulted some local bank officials, who informed him that such facsimiles clearly violate the national law and local regulations concerning RMB. According to the peddlers, it was indeed the realism of these new versions of otherworld notes that made them outsell the older versions, which included the simulations of American notes. The reporter noted that a stack of ten notes cost one yuan, and this is pretty cheap for ordinary people: "It is very easy for each peddler to sell several hundred stacks in a day." For these folks, at least, the traditional notion that paper money is inherently different from real money, is forgotten in the desire for realism through facsimile.

The next level of mimicry is the older fairly crude replicas of American $100 notes. One (L24726523A) replicates the old Franklin note; it was obtained from a vendor in Hanoi. The other (AL38730332 D) replicates the new Franklin note and came from a shop in Toronto. Each replicates the $100 bill down to the last detail except for the epigram, "Ngan Hang Dia Phu" (Vietnamese for Earth Bureau Bank), superimposed under "The United States of America" on the older version and substituted for "The United States of America" on the newer version. This newer version, however, leaves intact the epigram "In God We Trust" just below the "Ngan Hang Dia Phu".

For Hong Kong and its overseas networks the most ubiquitous paper note is the classic Hell Bank Note (No. A123456). I call it classic because it is the oldest extant paper note, at least in my experience (it is as popular today as it was when I first noticed it in the early 1960s). Although it is often referred to as *Měijīn* (American money) because of its uncanny similarity to the format and design of the U.S. dollar, its content is different. Its central figure, which varies somewhat among its various editions, is an imperial countenance in a quarter-right profile with the eyes cast in a sideward gaze looking slightly down at the beholder. This is similar to the Franklin head on the U.S. $100 bill and its facsimile (L24726523A), but different from most of the other paper notes, which have the imperial gaze straight ahead either facing front or showing a left profile. The classic Hell Note's emperor has a rather large nose, and because of this nose and that sideward gaze, he has always struck me as the sinister-looking "big-nosed foreign devil" of modern Chinese mythology. For those who entertain such a suggestion, the other aspects of the Hell Bank Note discussed in a previous section would fit an interpretation of these bills as allegory of the economic hell brought to China and presided over by the English.

Rénmínbì

Finally, the most provocative notes are those that resemble the real-world *Rénmínbì* (RMB), or "People's Currency," in ways that are obvious, painfully obvious, and not so obvious. What makes them less than obvious is not the crudity of their resemblance, however, but their sophistication. These ghost bills come in the ¥50 and the popular ¥100 denomination. The reverse sides of both ghostly denominations are an exact replication of the respective real-world notes. Again, it is the obverse sides that carry the principal message. Here the format and design conform to the respective real-world notes, but where the real-world RMB features the four great leaders of the People's Republic—Mao, Zhou, Liu, and Zhu—the netherworld notes feature the cloned countenance of four emperors. There is no attempt to make the imperial countenance look like the four great leaders. They do not, for example, depict the individual countenances of the four leaders wearing imperial garb—this would be an obvious mockery and not allowed. The parallel between the depictions of the real-world leaders and the netherworld emperors is nonetheless implicit. Being implicit, it allows for more than one interpretation. But however the interpretation is made, it must come to grips with the fact that the four imperial visages are all exactly the same, lined up like ducks in a row. The pertinent interpretation is that the four great leaders, who are seen as individual countenances in the real-world representation, become as one supreme countenance in the netherworld representation. The message is that what separated them in life—intraparty factionalism, political ideology, personal ambitions—is now history. Now they are one, and their rule is that of a single voice. This interpretation conforms to the common notion that persons who exercised power, especially charismatic or personal power, in the quotidian world are also likely, by force of that charisma, to exercise power in the spirit world, which relegates these four to the status of demigods. Part of the process of relegation was spurred by the uncanny circumstances of their demise.

An impertinent spin on these paper notes points to the four great leaders as mere incarnations of an imperial rule that lasted down to their demise, marked for the last three by the great Tangshan earthquake (1976). The emphasis of the sameness of things is striking. In this sense, the otherworldly notes can be read as a parody, a kind of mock money in the fullest sense of the term "mock"—both to replicate and to repudiate by means of satire—in a way that can claim complete innocence of conscious intent.

I once pointed to the note with the four emperors and asked my Hong Kong friend whether these could be interpreted as the four great leaders. Obviously the parallel had not occurred to him—he had never really bothered to reflect on these things—because he immediately broke down in fits of laughter, repeatedly sputtering the names and pointing to the imperial visages. The parallel was a revelation to him, and it was especially poignant because he could link his disapproval of the paper money tradition with his antipathy toward Mao's legacy. In my friend's world the paper money tradition and Mao's legacy were like mirror parts of the same insanity that held modern China in its grip. This points to the fact that the parody that paper notes inspire is for the benefit of nonusers. This is one of my theses in this book. The paper money tradition is more than the folks who use it ritually. It is also for those who ridicule it or use it for other purposes. My point is that as the paper money tradition adapts to the modern lifeworld—and these paper notes are the most obvious example of this process—it becomes evident that the tradition can be used in ways that make it look ridiculous.

Face Values and Inflationary Tendencies

The modern ghost bills betoken a paradigm shift that is well under way. The most radical aspect of the paradigm shift registered by these paper notes is the numerical specification of face values. Although other forms of paper monies can be counted, there is nothing so specific as an actual numerical value printed on the bill itself. This introduces a contradiction into the tradition, since largesse of offering is now a thing that can be calculated in terms of exact amounts: on the one hand, the amount needs to be small enough that it can be used for everyday expenses; on the other, the amount needs to be big enough that it suggests generosity, even abandoned giving. I think more than anything else, this second need accounts for the inflationary tendency in the face values of these notes (which is more than a reflection of the inflation of the real-world economy). Be that as it may, the tensions between realism and make-believe are manifest in the small and large face values and their accompanying rationales. The lowest face value is the one-yuan/dollar note (No. A123456), and the highest value is on a cluster of ¥8 billion notes (H-8573, HY-07888, YA94-08888). The median note (T-3088) is 50,000, its denomination unspecified. The median and the mean are far apart: the mean face value in my sample of one hundred notes is 529,556,737.26, which falls between a cluster of notes of ¥500 million and ¥800 million. The scale is definitely biased toward big face values. Of course, adding zeros after a number adds little or nothing to the printing cost, nor has it yet generally raised the commodity price of a pack of paper notes, although recently I have found isolated instances where it has (see the next chapter). Adding zeros only takes away from the realism, which as I have argued is entirely warranted, given the purpose of paper money.

Signs of Decommoditization

Numerical face values on paper go a long way toward making things into countable objects, signifying exchange values in a quantifiable, commoditized, and reified world that defeats what is traditionally signified. But as the face values inflate to surreal numbers, such as "8 billion," the signifier may trade its semantic function for its acoustic function—that is, trade in its exchange value for the magical effect in the sound of "eight" (*bā*) followed by nine zeros (*líng*): "*bā líng líng líng . . .*" The sound of eight (*bā*), with a shift of the initial consonant from a bilabial /b/ to a fricative /f/, signifies "increase" (*fā*) followed by an odd number, signifying an endless succession of zeros, the sound of which (*líng*) signifies the spiritual power to make the increase happen. This is Chinese reasoning, not mine. There are other signs pushing toward decommoditization and mystification. One note (YA94–08888) issued by the Netherworld Capital Bank features the Jade Emperor flanked on his right with the graph for *shòu* (longevity) and on his left the graph for *bǎo* (treasure). Each graph is embedded in a depiction of its corresponding personification and fetish objects: First is the countenance of longevity holding pomegranates in one hand, with a crane lifting off its perch on this shoulder, and holding in the other hand the dragon cane, whose scroll and gourd rest on that shoulder. Second is the countenance of wealth, with *rúyì* in one hand—*rúyì* is a rebus for "as you desire"—and a stack of first treasures in the other. The seals, titles, and signatures of the Jade Emperor and the King of Purgatory are also indicated in the usual position. The reverse side is captioned with "Hell Bank Note," but the picture depicts one of utter bliss: the generic scenes of the celestial city, with its ornate pavilions, and pagodas interlaced with pine trees against a background of mountains shrouded in mists, a veritable paradise (figure 7.5). This is of course an ¥8 billion note, and it is much bigger (35 by 17 cm) than the other notes, which approximate the size of real currencies.

Other notes are inscribed with Buddhist incantations. The $50 million note (No. 5-553139) has the Buddhist incantation for salvation of the soul, *ēmítuófó* inscribed along its right margin. The most remarkable note is the ¥100 RMB facsimile (AC8633863) issued by the Heaven and Earth Bank Ltd. This bill depicts the four emperors, with one removed to the margin

Figure 7.5 ¥8 billion bill (YA94–08888), 35 by 17 cm, obtained in Chengdu

(figure 7.6). The reverse side has a Buddhist sutra superimposed on the scene of pine trees and mountains. It is entitled "The Sutra for Blessing Paper Notes" (*chāopiào jīng*), and it reads in the traditional direction down each column from the right margin. The "sutra" is more remarkable for its rhyme in Chinese than for any meaning that can be gotten from its syntax of jargon either in Chinese or in English.

> *Foreign bills* (yángpiào) *ought to be blessed by scripture*
> *Every foreign note is like silver*

Figure 7.6 Simulated ¥100 RMB (AC8633863) with "sutra" on reverse, obtained in Shanghai

In the middle of foreign notes is the revered Buddha
Perfectly square shining brightly
Upon the five gold peaks revere the Bodi
Knowing the imperial reign of móhē xī[7]
Nāmó ēmítuófó *{Merciful Buddha}*

Serious or tongue-in-cheek or both, here indeed is a chiasm of the sacred and the profane, or perhaps the esoteric and the mundane or the ceremonial and chrematistic. Here is also a chiasm of the native and the foreign. The exogenous aspect of the bill is its "foreignness," even though it simulates the Chinese national currency.

It is the simulation of paper currency that makes the bill "foreign" or exogenous—its national identity is incidental. Second, although I don't know the provenience of its manufacture, the fact that I obtained this note from a shop in Shanghai, where the system of modernity and progress is most deeply rooted, bolsters my sense that in Shanghai more than any other place I visited in China, the paper money custom includes the desire to have its paper monies blessed by ecclesiastics. One elderly woman hawking her tattered bag of papers next to an upscale suburban Shanghai cemetery insisted that she had all her money blessed by the monks and, as if to reassure me, began at once to chant the Buddhist blessing as she handled the bills. Based on my experience, this seemed extraordinary, but entirely reasonable too, given that in no place I have visited do people consider paper money sacred—it is not sacred; it is of this world, a purchased commodity in most cases nowadays, and thus many people feel the need to consecrate the paper money (as noted earlier) by the way they handle the paper before offering it to the flames.

A Pedagogy of the Ghost Bills

The realism of the paper notes might place them in the same league as that of the paper binding offerings (*zhǐzhā*) of realistic-looking valuables and commodities (houses, cars, servants, etc.), except the pitched paper replicas are generally handmade by neighborhood artisans and scaled down from the real McCoy, while the facsimiles of monetary instruments and the like are generally scaled one-to-one and, if commercially produced (which most are), mass produced by machines. The two genres are also comparable in that both are offered to deceased members of a family or a deceased friend—spirits in the *yīn*-world that are conceived of as living in a world that is mostly the same kind of place that the living inhabit. Whether here or there, money is necessary for paying fees, patronizing and making relationships, and buying things. In the next chapter we will meet a woman who, wishing to send her deceased father on a trip to the United States, calculates the necessary plane fare and other costs in otherworld monetary terms and buys the amount of money (in ghost bills) necessary for the journey. This is obviously an extreme case and, when told in the satirical way that it is, seems surreal; but it is based on the rationale of the ghost bills. In the countless offerings I have watched, the paper notes are used in funerals and in cemeteries for recently departed members of the family. In funerals they are burned and/or placed in various ways in the coffin or on the corpse for use in the journey to the other shore. They may be placed in the shape of an open fan on the chest of the corpse. At the grave, for example during Qingming here in Honolulu, they are often mixed in with folded silver or gold *yuánbǎo*, creating a visually aesthetic sense; or they are offered after the bundles of *yuánbǎo* by individuals standing around the incinerator. Here they are offered individually by several members of the congregation, be it a family or a civic organization, in a mode that protracts the act of offering, allowing for some small talk. Often this task is assigned to the children.

An instructive example in the pedagogy of burning bills comes from the 2008 Winter Sacrifice in Yu County, Hebei, when I accompanied an extended family to a cluster of five family mounds on a high loess plateau. They brought a supply of paper monies, a few baskets of wheat buns—the fare seemed simple and sparse to me—and local incense sticks, plus armloads of dried cornstalks. The men lit the incense sticks on top of each burial mound, then took the paper monies out of the plastic carrying bags and, with no particular procedure and rather nonchalantly, placed the papers in front of the mounds, then placed the dried cornstalks over the bottom edge of the papers as "fire starters." The combination of papers at the main mound included paper clothes (to supply ancestors with winter clothes is the main purpose of the winter offerings), a bag of home-folded gold and silver *yuánbǎo*, a few of the traditionally folded "white paper" (signifying "silver"), and a stack of ghost bills face valued at ¥50 and ¥100 RMB and unceremoniously peeled off in small bunches. Women broke the wheat buns and tossed pieces on each mound. Although the cornstalks were described as "fire starters," I felt their use must have more meaning than their utility as tinder, since the paper itself is a ready tinder. I felt the dried cornstalks were their link to the earth, the agrarian source of all value, that which makes all the other things that stand for civilization possible. In some sense, if anyone had asked me, it was the cornstalks that stood for the necessary sacrifice. The fact that across the ravine two Han dynasty tomb mounds cast their earthen silhouettes against a blue winter sky added a certain emphasis, a certain momentousness to the ritual of this extended family. As for the cornstalks, whatever they may or may not signify, consciously or unconsciously, they added considerable flame and warmth, and an earthy domesticity to the whole affair. After the women broke the wheat buns and tossed them on the mounds, the cornstalks were turned into torches, and they gobbled up the paper clothes and valuables as ghost bills were dropped in to feed the holocaust. While one of the men stirred the fire with a stick to make sure the whole treasure was delivered to the other side, the little boy came by with a small fist full of ghost bills which he was urged to throw on the fire. He threw some on, then ran off to another fire to feed it in like manner. The boy had fun burning the ghost bills, and during the collective kowtowing, he went in front of everyone kneeling almost on the mound and mimed in a rapid and exaggerated way the bowing motion and prayerful up-and-down motion of the hands, which gave his elders much amusement. I did not see any formal instruction given to the kid; his elders simply told him in offhand ways what to do.

The kowtowing was the last part of the ceremony. All of the family members arranged themselves in a kneeling position in front of each burial mound in succession and on someone's command kowtowed three times. I was intensely aware of the unison and correctness of exposing the soles of the feet to the heavens—there was nothing offhand about this part of the service, and the only break in the totality of somberness and show of devotion was the antics of the kid in front of the little assembly. Taken as a whole, the service that cold winter morning was a combination of somberness, amusement, and play. Although children are often given ghost bills to burn, ghost bills are not children's toys. I have never met anyone who would allow a child to play with ghost bills apart from the whimsy of feeding the fire during the offering service—not because ghost bills are sacred, or really anything to do with the superstitious dread of contamination, but simply because it's not proper, and you don't want to get them tattered and dirty before you offer them to the deceased.

Ghost bills are the modern counterpart of the most original form of paper money, perforated sheets of money paper simulating strings of copper cash. With important exceptions, both the bills and the strings of cash are destined for the less exalted spirits: deceased members of the family, old friends, or other more or less anonymous ghostly figures. In theory, both bills and strings of cash are countable, but counting strings of cash requires a more arcane and variable theory of just what is being counted, whereas counting the bills is a simple matter of adding the numerical signifiers on each bill, which few if any do because it defeats the purpose of the offering. But it is precisely the close appearance to modern money that makes the ghost bills different from the simulated strings of cash. Devotees perceive the ghost bills as foreign, exogenous to their ageless custom, something like a toy, and for many a little bit ridiculous, which for some of the less devoted makes them an object of ridicule that calls into question the whole paper money custom. For me, the anthropologist, the ghost bills index a system that is somewhere between rationalizing the lifeworld and parodying it.

Conclusion

China has undergone enormous change in the past century and is currently hell-bent on the path of capital-intensive industrialization. The path of economic modernization has been widely theorized, according to the European historical experience, as promoting a civil society and a rational lifeworld that obviates magic and religion. Applied to China, this theory is clearly arguable in the case of the paper-burning custom, which has continued unabated from medieval times to the present day, across two chasms of historical formation, from feudalism to capitalism. While the custom clearly has not withered away in the face of modern economic forces, it has succumbed to them in various ways; for instance, paper money has become one of its products, one of its commodities; in turn, the paper money custom has incorporated facsimiles of modern bank and treasury notes (as ghost bills), a salient expression of modern (exchange) value, into its traditional corpus.

But these modern forms have not merely invaded the world of paper monies; in the last two decades, they have proliferated and expanded, and they have spearheaded a hypertrophy of forms along with a hyperinflation of face values (8 billion on one paper note). The inflation of face values on the ghost bills makes for a parody of the modern currency system, intended or unintended, and turns the process of rationalization toward the irrational in a way that Max Weber (1964) might have appreciated as a type of rationality aimed at gaining affective, expressive, or traditional ends; or the kind of pecuniary rationality that, according to Torstein Veblen (1953), disguises an increasingly predatory and irrational human nature in the sophistry of modern garb. Or, following the critical thought of Jean Baudrillard (1981), we might say that these new forms exhibit the change from the system of exchanging utilities into a system of exchanging signs and, thus, a system that no longer depends on production but instead relies on simulation. This shift in the rationalizing process augurs the much-heralded phase of human existence in which modernity and production of value seem to give way to the sheer replication of signs and a reality that is altogether simulated, making it a kind of unreal real, which reshapes the ideology of realism.

However we intellectuals play this paradigm shift, the "modernization of tradition" or the advent of a "postmodern simulacra" and new levels of alienation, the rationalization process has been greeted by ordinary people in China, even by devotees, with attitudes ranging from frissons of disbelief, to various forms of ennui, to outright disdain and laughter in different times and places: people say, in effect, that "ghost bills are not real" because, as a few of the more perceptive ones observe, "ghost bills are too real." This paradox of real and unreal echoes Elliot's attempt to return ET to his spaceship when he retorts to Greg's question about why ET can't simply beam up: "This is *reality*, Greg." Despite the qualms of a diminishing few, however, the ghost bills are increasingly incorporated into the potpourri of offering papers. In my view, the ghost bills entail a paradigm shift in the paper money tradition that more or less coincides with the shift in China's historical formation, from developed feudal to hypermodern in the space of a century or, with ever greater intensity and completeness, in the space of the last three decades.

CHAPTER 8

Burlesque

Yín sì wú fú [An unrestrained sacrifice brings no blessing]
—*Book of Rites*

The ghost bills described in the last chapter provide the opening wedge for a new category of paper monies that has increasingly penetrated the custom and divided it between the older, traditional replicas of value and the newer, modern, and exotic simulations of value. These simulations pay greater attention to realistic detail, the things of modern life—the commodities of the modern system—and its mode of reproduction in machined mimicry, with occasional accusations of forgery. Increasingly these items evoke not only the traditional desire for endless streams of luxuries, now a cornucopia of modern appliances, but more and more the stuff of entertainment, impulse release, sheer dissipation, even the antisocial. The mass media has labeled these things with neologisms: "exotic offerings" (*lìnglèi jìpǐn*) or "fashionable" or "faddish" offerings, and has thereby sounded the alarm that such things besmirch the original purpose of the paper money custom. Journalists from around the country participate in exposing and opposing the spread of exotic new-wave offering. A group of these squibsters, centered in Shanghai, accomplishes the work with artful effect (Blake, forthcoming). Of course nothing facilitates their work better than the ludic spirit of the paper money custom itself, for when push comes to shove, the paper money custom knows how to shove; under the wit and scrutiny of the modern media, the paper money custom turns to burlesque.

This chapter garners mostly online news stories from different places around China that represent themselves as factual news reports based in hard copy. The work of journalism in China is not reticent about hiding its didactic or propagandistic (educational) purpose. This does not make it merely the mouthpiece of the "communist" government, however. The hegemony here is not the old Stalinist monologue, but much more enveloping and insinuating and dialogic in its modus operandi, which is what makes it so much more effective than before. Many news stories include concurring and nonconcurring voices, while the whole thrust of the story is to cast aspersions on the exotic offerings—either to stigmatize the paper money custom as a whole or to show how ridiculous it looks from a traditionalist point of view. The dialogic of disgust and ridicule is augmented, indeed taken to another level, by the blogosphere and online chat rooms. Some bloggers, mostly global-minded younger folks, have suggested that the Qingming festival in early April (when paper money is prime-time) might as well be changed into April Fools'. Some bloggers view the new offerings as a conscious prank (*ègǎo*) on the recipients of the offerings. They play with terms such as *yúlè jié,* which convention refers to a festivity corrupted with fun and jollity, by invoking a neologistic homophone that signifies with even greater negativity, a festival of fools and morons. There is irony here: Just as the "communist" government recently turned Qingming into a national holiday by subtracting a day from the May Day (International Labor Day) celebrations, the Qingming becomes more and more a carnival of foolishness, thanks to the new trends in simulating paper money.

There are two forces changing the paper money custom. The one I just mentioned, the invasion of exotic objects, is the more spectacular. The other is more subtle, but in my estimation more significant: that is, the shift in the forces of production from hand to machine, which robs the product of its aesthetic qualities, causing many to complain that it lacks ritual effectiveness. Obviously the two processes are closely intertwined. Although the shift in the forces of production is less noticeable to the less attentive, it raises the question about the realism of paper money—or, more accurately, the authenticity of paper money—in ways that strike at the heart of the custom. Even if paper money is not real money, the question still remains, is what I am burning authentic? This is the question that a Mr. Huang was compelled to ask, as reported in the first news story we will examine, from Swatow, Guangdong (W. Liu 2005):

> A few days ago Mr. Huang observed the first death anniversary of his father. Mr. Huang lives downtown. His father's spirit tablet was kept

in a temple in the suburbs. Following Chaoshan [Swatow] custom, Mr. Huang prepared incense, candles, offerings, otherworld bills (*míngbì*) and paper bindings (*zhǐzhā*), etc., to bring to the temple to convey his feelings of sadness and longing. . . . Accordingly, he went to a special store selling sacrificial materials and otherworld notes to buy the offering stuff.

He found that the paper money sold in this store was much more "beautiful" than before. The paper appeared not only more refined, but also more colorful and lustrous: the gold and silver foiled papers were extremely bright and shiny. Moreover, the price was a little lower than usual. He bought several thousand (ingots) on the spot. Including other offerings, such as incense and candles, he spent about one hundred yuan. One hundred yuan is a considerate sum for a father's death anniversary, but as Mr. Huang approached the incense burner to burn the armload of paper monies, an old man who worked at the temple suddenly informed him that the paper money he was about to offer was fake and would not circulate in the *yīn*-world. It would be useless to Mr. Huang's father.

> The old man continued to explain that the customary gold and silver foiled papers were made by hand-mounting tinfoil onto sheets of paper. But the gold and silver on Mr. Huang's paper sheets were merely printed on the paper, the same as gold and silver wrapping paper. Colorful as they appeared, they were worthless indeed.
>
> The old man's remarks made Mr. Huang hesitate in his offering service. Finally he burned all the "fake paper money" that he had bought; but he was flustered and determined to check out what the old man had told him. Upon returning to the downtown, he made inquiries among several vendors of otherworld notes and sacrificial materials. They told him exactly the same thing that the old man had told him. He was so bothered that he asked this journalist with a perplexed look on his face, "Can people cheat even when it involves showing respect for heaven and earth (*tiāndì*) and making offerings to spirits?" When hearing this, we do not know if we should laugh or cry.

The reporter does not appreciate that Mr. Huang is questioning the authenticity of the artifice by which the paper money is replicated. When it comes to such exotic new-wave simulations as ghost bills, the question of authenticity is complicated by the extent to which the simulations are expressly made to look "realistic," sometimes to the point of counterfeit. What is more interesting in Mr. Huang's case, however, is that the traditional offerings, the gold and silver foiled papers, no longer bear the aura of authenticity, which makes them ritually ineffective. Mr. Huang's reasoning seems identical with what Walter Benjamin (2010:19–20) wrote about the work of art in the age of mechanical reproduction:

> The work of art with reference to its aura is never entirely separated from its ritual function. In other words, the unique value of the "authentic" work of art has its basis in ritual, the location of its original use value. . . . But the instant the criterion of authenticity ceases to be applicable to artistic production [by mechanical reproduction], the total function of art is reversed. Instead of being based on ritual, it begins to be based on another practice—politics.

Or, as I have argued, ideology.

Although inauthentic, these newer *printed* forms of gold and silver are truer as "paper money"—they are all paper—and they seem more real in the shine of their gold and silvery colors. Making them (seem) more real, however, makes them less authentic as artifices. The realism diminishes their aura of originality. The inauthentic printed forms of gold and silver are the effects of a mode of reproduction that drowns the aura or aesthetic of the rustic in the kind of refinement, smoothness, evenness, brightness, and shininess that is the product of modern machined technologies. These include manufacturing processes that transfer the labor from hand to machine, from flesh to steel, from nervous energy to electrical energy, from renewable fuels to fossil fuels. They lose the domesticity and rusticity of artifice in their mass production by an industrial order. What is more, it so happens that the paper-money-making machines are themselves manufactured in Mr. Huang's hometown, Swatow.

An array of Internet sites advertise machines that make paper money, and not just facsimiles of modern banknotes or ghost bills (chapter 7), which has been going on for many decades, especially in the Hong Kong region: now the old-fashioned paper monies described in chapter 2 are being subjected to the machine. Referred to as "superstitious-paper-making machines" (*míxìn zhǐqián jī*), they are built in factories around the port city of Swatow, Guangdong, and sell for around ¥50,000 RMB. There is an impressive variety of models, each with a different purpose. One of them irons on the stannous and smears the pigment over the surface, a process that only a few years ago was a sweated task in Xu village (chapter 2). Even more remarkable is that the advertisements for these machines address the fact that people desire paper money that is made by hand; these ads assure potential customers that their machines produce paper monies that have the appearance of handmade, that is, the kinds of qualities that made Mr. Huang question the authenticity of the paper he was offering to his father. And for the truly devoted, the advertisements even promise that its machines process the paper in such a way that when it is burned it produces an ash that has the most propitious color and texture.

Reification in Ghost Bills

In modern times, driven by the accumulation and circulation of capital, the mysterious is changed into the natural or real (what Marx parodied as a fetish and Lukács called reification, the foundations of ideology). We can see how deeply the reification insinuates itself in the ghost bills and other exotic offerings. Nothing is more reifying than the face values printed on the ghost bills. Stories are rife with how vendors and buyers of ghost bills play with the face values printed on the bills. In one news report (Yang 1995), a Shanghai woman purchased enough American ghost bills to pay the ¥80,000 price tag for her deceased father's trip to America (a fuller account is in Blake, forthcoming). Though this story, presented as a factual account, seems utterly discordant—because ghost bills are not purchased in this piecemeal manner based on their face value—it is plausible because the whole point of the simulation is to be realistic. Usually the actual cost of the ghost bill does not depend simply on the monetary value printed on its face. But now we have a story from Xinyang city, Henan, during the 2005 ghost festival (Guǐjié) in which the monetary values printed in the bank deposit book determine the price of the bankbook. The reporter (Qu 2005), disguised (as usual) as a customer, visited several makeshift paper money stands at the gate to a temple located in Zhongshan Road. The peddlers showed him several new kinds of paper money, among which there was a bankbook. The inscription "Heaven and Earth Bankbook" (tiāndì yínháng cúnkuǎnzhé) was printed on the cover. The inside pages recorded detailed entries of the deposits. According to the peddlers, the deposits in the bankbook ranged from ¥100,000 to ¥200,000. The price of the bankbook changed with the amount of deposited money.

The proprietors of several funeral supply stores told the reporter that the bankbooks were selling well these days.

The more money on deposit in this simulated bankbook, the more the bankbook costs in real-world money. The notion that the imitative face value printed on a piece of money should fetch a higher price in real-world money is new. The next paragraph discloses the chain of complicity in the recurrence of this pretense:

> Due to the soliciting of the peddlers and the store owners, there were a lot of people who bought this kind of paper money, and this included a lot of young people. When asked why they bought paper money, an eighteen- or nineteen-year-old girl said, "My folks asked me to buy it. The new kind of bankbook is quite interesting; it's the in-thing." Some other people said they bought these for the older folks in their families. It is mainly for entertaining the old folks; but actually we have to laugh at the sight of such oddities.

Thus, the reproduction of this custom begins with advertising or soliciting. It has entertainment value for old and young alike, although the entertainment value seems to resonate differently—it amuses the old folks, while for the young it is simply laughable.

There are numerous stories about how the desire for realism (in effect, a ritual of Marx's fetishism) is realized. In many places, folks answer John McCreery's question "Why don't we see some real money here?" with offerings of real money. To make the simulation of modern banknotes more real, thus more effective, some people employ a new kind of sympathetic magic. In a report from Jianghuai, Anhui, the reporter (Ji 2001) visits the Taiping Cemetery in Wuwei County, where amid the hubbub of people performing traditional offering services, he notices to his surprise two young people holding yellow paper and stacks of otherworld notes covered in a haphazard manner with real money. They told the reporter that by burning some real money atop the otherworld notes, according to what the old folks told them, they could increase the realness of the otherworld notes. "Thus, what the people underneath [in the *yīn*-world] receive must be real money. When asked how much real money they burned with the otherworld notes, the young people explained casually that it was not necessary to burn a lot, and it was mainly a gesture. Each stack of otherworld notes only had several pieces of five-*jiǎo* or two-*jiǎo* bills, altogether less than five yuan." The reporter went on to note how this practice of burning real money with otherworld bills has become increasingly popular throughout the province. And it's the old people who seem to be pushing the practice: "Usually they make change to get the one-*jiǎo*, two-*jiǎo*, or five-*jiǎo* bills, and put them among the otherworld notes with face value of several hundreds, ten thousands, even several millions. It is said that some people who are reluctant or cannot make change to get the small face value of a *jiǎo* bill are already burning one yuan bills." Traditionally real money may be used to infect plain paper (i.e., money paper: unmarked sheets of coarse yellowish-brown paper) with the magical power to circulate wealth by bringing the real bills (nowadays the ever-popular ¥100 RMB) into physical contact with plain sheets of paper. But the case above reverses the production of value: the transfer of magical effect is made by burning real money of low face value (*jiǎo*) with ghost bills of much higher face value. Burning the real bills of low face value with the ghost bills of high face value is done to increase the realistic value or *realism* of the ghost bills. This practice complicates the traditional logic of sympathetic magic. It is a short hop from this confabulation of magic and realism to outright realism or reification in making offerings of real money, which defeats the tradition and genius of paper money.

There are numerous reports of people burning real money as offerings. Each report gives the reason for using real money, which include mistaken identity, showing off a family's wealth, and striving for efficiency. Reports and stories about mistaken identity are rife and usually entail a young boy imitating his parents, but using their stash of real cash instead of their stash of otherworld notes (e.g., Chen Dachao 1997; Zhou Kailing 2000; Blake forthcoming). Equally often, it is an oldster who due to poor eyesight or loss of touch with reality makes the disastrous mistake. The *Changchun Evening News* (Li 2000) reported that in Huang Jin village, Nong'an County, Jilin, an old man mistakenly burned ¥5,000 budgeted for the spring planting.

> On the morning of the 21st old man Zheng planned to go to the tombs to make offerings, so he asked his son to go to the village store to buy paper money. At that time, the oldest daughter's husband, who lived in Songyuan city, brought five thousand yuan of spring planting money. The old man took the money and casually put it into the drawer. Shortly thereafter, the son returned with the paper money. Old man Zheng put the paper money into the same drawer. Around 11:00 a.m. . . . . the old man took the paper money out of

the drawer and went to the tomb. Because the money brought by
the son-in-law was the new version ¥100 notes, and the color was
off-red, the old man did not recognize it and mistakenly took the real
money to the tomb and burned it. The following day old Zheng's
son was going to buy fertilizer. As old Zheng took the money from
the drawer, the son found that money was otherworld cash; then old
Zheng realized that he had burned the real money by mistake and he
was filled with regret.

These stories evince the persistent anxieties around how a person, usually a
child or an oldster, might mistakenly burn real money. But there are many
creditable news reports of intentional burning, some out of desperation, lacking a ready-at-hand supply of ghost bills; or, quite literally, giving a son a
lesson in realism: the *Haikou (Hainan) Evening News* (Peng, Ouyang, and Luo
2005) reported a case from the Fulingshui cemetery of a family's Qingming
observances: First "they lit the incense in front of the tomb, then they burned
stacks of otherworld notes, a paper house, a toy car, whereupon a middle-aged
father even asked his son around seven or eight years old to light two pieces of
¥10 real cash. Confronted with reporters' questions, the father tried to mini-
mize his malfeasance by telling how he observed 'some families even burning
waitresses and young ladies when they made offerings.'"

From Hong Kong we have Mr. Tony Chan (Chen Zhencong), a geomancer
who credits his father with having taught him the practicality of burning
real money in lieu of ghost bills. Mr. Chan, allegedly following this fatherly
wisdom in advising a client, Gilbert Leung Kam-ho (Liang Jinhao), well
known as a former Hong Kong legislator, to burn real money in order to
change his fate stemming from his arrest for election bribery in 1993. The
story came to light in the midst of a protracted lawsuit between claimants to
the multi-billion-dollar HK estate of a deceased mutual friend, an eccentric,
Nina Wang (Gong Ruxin). Court questioning Chan's and Leung's relationship in the matter turned up a lot of racy scandal plus the newsworthy tidbit
that Leung had been advised by Chan to burn real silver paper (*zhēn yínzhǐ*)
to the tune of $1,500 HK every night for a year. By the time of Leung's sen-
tencing for corruption in 1993, Chan had turned half a million dollars to ash.
Chan defended himself by asserting that Leung had asked if burning real currency would help him avoid a bad fate, and Chan responded, "As you will."
Chan admitted that his own father had taught him that since the dead can
see, they can see the money being burned for them, and so it's better to just

burn a single ¥100 bill of real RMB than to go to all the trouble and waste of buying and burning ¥100 worth of otherworld currency (*Dushi ribao* 2009).

I have asked people in many parts of China, "Why not burn the amount in real money that you would spend on paper money?" No one seems to have thought of it, and in that sense it is unthinkable—no one mentioned that it is not legal—but the question does evoke a plausible practice. Most folks answer that burning a single bill misses the point of burning a lot of paper. Many cite the customary rule that the two kinds of money are not transposable (except, of course, in the exchange of a worldly market), that real-world money is no good in the *yīn*-world. Of course, this rule made more sense in the long history of burning replicas of precious metals and fabrics; but now that the paper money increasingly simulates *real* paper currencies, and now that the desire for realism is creeping into the discourse of burning money, the old reasoning based on keeping the two kinds of money separate seems a bit pointless. The new forms of paper simulations are so "realistic" that they are not so different in their form—and here form is everything—from the real money or item. On another level, the fact that the accusation lodged against Mr. Chan was added to a lawsuit is entirely reasonable, since it is illegal to exploit superstitious fears, especially with the intent to make a financial profit or do psychological harm. There are reports from Anhui and from Henan of persons placing offerings of paper money on the doorstep of an adversary for the purpose of striking terror and doing personal slander (Meng 2006; Liu and Li 2002). Treating a live adversary as a dead ghost by burning paper money on his doorstep is the tangible equivalent of the English curse "I worship the ground you have coming to you." This kind of terroristic threatening is treated seriously: police are summoned, and offenders are arrested and prosecuted in the local courts.

Vanities and Fantasies, Fads and Fashions of Desire

The realism and questions of authenticity wedged into the custom by ghost bills is intensified by additions to the replicas of modern commodities. These replicas (paper bindings or *zhǐzhā*) are not new in the sense that they replicate the world of material artifacts (see Scott 2007), but they are new to the extent that they represent modern commodities in their realism. These include, more or less in order of historical appearance, replicas of modern appliances (computers, air conditioners, refrigerators, microwaves, color TVs, cell phones, etc.); other forms of "symbolic" capital (diplomas, IDs, credit cards with unlimited overdraft, stocks, bankbooks, checkbooks, etc.); big-ticket luxuries (villas, limousines, yachts, etc.); games and gambling devices (mahjong sets, checkers); weapons, famous brands of electronics, cigarettes, wines, watches; mannequins of servants, private bodyguards and guard dogs, pilots, and doctors; and now mistresses, including beautiful ladies and famous actresses! The most recent additions are "sex supplies" (*xìng yòngpǐn*): Ecstasy, Viagra, and various types of condoms.

Although the mahjong set is hardly part of the newest wave of offerings— it has been available in the Hong Kong orbit for many years—it is invariably elevated to an exemplary exotic position because it has been and remains arguably the most salient symbol of decadence, rivaling in popular appeal and social stigma the paper money custom itself. In the report cited below (*Xin kuai bao* 2005), the reporter itemizes the exotic offerings put on prominent display by peddlers at the Silver River Cemetery in Guangzhou; not to be left out is the dominant symbol of decadence and dissipation: "Mahjong sets neatly displayed can be seen on every stand." Mahjong plays a prominent role in the lampoonery of the paper money custom (see Blake, forthcoming). There is a virtual continuum of exotics, beginning with the older and now ubiquitous ghost bills, then other such monetary instruments (credit cards, now bankbooks), running through entertainment and gambling devices (mahjong), and ending most recently in firearms and sex supplies. With each addition to the list of exotic fads, there is an increasing sense of scandal and degradation of the custom. They not only offend the traditional mores of many devotees, but also provide grist for scoffers and satirists to squib and burlesque the paper money custom. I hasten to remind the reader that squibbing and burlesquing the paper money custom is not simply the heavy hand of (state-sponsored) hegemony pushing down a venerable, vulnerable folk custom, but is endlessly complicated with the capacity of the folk custom to push right back, and in all directions, with plenty of allegory, nostalgia, irony and sarcasm, and fun and foolishness to go around.

Reading these news reports sometimes gives me the uncanny feeling that Qingming has become for Chinese journalists what Christmas is or was for American kids—it's the approach of the Qingming festival in early April that lights up the news services with reports about the new items for sending to the dead. Reporters fan out in many cities—a Guangzhou newspaper refers to their reporters "patrolling" the city—to find the new, exotic, outrageous fashions in offerings. I find remarkable that people can experience a medieval folk custom as exotic (foreign, Occidental) and fashionable partly because its momentum keeps pace with the "pop" of popular culture and, in the larger sense, with modernization—but, as we continue to witness, they do so with considerable consternation, and often with devotees and scoffers standing together on the side of tradition!

Private Planes and Villas

At the gate to the Silver River Cemetery in Guangzhou, a reporter encountered (as the accompanying photograph shows) row upon row of makeshift stands selling offerings for the four categories of human needs: clothing, comestibles, accommodation, and transportation. Among the big-ticket items: villas, limousines, and, this year (2005), airplanes. "This reporter asked the price for a limousine. The vendor could not wait to solicit in an obsequious manner the more expensive airplane. 'The limo is already dated. The airplane is hot this year. Let the dead forbears enjoy it down there'" (*Xin kuai bao* 2005). Costing from ¥8 to ¥12, the planes were selling well, according to the old peddler. This claim would be confirmed later when the reporter visited the Renji Road paper money wholesale market, where Chaoxing Street was jammed with cars carrying paper offerings, and according to the boss in one store, "the airplanes sold out yesterday." Back at the cemetery, the peddler went on to say that "a lot of people are buying airplanes, and some request a pilot to go with the airplane." Asking for a pilot to fly the airplane indicates that the airplane is a private vehicle, which makes sense: dead dad can't fly an airplane—he probably never flew in an airplane, so he needs a pilot to fly him. But requesting a pilot also evokes a sense of hyperreality in what Umberto Eco (1986) calls the authenticity of the fake, and it offers material for Fredric Jameson's (1998) theory of a schizophrenic disconnect in the cultural productions of consumer society. There is, nonetheless, a saving grace, at least for the anthropologist reading all this: "This reporter took a close look at the paper airplane and found it very crudely made, with poor-quality paper. The designs on the fuselage were illegible." The reporter implies that the crudity of the paper replica detracts from its worthiness as an offering. But this observation misses a crucial point: the "crudeness" of the paper replica does not detract from its authenticity as an artifice of the paper money custom. On the contrary, its authenticity is somehow enhanced by the coarseness, the rusticity of its artifice. It becomes more original as an artifice, which is more acceptable to many people than what seems real but is manifestly unreal or fake.

Three years later, the same market featured the "nine springs villas" as the fashionable offering of the Qingming season. "Nine springs" is a euphemism for netherworld, and there is nothing new or exotic about providing one's deceased forbears with a netherworld residence. After all, the idea of a netherworld residence begins, as it always has, with the tomb itself, but it doesn't end there. The imaginary world of paper offerings renews on a seasonable basis the respite of the tomb in dispelling the gloom and doom of the dead zone. The thing that makes these villas exotic is their association with modern luxuries. Back on Chaoxing Street in 2008,

> some of the four-story villas were as high as two meters and they had doors, windows, pillars. There were pavilions on the terraces, and there were nurses and waitresses indoors. Some of the villas even had security guards and cars. All kinds of modern household facilities were drawn in the villas, so that the deceased forebears could live a comfortable life. . . . [T]he small villa cost ¥15 and the one about two meters high cost ¥128. (*Guangzhou ribao* 2008)

The prices for villas seems fairly stable. The 2006 prices for villas in the Yinzhou District of Ningbo (Zhejiang Province) were about the same as those in Guangzhou the year before: "Here, this reporter noted, one so-called simple small villa about 30 centimeters high cost ¥15, whereas the bigger luxury villa about half a meter high with a garden and limousine cost ¥50" (Zu 2006).

Sex Supplies, Guns, and Beautiful Ladies

As we move to "sex supplies" and "guns" and "beautiful ladies," we encounter ostensibly new items in the galaxy of paper offerings. Sex supplies have captured a disproportionate share of the press in recent years. The sex supplies receive the most limelight, even though their inclusion in actual ritual offerings tends to be furtive, motivated more by the spirit of self-gratification than by public self-aggrandizement, and of course they are the least ubiquitous in their public presence in shops and offerings. For instance, from the 2005 Guangzhou report cited above, the reporter visited a funeral store on Yingyuan Road near the Sanyuangong Temple, where he noticed airplanes, cars, villas, and beautiful ladies on display,

> so he probed further to learn if he could purchase condoms and beautiful mistresses [*měinǚ èrnǎi*] to be burned for the dead. The proprietress called the wholesaler and asked if they have such things

as beautiful mistresses and Viagra and condoms. . . . The wholesaler
told her they had these kinds of offerings a short time ago. However,
agents from the government bureau that handles these matters
enforced the regulation, so the wholesalers don't offer this stuff
anymore. (*Xin kuai bao* 2005)

Then the proprietress uttered the perfect repartee to the reporter: "You might
as well burn a real condom; they only cost several yuan; for sure your ancestor can use it." This recourse to the real McCoy raises the possibility, rare
though it may be, that a paper replica (such as a matchbox-size box of paper
condoms for ¥20) costs more than the item it replicates. The likelihood of
this happening probably increases when the paper replica has to be special
ordered and made by hand![1] The proprietor in another store told this same
reporter that condoms, Viagra, and beautiful ladies need to be ordered from
the factory. But those things are not in great demand, even though there
are always some people asking for them. In northern China, the reticence
to countenance such things is greater: a vendor in Hebei, mistaking us for
newspaper reporters, denied that such offerings as condoms and guns even
exist, since they are contrary to the spirit of the custom. The Internet, for its
part, certainly tests my willingness to believe that some sex supplies, such as
the "G-spot device" (*G-diǎn tào*), are anything more than figments of virtual
reality—copied and pasted from one blog to another enough times to make
them "real," or, in Baudrillard's terms, "hyperreal." But it seems that some
people take such things seriously. Here, for instance, an official Chinese Web
page displays a box labeled *G-diǎn tào* amid other "sacrificial offerings to the
ancestors." The other offerings include a box of Viagra and a box of ordinary
condoms. The caption under the picture of the three boxes reads (in Chinese):
"'Viagra' and 'condoms' and other quite-enough-already sacrificial offerings
for the ancestors." The boxes all appear to be facsimiles (counterfeits) of real
commodities; they all are stamped with the official seal of quality control.
In the real world, they are part of a mushrooming industry and trade in
"sex supplies"—toys and tonics. Although such things are nothing new to
Chinese civilization (Gulik 2003), now they are products of modern science,
technology, and merchandising, and increasingly part of the capitalist-based
discourse (ideology). One marketer advertises the actual *G-diǎn tào* as a device
that enables a woman to experience orgasm, harmonize her menstrual period,
strengthen her nerves, and stave off illness, and, when it is *used in sequence*
with its own newer, scientifically engineered "three-dimensional" condom,

enables a woman to experience much more (*You'a* 2010). If we take seriously the offering of a condom, not to mention one specifically designed to facilitate female orgasm, we have to wonder who would donate such a thing, and to which of his or her ancestors, and to what end? What possible role could the offering of a condom play in a sacrifice to ancestors?

Many of the folks I have talked to in China plus participants in online forums and blogs "accept" the possibility that there are people who offer these exotic things to their deceased loved ones and ancestors.[2] (My only participation in the online traffic is reading what others write.) The online discussions express a panorama of attitudes and rationales. To a blogger's question (*Qixing de boke* 2010) "Can there be fewer appalling sacrificial offerings?" some respond with outright expressions of skepticism that such offerings as condoms exist, while others use the opportunity to have fun with the possibility that they do: "Offering condoms to a deceased father is a way to alleviate the fear that deceased father might sire a younger brother (to the donor) in the y*īn*-world." Or, as another puts it, offering condoms helps "the deceased to observe the one-child policy, which prevails even in Purgatory." Others point out that such beliefs could be inspired by popular ghost stories in which ghost children are sired by the deceased, which is bound to have a bad end for the living.

The appearance of such "unrestrained sacrifices," especially if they are hyperrealisms of cyberspace, pales against the widely observed phenomenon of strip dancing and live sex shows staged on modified trucks at funeral wakes and memorial services, which developed in Taiwan from the late 1970s to the early 1990s and more recently was reported in some villages of Donghai County, Jiangsu. "Striptease used to be a common practice at funerals in Donghai's rural areas to allure viewers, as local villagers believe that the more people who attend the funeral, the more the dead person is honored" (Zhu 2006). Once alerted, though, Jiangsu officials stopped the practice, declaring that it was "antisocial, destroyed tradition, made a mockery of the living and showed enormous disrespect for the dead." In Taiwan, where the practice has been more extensively documented, it developed around the "show truck" business as part of a broader shift in the forms of entertainment, from traditional folk ensembles, operas, and puppet shows, to popular music and dance performances with increasingly explicit erotic displays at many kinds of gatherings, including temple and deity anniversaries, weddings, and funerals (Chen Shihlun 2010). The entertainment at such gatherings, whether traditional folk opera or modern strip dance, was always intended to maximize the size and boisterousness of the gatherings. Boisterousness (*rènao*) signifies feelings of joy and vitality, which gain face and status for the sponsor. In the context of major changes in Taiwanese society, the puppet shows had become "vapid," while strip dancing and, in more sensational cases, live sex shows on a mobile stage were by comparison lively and profitable. The various kinds and levels of entertainment, including the explicit sexuality at funerals and memorial services, varied in the way they were sequenced in the ritual service. As we saw in chapter 4, the ritual service begins with gravity and solemnity and gradually shifts to boisterousness and jest, and if the final mood extends to jouissance, the inclusion of strip dancing does not seem so far-fetched. In fact, expressions of sexuality in contexts of death can be found in many cultures, and they can be expressed philosophically: "Death is the sexualisation of life" (Baudrillard 1993:185), and "sexuality and death . . . are simply the culminating points of the festival nature celebrates" (Bataille 1977:61). Anthropologists, who neither wax so philosophical nor register much shock at what others view as a violation of tradition, rather look to that same tradition for the social, political, economic, and symbolic connections to explain the apparent changes. In the matter of strip dancing, we note the link between sexual symbolism and symbols of fertility and longevity that are traditional in marriage and funeral rites, not to mention the whole fabric of the paper money custom. The symbolic link between male longevity and immortality, which depends on sexuality, and the female capacity to bear progeny (the source of immortality) is deeply etched into the patriarchal formations of Asia, not to mention the human male psyche in general. In Asia, the link is enacted in all manner of public ceremonies. In Honolulu, for instance, the Qingming memorial gathering at the tomb of the Grand Ancestor includes the trustees of the Lin Yi cemetery association and Chinatown dignitaries, mostly old and middle-aged men having their official group photograph taken with all the contestants of the Narcissus beauty pageant (all young, beautiful, talented ladies dressed in stylish *qípáo*). In my mind's eye, this scene is but a prelude to burning effigies of "beautiful ladies" for the ancestors that have become a topic of so much discussion in China. Of course, Viagra and condoms are new symbols that signify sexuality but do not signify fertility. Rather, they signify longevity in ways that reify sexuality under the sign of "pleasure." In other words, the signs of sexuality and longevity are less about fertility—they move away from the podal symbol of labor, production, and reproduction in bound feet—and more about sensual pleasure (consumption and dissipation) as the basis of *social* reproduction, which is in another, perhaps older sense, antisocial. The condoms signify a new kind of antifertility pleasure-oriented reproduction, the reproduction of sensual pleasure (especially for women) without "children to foul the bed," while the other, Viagra, connects sexual pleasure with longevity in ways that undermine reproductive intentions, Viagra being age-related. Without "children to foul the bed," however, there is no paper money to recompense the ancestors (Smith 1894:185).

A reporter in Tangshan, Hebei (Jin 2009), visited a number of funeral stores in search of exotic offerings, including effigies of beautiful ladies. As he went from one to the next, he found mostly conventional things. The boss in one shop told him that the modern luxury offerings such as paper TVs, cars, and so on were all put in the rear of the store due to their large sizes, although, reading between the lines, it is just as likely that these things are put in the back to keep them out of sight. But a peddler selling paper money beside the road told the reporter that if he needed "beautiful ladies," he could order them from the shop. In Guangzhou, Guangdong, a volunteer student who was working in the Silver River crematory told a reporter that this was really an eye-opener for him: "Not only did he see people burning servants and body guards, but he also saw mistresses burned as offerings. 'Some people who brought these exotic offerings burned them furtively, and today I saw a family standing around a big pit burning a big pile of high-status luxury offerings which included a particularly conspicuous paper mannequin with colorful makeup'" (*Xin kuai bao* 2005).

The beautiful ladies (*měinǚ*) and mistresses or secondary wives (*èrnǎi*) are perhaps the most provocative of exotic offerings in China today, perhaps because these effigies strike so close to real-life anxieties. An official online forum (*Han feng gu yun* 2010) posed the question in almost Confucian terms: "Is burning mistresses for the ancestors a licentious way to show mourning?" Many responses to this question observe how burning mistresses reflects the sorry state of social reality: "It is a reflection of the reality in China. It is a kind of Chinese humor." "It's making fun of society." "It just shows how many stupid things there are and how many stupid people there are." "These people's actions are really vulgar; however, [we] have to admit that this is the social climate today. Sigh . . ." "It accurately reflects the vulgar and morbid society we live in." One alluded to burning mistresses by paraphrasing "the chairman" (i.e., Mao) to the effect that there is nothing new here, since taking a mistress is a form of private property which for several thousand years got China nowhere. Some put it in terms of social class: "It epitomizes the

way officials and rich people actually live." To paraphrase another, "it's a way
the poor people finally get to enjoy the exotic things that rich people enjoy
in real life." In other words, after death, when everything is "free of charge,"
there is a "second allocation" that benefits the poor. Burning effigies of mistresses—"what a lot of nonsense! You can make whatever you want, except
for a mistress. When you burn a paper mistress, over there [in the *yīn*-world]
it is still a paper mistress; she can only be looked at, she can't be used, which
can only make the ancestor very frustrated." Clearly, many online responders
have fun with what they perceive as the logic of the money burning custom.
From its inception in April 2010 until the last time I looked in August
2010, there were almost twenty-eight thousand hits on this blog. There have
always been mannequin-like human figures among the items of the paper
money galaxy. In a previous chapter we traced the use of human figures in
mortuary rituals back to Confucius' purported affirmation that the tradition
of using straw effigies of humans for graveside sacrifice be done with attention to the effigy lest the desire for using real humans be reinvoked. "Paper
offerings traditionally include papier-mâché domestic servants; but now we
see more personal body guards, even guard dogs. We can also expect that
paper pilots will be available to fly our private jets. And the female servants
have begun to look prettier and prettier with scantier and scantier clothing,
so now we have life-sized scantily clothed beautiful ladies for graveside sacrifices" (Jin 2009).

   While the beautiful mistresses seem to be the most provocative item,
guns and corporate logos are more significant for my thesis. A 2006 report
from Yinzhou, Ningbo, describes the crowd of people making offerings in
a nearby cemetery. They displayed the usual offering materials—the otherworld notes, incense, and candles.

> Some peddlers asked each customer with an air of mystery, "Boss,
> would you like something more valuable?" This reporter asked,
> what else is new? The woman in her fifties said, "There are some
> offerings we dare not sell in public, but we have them close by. If
> you're serious, I'll take you there for a look." In the residence not far
> away this reporter saw piles of paper buildings, cars, servants, and
> also young beauties, and even airplanes, tanks, and assault rifles.
> The reporter pretended to be curious and asked: "Previously people
> burned the cars, I can understand that, but how come you sell those
> tanks and assault rifles?" The woman answered, "Nowadays, it's not

so secure, even in the *yīn*-world. If you burn some weapons and send them down to your forebears, they won't be bullied." (Zu 2006)

In another report (*Fazhi wanbao* 2008) the Beijing hawkers' reputation for glibness is manifest:

> In the lane close to Shijingshan Moshikou morning market this reporter encountered two peddlers selling sets of paradise mahjong, paradise checkers, and heavenly kingdom handguns, etc. All of these mahjong and checkers are made of paper and were packaged in dictionary-size boxes costing ¥15 per set. The two peddlers were shouting: "Buy these sets of mahjong and checkers for the deceased old people in case they are getting bored there!" When a young man bought a paradise mahjong set, the peddler recommended that he also purchase a Heavenly Kingdom handgun. It's a "54 handgun" [7.62 mm. sidearm made in 1954] about the size of a matchbox, costing ¥3 each. The peddler said, Why don't you buy a gun for the deceased old man so when he plays mahjong and the loser tries to cheat him, he can use the gun to deal with the cheat?
>
> Someone asked the peddler in a joking way, do you have any missiles? The peddler answered, I can make an order for you. We have whatever you want. Even if you want an American aircraft carrier, we can make it for you. According to the peddler, because the paradise mahjong is a new item, a lot of people think it's entertaining and accordingly it sells well.

On a government-licensed Web site, under the forum on society (Tiexue Net 2009), the discussion pivoted on the reasons for including guns and other weapons in an offering to deceased loved ones. One person questioned the habit of transferring huge amounts of wealth to the other side, given the possibility that deceased loved ones could be robbed. Others argued that transfers of huge amounts of wealth need to be protected by weapons such as handguns. Another man included a handgun to protect the deceased with his money on the journey to the *yīn*-world, lest he be robbed. One person actually strapped replicas of guns around his deceased father's waist before sending him off to purgatory. Sometimes it's hard to tell how far into their cheeks their tongues are pressed when bloggers and chatters are declaiming their or others' paper money practices. Talk that brackets off the real world can of course be serious, more or less. Traditionally people simply relied on cash money to purchase an easy passage to the other side, but now some reportedly carry guns to protect their treasures. Much of the back-and-forth takes the absurdity, be it sarcasm or another kind of foolishness, to extremes by adding one system of make-believe to another system of make-believe: "You can burn a Superman or Spiderman outfit instead of ordinary clothes, then the dead ancestors won't be afraid of anyone." Or "Just burn the earth globe so they will be king of the earth!!!!!" One example in effect does this very thing. Ostensibly discussing a real case, and in a more ominous tone, one blogger reports that a couple of years ago, a neighboring family burned a whole arsenal of paper weapons for a young family member:

> The dead kid's parents burned a big stack of paper for him. Can you guess what was inside? If I tell you, you will be really aghast. There were all kinds of self-defense weapons like handguns, assault rifles, automatics, machine guns, mortars, tanks, fighter airplanes, aircraft carriers; and there was one big elliptical thing, which I could not identify. I asked the dead kid's brother. He told me that it was a thermonuclear bomb because his brother had been a military freak and he liked the hydrogen bomb the best. I was really scared and at that point I said to myself, with all these weapons in the otherworld, the kid could set up the Republic of Yellow Spring [euphemism for the otherworld].

As I read this, it occurred to me that not only is the *yīn*-world becoming reified and commoditized and inflated; it is also experiencing a proliferation of nuclear arsenals!

The fact that most of these stories about guns, condoms, beautiful ladies, mistresses, and now movie stars tell how these things can be special-ordered from the factory in the spirit of "whatever you desire" begs the question of exactly how common these items are in actual use, a question we must keep asking. Clearly there is some exaggeration on the part of the mass media, but to what end is not entirely clear, other than a sincere attempt to reform and educate. But it is probably more complicated than this staid formula. While most news stories end by abjuring the new-wave exotica and suggesting the more dignified—they use the term "civilized"—alternatives (fresh flowers, tree planting, online memorials, etc.), the paper money custom is becoming harnessed to a new, urban folklore that satirizes and allegorizes the tensions in modern society. The current hype of a perennial, often acute anxiety around male potency, the common assumption today that every man has a mistress outside marriage, the debate over whether condoms should be easily available in dispensing machines in hotel rooms and universities (to reduce the use of abortion for contraceptive purposes), the growing resentments between emerging economic classes (the nouveau riche, especially the ones who profited from the privatization of the collective economy, versus the masses of ordinary folks who didn't), is being told and retold in the idiom of paper money.

New Outlets and Marketing Strategies

Paper money has become part of the modern consumer economy on at least three fronts: first, the appearance of brand labels on offering items; second, the extent to which paper monies depend on marketing strategies to increase the volume of their sales; third, the extent to which marketing of paper money is being commercialized. News reports give evidence for all three of these processes. A report from Fuzhou, Fujian (*Dongnan kuaibao* 2009) describes how the approach of Qingming finds the incense and candle stores stocked with all kinds of traditional paper monies. Some of the stores along Fuzhou Street showcase the new-wave offerings by placing them in conspicuous places.

> What is different is that the offering industry has enhanced the
> awareness of brand names. . . . not only has the kind of offering
> changed, but now the offerings carry such famous brand names as
> Mercedes-Benz, XO cognac, Nestle, Lenovo, etc. . . . The incense and
> candle store located in the Junmen community of Fuzhou's Gulou
> district showcased famous makes of automobiles, gift boxes of food,
> and mahjong sets. The elaborate gift box of food includes Three-
> Five brand cigarettes, which uses revamped packages. There is also a
> bottle of XO cognac, a jar of *Tie Guanyin* tea, and a jar of Nestle milk
> powder. But all of these things are paper counterfeits. The boss told
> this reporter the price of these famous brand offerings is relatively
> high. . . . It is more profitable than the traditional line of offerings.

Putting a brand name even on a facsimile or paper effigy, or using a revamped logo, jacks up the price; and the idea that the brands are "counterfeit" (*wěi-zào pǐn*) implies the malfeasant use of a corporate logo. I can hardly imagine that a modern corporation would be glad to have its logo used to enhance the profits of tradespeople pandering superstition, especially if it gratifies the desires of the dead. (This may be a naive assumption about what corporations are glad of.) On the other hand, the logic of such a destination for corporate logos is more than plausible. It is downright compelling if we follow the peroration of Jean Baudrillard (1993) that nothing is more "deadening" than the political economy of the sign, in which the process of simulation has replaced production, the ultimate expression of which, in my view, is the corporate logo.

Continuing in the vein of that which deadens, the *Beijing Daily* reported a case in which famous-brand-name cigarettes were being marketed under the authority of the Office of the Otherworld Tobacco Company. "In Tonghui Cemetery . . . , one businessman was selling paper cigarette packs printed with the characters for famous brands, such as 'China,' 'Little Panda,' 'Fortune and Longevity.' Except for the name, 'Under the Authority of the Office of the Otherworld Tobacco Company,' the colors and decorations were exact copies of the real cigarette packs" (Dou 2009). The story goes on to report how the Industrial and Commercial Department confiscated many sacrificial offerings tinged with "feudal superstition" in three local cemeteries and revoked the licenses of two fireworks vendors. It was in fact (and, we might add, indeed) the Tongzhou district government's Industrial and Commercial Department that alerted the news reporter to the story. As I read the story, I wondered if anyone, including the reporter, saw the irony in famous brands of cigarettes, which are government monopolies, being marketed under the authority of the Otherworld Tobacco Company, or was the sarcasm so obvious that it provoked official interdiction under the cover of "feudal superstition"?

Another marketing strategy is to package the paper money materials into a kit so the buyer or even the vendor, who is not otherwise knowledgeable or who has lost touch with the tradition, can feel confident that at least she is using the correct materials for the purpose at hand. Within the far-flung orbit of the Hong Kong paper money products, there are the prepackaged kits for each domestic and public divinity, for ancestors and various demonic spirits. One of the popular kits, even in my hometown of St. Louis, Missouri, according to the grocery vendor, is the kit for exorcising (literally worshipping) the petty person (*bài xiǎorén*). More colloquially it is called "beating the petty person": either by worshipping—in effect, buying off—or beating to shreds, or both to be on the safe side, one can cast off the baleful effects of a husband's mistress, or some other nemesis or demonic bother. The package contains the necessary charms, effigies for beating to shreds with an old shoe (the old shoe does not come with the kit), paper monies, candles, and incense to conduct the exorcism. I digress! The prepackaging strategy has also come to Beijing. A report from the *Beijing Morning News* (*Beijing chenbao* 2008) tells how a Qingming Gift Box, which includes paper money, is being sold by the Bianyifang Anhua Roast Duck Restaurant.[3] Disguised as a customer, the reporter noted that

> in a conspicuous spot just inside the door was the display counter for the Qingming Gift Box. Realizing that the "customer" was interested in the Qingming Gift Box, the waitress came up promptly to introduce it. This journalist noticed that the wooden Gift Box had two layers. The top layer held apples and oranges, distilled spirits, and two packages of baked pastry. "These are offerings, and they all convey good meanings," the waitress said. The lower level held the stuff used for sacrifice. Other than the gold paint used for painting the tomb stone, writing brush, incense burner, and incense, there was golden yellow paper money, about ten bundles. The waitress said the paper money was also an offering. Besides these, there was a bottle of Peasant Spring Mineral Water. The waitress explained that the bottled water was not for drinking but for wiping down the gravestone. (*Beijing chenbao* 2008)

The reporter gives a separate paragraph to a Mr. Ma, who as a customer at the restaurant had been introduced to the box and upon opening it was surprised to find paper money: "Paper money is feudal stuff, isn't it?. . . Since the government doesn't allow it to be sold, how come businessmen can sell it in public?" Mr. Ma then waxes politically correct: "Nowadays people promote the civilized way of making offerings and sweeping tombs, without burning paper; every citizen should abide by this, especially the businessmen." The next paragraph includes customers with different points of view. One customer said that he still burns paper, makes offerings, and sweeps the tombs every year. "However, it seems that wiping the tombstone with Peasant Spring Mineral Water is too extravagant." (This customer did not stop to wonder whether the water in the Peasant Spring Mineral Water bottle was actually from a mineral spring or simply from the tap in the kitchen!) "The waitress said that the Qingming Gift Box was sold exclusively by Bianyifang Anhua Roast Duck Restaurant; they started with a total of fifty sets, ten of which have already been sold for ¥199 each." As the reporter turns to the assistant manager, he seems to exchange his masquerade as a customer for the countenance of a Mike Wallace type: Ms. Wang is impelled to explain how "the ten bundles of yellow paper are not coins, but are just cut to resemble the shape [of coins], and that this is not paper money": "They are nothing but what's placed on top of tombs when people sweep tombs and make offerings." She also explains that the Qingming Gift Box was mainly for display not for making profit—she obviously knows the regulations and is maneuvering around the letter of the law—and neither did she think it contained *superstitious* items. Rather, the paper money is a *customary* item. "If the customers view the boxes as feudal superstition," said Ms. Wang, "then I will remove them."

The next day, the reporter visited the Funeral and Burial Office of the Beijing Department of Civil Administration, where staff provided him with both the national and municipal regulations that banned any company or individual from making or selling feudal superstitious funeral and burial stuff like otherworld notes, paper dolls, and paper horses. "Paper handgun also belongs to this category." (Another report adds that otherworld notes are not allowed to be sold unless licensed by the Civil Administration Department.) Citizens can report infractions of these regulations to the relevant authorities, which is what the reporter did on the following day. The subadministrative department of Beijing's West District promised to investigate the roast duck restaurant's Qingming Gift Box.

The lesson here is that the regulations concerning paper money may be enforced when complaints are lodged. And as the paper money custom becomes increasingly part of the industrial commercial big-time, and out of the hands of seasonal street peddlers, it will become a point of increased contention. The reputable Oushang superstore is a case in point. Part of its reputation is its foreign origin (France) and its location in Sijiqing, Haidian District, a Beijing district reputed for its many institutions of higher learning and burgeoning affluence. Two reports focus on the discovery that Oushang is stocking shelves with paper money. Beijing's *Jinghua Daily* (Zhou 2009) reported that the multitude of Sunday shoppers found shelves close to the main aisle displaying a lot of colorfully printed materials that resembled real paper notes. A closer look revealed that these materials were otherworld notes used as offerings. "Here, they were obviously treated as a commodity: the bar codes were pasted on the packages, the price was marked out, and the characters for 'Shanghai Yiyuan Office and Stationery Supplies Limited' were also printed on the packages. The adjacent shelves held bundles and bundles of round-shaped paper money and yellow paper" (Zhou 2009). The reporter goes on to describe the reactions of shoppers passing by: most were bemused at first, then they realized that this stuff was actually paper money, so they wondered why it was being sold in the superstore. Some disapproved: "One female shopper passed by muttering to herself." A few minutes later, a couple discovered the otherworld notes, and, looking very surprised, the woman blurted out, "The superstore sells this kind of stuff when it is barely allowed to be sold outside. The Qingming festival is coming soon; we may as well buy some here." And with this, she grabbed two stacks of otherworld notes and put them in her shopping cart. After interviewing quite a few shoppers, the reporter concluded that everyone felt surprised to see otherworld notes sold in the superstore. Most held that otherworld notes are superstitious stuff, but the practice of burning paper at Qingming is a special occasion that won't end anytime soon. Still, as the reporter continued to summarize his poll of public opinion, he concluded that significant public places like this superstore should not be selling otherworld notes in the form of a commodity. Mr. Yan, manager of the household goods, wriggled out of his encounter with the reporter by claiming that he "was not very clear concerning the policy of selling otherworld notes"; he asked the reporter to contact the assistant manager of the superstore. After a lot of procrastination, the staff finally informed the reporter that the assistant manager was taking that day off from work and they were not able to contact him.

Another report from the *Beijing Daily* tells the serious consequences when the above revelation came under the purview of the local authorities (Dou 2009). Noting the French origin of the Oushang superstore, with its shelves of paper monies, this reporter invoked the old quip "When in Rome do as the Romans do"—sarcastically, of course, but at whose expense is not entirely clear:

> Agents from the Sijiqing Office of Industry and Commerce informed the managers of this superstore that according to "Administrative Regulations Regarding Funeral and Burial in Beijing," companies and individuals are banned from making or selling feudal superstitious stuff such as otherworld notes, paper dolls, and paper horse [charms]. The staff [of Oushang] will temporarily forfeit the unsold portion of feudal superstitious funeral and burial stuff, and they will also be fined a sum that is more than the total income but less than

three times the income made from the stuff that was sold. (Dou 2009)

The agents temporarily confiscated 670 packages of unsold otherworld notes, 332 packages of First Treasures (*yuánbǎo*), and 784 packages of yellow paper; then they went on to inspect and confiscate materials from other stores and cemeteries under their jurisdiction.

The New Criticism

Most news reports reveal how the paper money custom is becoming more and more popular as it seeps and spreads into the industrial and commercial infrastructure, and how strangely it exudes its own animus of exotic fads and fashions. The surprise of the reporter often takes the voice of a likely customer—the politically correct Mr. Ma, who remarks that he thought all this superstitious stuff was illegal. Or the woman who expressed surprise that the superstore sells this kind of stuff, then grabbed two stacks of otherworld notes and put them in her shopping cart. Now places such as restaurants, grocery stores, and foreign superstores are marketing the stuff, and the seepage is moving northward into the nation's capital, where the circumspection seems most vigilant and lacking of a funny bone. Many reporters, especially in Beijing, find astounding and newsworthy things that have been around for many years outside Beijing, especially in the southern part of the country— the types of things I described in the previous chapter, except for the guns, sex supplies, and mistresses!

The criticism that is expressed through the mass media is pretty uncompromising, especially toward the new-wave exotic offering materials. There is considerable give on tolerating the more traditional, less ostentatious offering materials, especially as we get farther away from Beijing (see Blake, forthcoming). The criticism, which comes at the end of most news stories, is not a blanket condemnation univocally emanating from "the broad masses," as was the practice in the Maoist years. Now the criticism is on behalf of "civilization," which points the finger at "ordinary people and businessmen [whose] fascination with these exotic offerings reflects a vulgar and vicious worship psychology [which] if pampered puts into peril prevailing tastes and customs" (*Guangzhou ribao* 2008). The finger pointing is often attributed to other ordinary people in the vicinity who feel that these exotic offerings are "not only a waste of money, but also make the originally serious customary festival appear ridiculous and vulgar" (Jin 2009). But we also get the occasional voice of a customer such as the one from Beijing who said he still burns paper, makes offerings, and sweeps the tombs, but finds the Peasant Spring Mineral Water in Ms. Wang's Qingming Gift Box too extravagant for wiping down a gravestone.

But all the evidence, even if only the preponderance of the news stories themselves, suggests that most ordinary people observe various aspects of the paper money custom. Some news services have polled members of their community on the acceptability of the custom. Despite the limitations of survey results, some of the data are nonetheless revealing. For instance, residents of an unspecified sample from Yingkou, Liaoning (northern China), were surveyed for attitudes toward the exotic offerings (paper house, paper cell phone, paper beauties, etc.): Using round figures, 34 percent responded that they buy these exotic kinds of offering materials, depending on the situation. Twenty-four percent of respondents asserted that they did not purchase these kinds of materials because they are not traditional. Seventeen percent objected to exotic offerings because they distort the meaning of sacrifice. Almost the same percentage consider buying these things out of a felt need to express their filial piety. Seven percent consider buying these things to keep up with changing times, and almost 3 percent consider buying them for curiosity's sake (Hui 2009).

Moving from Yingkou in the far North to Haikou in the far South (Hainan), we find the *Haikou Evening News* (*Haikou wanbao* 2009) reporting in a long article that identifies its sample as random interviews of 100 residents in Jinniuling Park, Renmin Park, Donghu Road, and Bo'ai Road. Seventy-four percent of these respondents held that the exotic offerings profaned and disrespected the deceased; 21 percent held that Qingming offerings should advance with the times; and 5 percent said the exotic offerings are astounding but very creative. These survey responses from the northernmost and southernmost parts of the country indicate that (1) the vast majority of respondents recognized the category of exotic offerings, and (2) a sizable proportion are able to rationalize the exotic offerings. Indeed, the 2008 *Guangzhou Daily* (*Guangzhou ribao*) report cited earlier recognizes the extent to which the paper money custom, in particular the exotic element, has insinuated itself into the ordinary layers of society, which is what alarms the officials in the Guangzhou Funeral and Burial Administrative Bureau who oversee the offering market. Finally, the third conclusion we can draw from the surveys just cited is that there was no category of respondents opposed to the *traditional* paper money custom. The 2009 *Haikou Evening News* survey also reported the stated expenditures for paper monies during the recent Qingming festival: 63 percent of households spent between ¥100 and ¥200. Twenty-nine percent spent ¥200 to ¥500. And 8 percent expended ¥500 to ¥1,000. These kinds of estimates and numbers are typical and frequent in the news reporting of the past several years.

Conclusion

I am not prepared to follow my intuition and predict that the burlesque of the paper money custom is its last hurrah. I once thought the Great Proletarian Cultural Revolution would extinguish the paper money custom. I hate to be wrong twice. The fact that the Maoists did not extinguish the custom left echoing in my brain *The Communist Manifesto*'s declaration that international capital and technology is the most destructive force of all things sacred. The Cultural Revolution's attempt to accomplish this with its application of ideology and organization (Schurmann 1968) proved insipid by comparison to the capitalist juggernaut in its drive to make the world real, or seemingly real, instead of mysterious.

In this chapter I have given the last word on the topic of paper money to its opponents. These are Chinese voices, even if it is obvious that I play a part in bringing them to the reader's attention and placing them in the penultimate chapter of my book, the point being that too often we ethnographers (including myself) get caught up in the mysteries and reifications of our subject matter; we labor under a misguided version of cultural relativism and fail to see the native capacity to satirize and oppose their own customs, or we dismiss the native satire, or cover it up, or deconstruct this form of opposition as exogenous or hegemonic. This kind of "ethnographic refusal," to borrow a term from Sherry Ortner (1995), denies the ability of ordinary people to "see through" the mysteries that they themselves create, a point that Helen Codere (1956) demonstrated with the Kwakiutl potlatch and that David Graeber (2001) has enlarged upon with great insight.

I have argued throughout that the paper money custom belongs as much to the scoffers as to the devotees; but, more importantly, this polarization is purely heuristic, since I cannot remember ever meeting a devotee who took the custom so seriously as to be completely unable to recognize its humorous side—although we have encountered some pretty grim-faced devotees in the mass media who might qualify for the part—nor do I recall meeting more than one or two whose scoffing was so embittered as to surrender that certain twinkle in the eye that conveys another sensibility, of "a spirit in a world without spirit"; although the reporter who brought Ms. Wang's Qing-ming Gift Box to the attention of the local authorities might be one of many exceptions to this rule. But for scoffers, the humor provides traction to their purpose; indeed, it is the only traction they have; and besides, many a scoffer can be seen participating in the paper money custom. We saw in my survey results reported in chapter 1 how even persons who denied the existence of the *yīn*-world show a tolerance for paper money burning or a willingness to burn paper money on certain occasions. There is a disconnect, after all. For me the typical person—for the sake of argument, let's say there is something we can label as "typical"—would be the Shijiazhuang retired truck driver who said he didn't believe the spirits receive the burned paper but he burns the paper anyway. His meaning was somewhere between denying the existence of the spirits and denying the effectiveness of the ritual, plus somewhere between affirming the force of habit and affirming the sense of obligation. This is not prevaricating or equivocating, in my book. This is the essence of the custom and the material spirit of the Chinese lifeworld.

CHAPTER 9

Value

Toward the end of *Argonauts of the Western Pacific* (1922) there is a passage in which Malinowski summarizes his study of the Trobriand kula with words that I take as the epigraph for *Burning Money:*

> Thus, in several aspects, the Kula presents to us a new type of phenomenon, lying on the borderland between the commercial and the ceremonial and expressing a complex and interesting attitude of mind. But though it is novel, it can hardly be unique. For we can scarcely imagine that a social phenomenon so deeply connected with fundamental layers of human nature, should only be a sport and a freak, found in one spot of the earth alone. Once we have found this new type of ethnographic fact, we may hope that similar or kindred ones will be found elsewhere. (Malinowski 1984:513–514)

No less than kula, burning money is a novel ethnographic fact, a "type of phenomenon, lying on the borderland between the commercial and the ceremonial" and "deeply connected with fundamental levels of human nature." Malinowski might have added that what is for us "a borderland" is for Trobrianders a prototype.

The paper money custom is a large network of industrial and commercial enterprise that produces money and things for the purpose of undertaking commerce with the spirits. But the commerce with the spirits is conducted according to ceremonial giving. This "ceremonial commerce" sublates the two aspects of human nature that Chinese otherwise relate to one another by telling them apart. The one that seeks profit (*li*) motivates ordinary persons to nickel-and-dime each other. The other, which cultivates giving, sacrifice, and etiquette (*lǐ*), motivates people to give themselves to others. The *lǐ* of etiquette makes ordinary persons who are merely human (*rén* meaning "human") into humane persons (*rén* written with the graph for "human" compounded with the graph for "two") by making the body ever more mindful of its obligations to others over and against the profit to be derived. This begins with parents. As the Reverend Arthur Smith (1894:185) bluntly observed on the basis of a popular Chinese proverb: "Neither parents nor children are under any illusions upon this subject. 'If you have no children to foul the bed, you will have no one to burn paper at the grave.' Each generation pays the debt which is exacted of it by the generation which preceded it, and in turn requires from the generation which comes after, full payment to the uttermost farthing." In some elemental sense, the money-burning custom turns the ordinary means of trade into the ceremonial means of showing one's piety (*xiào*) and, hence, humanity (*rén*). Behavior that is motivated by ritual, ceremony, and etiquette is of course pure artifice, which is the thing about becoming human(e) that Chinese cherish, but which also opens complicated and vexing questions about the originality, authenticity and deception insinuated in artifice, a discussion that, based on my reading, pervades the Confucian classic *Book of Rites* as much as it does the everyday language of politeness (Stafford 2000:104). The money burning custom in important ways allows plebes to act as patricians.

If the object of kula was fame (Munn 1986) and the principal object of burning money in commerce with the spirits is filial piety, the quest of the Kwakiutl potlatch, another prestation ceremony, was yet another quest for immortality. In potlatch, as described originally by Franz Boas and George Hunt (Boas 1897:341–357), men bestowed vast stores of property on other men or destroyed their own stores in a frenzied gathering that attracted an assembly of spirits and gods: "It is not only in order to display power, wealth and lack of self-interest that slaves are put to death, precious oils burnt, copper objects cast into the sea, and even houses of princes set on fire. It is also in order to sacrifice to the spirits and the gods, indistinguishable from their living embodiments, who bear their titles and are their initiates and allies" (Mauss 1990:16). With some obvious and not-so-obvious differences, Chinese still do this, albeit with paper replicas. It is possible that ancient China passed through a phase that was similar to the Kwakiutl potlatch (Cooper 1982), although the question of how this ancient potlatch might have been connected with the much later money burning custom—for example, as an evolutionary homologue or cultural survival—has not been addressed, to my knowledge. Be that as it may, the similarities between the Kwakiutl potlatch and the Chinese money-burning custom are offset by some obvious differences: the money burning custom is prestation directed *toward* indemnifying the spirits of the dead and honoring them as gods, and the wealth (servants, houses, coppers, and gold bars) takes the form of paper replicas. In other words, the Chinese custom is not about abandoning worldly possessions per se; or, ipso facto, the realization of Eros or divinity in oneself; and the animus in giving is more subtle, often couched in or hidden behind outward forms of etiquette. With some exceptions, the gift of paper replicas is not the behest of the spirits and gods personating the actions of human donors; on the contrary, the gift is explicitly from human donors to the spirits of the dead and of the gods. That is, unless real money is being handed out to living people under the guise of "spirit favors." For the logic of paper money is that money (and all wealth and valuables) belong to the spirits; when sending money from this world to the world of ancestral spirits, at least in Shanghai, it is good to have it blessed by the high divinities, especially those of the Buddhist pantheon. It is also possible for the living to receive real money from the deities impersonating a living person. At the ecstatic finale of a Dao Mau temple ceremony in Hanoi, that part of the Taoist-based ceremony that is most characteristically Vietnamese, the patron host of the ceremony, possessed by her patron deities, dances and passes out "spirit favors" in the form of real money to the assembled participants. The money or "favor" has been transmuted into a "lucky" charm—or perhaps we should say its original charm has been restored and enhanced by the spiritual host. The charm of the money-favor is more procreant than ordinary money and is used to buy offerings for other spirits or to invest in a business. The money-favor comes from the host's own expense account and contributions of assembled guests (Vu, forthcoming). This "redistribution" has some earmarks of the potlatch, but is otherwise different, since the host is not expressing her abandonment of worldly property, and there is no explicable intention to humiliate her guests, although I would argue that there is a definite social animus in this redistributive, sharing gesture. The money is returned to the spirit world, washed in the sacred, restored to a community of goods, and, with its original charm restored, redistributed to that community. Thus, paper money is designed to be given to spirits by living persons, whereas "spirit money," or, more accurately, spirit favors that include forms of "real money," are given in the name of and by means of a spirit or god possessing the donor-patron of the ceremony.

Social Economy

I have pointedly chosen to compare burning money with kula and potlatch because they are celebrities in the world of ethnology and thus familiar to most readers. Their celebrity is not only their originality, but also the work of a little book entitled *The Gift* by Marcel Mauss, which has been rightly characterized as generating "more debate, discussion, and ideas than any other work of anthropology" (Graeber 2001:152). Mauss used the original ethnography of these prestation ceremonials to theorize the nature of societies in which production and circulation take the form of reciprocal gift-giving. Mauss's focus on the spectacular nature of kula and potlatch allowed him to disclose the "spiritual" aspects of reciprocal giving. I mean by this that giving stuff away entails or arouses in humans a certain agonistic spirit, or, in my terms, "a human social animus," and this is often expressed in stylized ways, including stylized forms of animosity and ritual insult typical of potlatch and kula. The other spiritual aspect of a reciprocal gift-giving way of life is the involvement of otherworldly beings, since "indeed, it is they who are the true owners of the things and possessions of this world" (Mauss 1990:16), which in my view amounts to the mystification of a social economy.

Mauss's purpose was to broaden theories of exchange by comparing the circulation of valued things in cultures that were radically different from modern Europe. Mauss theorized that societies such as the Trobriand and Kwakiutl produced things of value by giving them away in such a manner as (1) to constitute persons as social beings or collectives rather than "individuals" or "utilities" and (2) to insinuate the donor's social animus in the gift such that something equivalent would necessarily be returned. Acts of giving instilled an obligation to give back. These were "gift economies" to the extent they were *socially* embedded economies, or what I simply call "social economies." Thus from many points of view (including my own) they were *social* formations that accomplished economic purposes in which the acts of "producing" and "giving away" and "getting" were *continuous* processes that instilled the value of the donor's person in ways that obligated a return. Other ethnographers took up the task of enlarging on questions concerning how exactly value is realized.

One of the most insightful is Nancy Munn's *The Fame of Gawa* (1986). Although Munn does not use the term "lifeworld" (i.e., the encompassing world of immediate experience), she in effect theorizes the Gawan lifeworld by describing a manifold of intersubjective spheres in which actors engage and finesse each other by producing, giving, taking, and consuming. The lifeworld of intersubjective engagements is predicated on an aesthetic of embodiment (with its emphasis on bodily presentations and décors) that finesse relationships in giving and getting things and fending off demons and witches that disappear things and persons by consuming them. "The witch is the prototypic consumer" (1986:14).

The higher and more positive values are the producing and gifting endeavors that make things appear by bringing them to light, while consuming, making things disappear, is fraught with ambiguity, since disappearing things covered in the darkness of interiors reverses and negates and, sometimes in the form of witchery, subverts that which is valued. Here, the *balouma* ("life force," or what I refer to as the mystified human social animus) loses its social, giving, creative capacity and becomes a kind of pure animosity in acts of consumption and destruction. The dialectic between light and dark, appearance and disappearance, is also associated with life and death, collective and individual, a dialectic that personifies the senses with greater alacrity than does Chinese *yīnyáng*. The whole of the Gawan lifeworld strains toward the aesthetic work of bringing things to light (*yáng*) and, by that effort, realizing that which gives value. Differences in value are related to the quality and scale of an actor's intersubjective sphere of "space-time"; sleeping off a glut on one's own larder produces no value, brings nothing to light; giving food and things over longer distances produces ever greater value; the critical limit of space-time seems to be the neighboring islands in the kula ring. It is in this interisland sphere of space-time that having one's name attached to a kula valuable circulating along a path that the donor himself has not traveled, but has otherwise worked, produces the highest Gawan value: fame.

Holistically, the implicit Gawan theory of value and personhood compares with Chinese *yīnyáng*. Even perhaps in more specific terms, China's ceremonial *lǐ* can be understood as the intersubjective space-time sphere, in which its intersubjective capacity (*rén*) to recognize the moral significance of others is rooted in the intercorporeality of parents and children, from whence it may be transposed into an aesthetic in the form of etiquette (*lǐ*). It is by this particular form of the aesthetic that intersubjective relationships with those near at hand (the intercorporeality of parents and offspring) or in ever-expanding circles of influence are formed and finessed. Among the ranks of literati (the essence of masculinity), this particular mode of the aesthetic, this etiquette, was produced and circulated by means of the written word (*wén*), which, following Zito (1997), can be understood as "cosmic text-pattern" with its mystical power to make things appear (beginning with bringing words to light) over vast differences of "space-time" through the embodied prowess of the writing brush. The writing brush was to Chinese what the kula voyaging canoe was to Gawans. Both were encumbered with taboos, and both mystified the masculine world of rank and prowess and extension and influence and fame because both produced the most comprehensive patterns of space-time—the brush produced cosmic pattern, and the canoe the "interisland kula pattern." And both were integrally related to other spheres of making things appear and disappear. For instance, the appearance of words (on paper) created a space-time horizon of control on an immense scale. The written word, the materialization of the cosmic text pattern, was every bit as talismanic as was the kula valuable.

Even today, I know folks in China, in particular in Qinghai, who still act on the old adage that if you improperly dispose of written words, you'll go blind in the next life. How things are disappeared also matters. Paper money carries many kinds of signs; many are worded with ordinary and mystical graphs demanding and requesting help and transmitting wealth into an unseen future located in the past, or what amounts to a cosmic horizon of space-time. The writing brush, with its ability to make words appear just to have them disappear over geographic and cosmic spheres of influence, was to the masculine body what bound feet were to the feminine body. Binding feet made the flesh disappear by hiding it in order to make its disappearance appear with greater brightness and value, the fetishized object of masculine desire, which the one doing the binding produced and finessed. Where the writing brush extended spatial being (the materialization of words) into time, the bound feet contracted or concentrated time into spatial being. As far as I can see, the main difference between Gawan and old Chinese lifeworlds is the sheer scale of intersubjective space-time spheres. I think both lifeworlds were structured around the human ability to mediate the appearance and disappearance of things, which is predicated on the notion that the critical aspect of reality is its form and pattern, which raises questions of authenticity and the mysteries of producing and reproducing and re-presenting it. This is the "superstructure" of a social economy that finds its highest values produced by means of a BaMbuti *molimo* (Turnbull 1961), a Gawan canoe, and a Chinese brush, convivial tools in the hands of men that resonate and depend on ever more basic productions and reproductions and re-presentations in the hands of women, but always in the hands of persons: in other words, person-centered worlds.

Mauss's work and its splendid legacy (e.g., Munn 1986; Weiner 1992; M. Strathern 1988) has helped to brighten the line others (e.g., Polanyi 1944; Heilbroner 1962) have drawn between social formations that circulate things in capitalist markets and those that don't. Mauss thus theorized how those that don't did, as matters of fact, produce and circulate things of value by reciprocal giving. In these social economies the things that people put into circulation are largely extensions of their personalities and workaday lives— things that have personality—as opposed to the commodity-based capital- ist system of exchange, where the inherent connectedness between persons and things disappears in the exchange (see Gregory 1982). In the capitalist system, a *human social animus* is simply obviated by a pricing mechanism, a system of exchange that explains itself in the substantive scientific terms of nature. This distinction, which is by no means absolute, nonetheless forms the foundation for my distinction between social economies that fetishize pro- ductions of value by means of mystification of form (ceremony) and commod- ity economies that fetishize production by reification of substance (ideology).

There is nothing simple or idyllic in the concept of "precapitalist" or social economy, especially in the thinking that follows the work of Marx and Engels, who hailed the "progress" of capital as much as any of the other clas- sical economists did. To the extent that they theorized precapitalist forma- tions (social economies) they found different ways that humans exploited and oppressed each other (T. Turner 1986). Each precapitalist formation (I prefer "social economy") constructed its own theory of personhood and motivation and human nature (see Wilk 1996). Nevertheless, I argue that as different as they are (that is, for example, as different as the unhistoricized lifeworld of foraging bands such as the BaMbuti is from the highly developed feu- dal formations, including the agrarian Chinese), precapitalist social econo- mies share(d) at least one thing in common: a common sensibility that value derives from a human effort that traces back to a mystified social animus and expresses itself in all kinds of creative endeavors experienced in the continu- ities of producing, reproducing, presenting, and getting things of value (see Belk 1983 for a similar argument). Once again, production-exchange-repro- duction are all continuous processes, and it is from this *continuum* that value is realized. The paradoxes or resistances include the fact that things consciously imbued with the life-force or animus of their makers and donors have a prob- lem with being "alienated," to use a modern parlance (Mauss 1990; Weiner 1992; Godelier 1999, 2002). Another paradox of social economies, precisely because of the animus in giving, is how egalitarian or "generalized" forms of reciprocity (what I prefer to call "sharing") can only work to the extent that a community of sharing is structured, that is, where some members "are more equal than others" (see Graeber 2001:221).

In small-scale formations, or complex formations at the domestic level, this structure usually begins with the asymmetrical position of women. This has become a cutting-edge topic of research and debate in recent decades, especially centered in Highland Papua New Guinea (e.g., A. Strathern 1979; Josephides 1985; Sexton 1986; M. Strathern 1988). Here, in another prestation ceremonial called *moka,* men form long-term reciprocal relationships with ceremony-occasioned gifts of pigs and strings of shells that increase with every reciprocation in the donor's quest for name and fame; at times the gifting is organized by a "big man" on a grand scale. Much of the ethnography on *moka* centers around the differential roles of men and women, which seems to be a point of high social salience among the participants themselves. The linkage between women's part in the production of wealth in pigs and men's part in giving them away in the quest for fame is so obvious that the men seem to go out of their way to deny the contributions of women, while women either take such denials in stride, in good humor, or, with the arrival of a cash economy, take measures to gain recognition for their contributions or even for themselves. For me, the important point is "the necessary linkage between production and exchange which enables *moka* to take place" (A. Strathern 1979:534) and which men seem pressed to deny. It is at this linkage point that Lisette Josephides (1985) argues the exploitation of Kewa wives by their husbands in the same terms that Marx used to analyze the appropriation of surplus value under conditions of modern capital. This has the effect of dulling the line between gift-bearing social economies and the modern system of capital production. This obfuscates how value is produced in different kinds of social formations, which some feel is the crux of the anthropology, not to mention Hegel- and Marx-based studies (see M. Strathern 1988; Gregory 1980, 1982, 1983; Graeber 2001). The connectedness of production and "exchange" in social economies is ritualized and mystified in cosmologies, norms, and theories of *relatedness* (as in kinship) that entail a different mode of valuation from the one that the system of commodity production and exchange entails. Which is not to say that there is no "exploitation" in social economies.

There is no question that "exploitation" based on the *implicitness* of gender is an organizing feature, often a highly dramatized (ritualized) feature of social economies, but what makes this significant in my view is how it differs from the way that the modern capitalist formation hides the exploitation in the reifying process of ideology. In *The Philosophy of Money* (1907) Georg Simmel (1978) argued that the cultural dynamics of capitalist development best explained the rise of demands for women's rights. He noted, in Muller's words (2002:57), that as women developed a greater consciousness of themselves *as women* they were becoming more like men. Does this explain what has happened in the shift from a "shell *moka*" to a "cash *moka*" (which includes gifts of modern monies and commodities) with the penetration of a commodity-based economic system in which women have increased visible participation in the economy (A. Strathern 1979)? Back in the paper money custom, we have a new "exotic" commodity, the "G-spot device" mentioned in the previous chapter. At first glance, the term is ambiguous because "device" suggests a protective "covering" for the male organ, for which the hypostasized G-spot is the supposed homologue; but in the real world of advertising, it is a "condom" worn by the male and designed to give the female a level of genital gratification that is equal to his. This is based on the modern ideology that transfers the anatomy of the fetishized phallus from the organ of tractable labor (the foot) to the organ of genital gratification, that is, the medical-science-mediated reification of a hypostasized G-spot that produces a genital-based orgasmic release equal to the male's. There are two important points here: first, that there is a difference between how the phallic signifier is fetishized in women's bodies, which has much to do with the historical formation's mode of production and mode of being-in-the-world; and second, whether that mode of being-phallic-in-the-world is made dramatically different in the ritual aesthetics of pain (footbinding) or is reified in the form of a homologous simulacrum ("G-spot"), the world women make bears a direct relation to the world men make in the overall reproduction of the social formation.

Published over twenty years before Mauss's little book, Simmel's daunting tome *The Philosophy of Money* analyzed the social and cultural function of money in modern society. A key function of money was its capacity to realize different notions of value as a phenomenon of exchange, which for Simmel was the irreducible given of (human) social existence and persons as social beings. In assigning such historical and existential importance to the phenomenon of exchange, Simmel seemed to foreshadow Mauss's work on the gift. But in my view, Mauss's whole point was quite different: that in a gift-based social economy, exchange is continuous with production in the work of making value. Even more explicitly, Simmel moved away from Marx's thesis that the irreducible given of human social existence and personhood is the work of production and reproduction. Where Marx saw exchange as a derivative of production (because in Maussian terms the two were originally continuous with each other), Simmel held that exchange envelops both production and consumption as money and things circulate and articulate multiple realms of value and different modes of valuation. (Simmel's theory definitely anticipated the current thoughts of Arjun Appadurai on matters of value defined by exchange.) Simmel wrote of the "spiritualization" of money in a way that echoed Carlyle's "cash nexus," a money-based lifeworld that connects countless numbers and types of people in anonymous ways they do not perceive, much less understand, but in the balance, despite some notable misgivings, in Simmel's opinion, augurs well for humankind.

Fetish

Simmel understood the depths of individual desire, and how it and the will to "sacrifice" one valued thing in exchange for another, more valued thing were definitive moments in the manifold of monetary value and of value per se. For Simmel, the nonpresence of the desired thing was, however, a consciousness of "distance" between individual desire and the "resistance" of the thing desired. These were terms of the then-emerging "marginalist" and "neoclassical" economics that soon dominated the capitalist system's scientific understanding of itself.

Simmel could not appreciate Marx's concept of a commodity and money fetish that was shaped by a deception of historic proportion. Fetish is the avowal of a generative or living presence in a material object that has been separated from its actual generative substance—that is, the material force and social relations that actually produced it. For Marx, the historical deception was separation or alienation of the social relations of production from the commodity relations of exchange, a separation and inversion rooted in exchange ideologies of reason, fairness, equivalence, and equality and enforced by the nation-state. In the system of exchange, the commodity was freed of its mystical social animus and became the reified object that as a matter of mathematical laws can be shown to "grow the economy" by the sheer velocity of its circulation as "capital" in an unfettered system of exchange. The idea of free, fair, and equal "exchange" is so omnipresent in the discourse of capitalism and anthropology—exchange is synonymous with what it means to be free and human—that it infects all our thinking, even to the point where some who avow Marx's ideas, according to Terence Turner (1986:108), have

not fully appreciated Marx's concept of commodity fetish, to the extent that
they orient the impetus of the "mode of production" to the *form of exchange*
rather than to the central relation of exploitation in production.

Turner's comment was made in reference to the peripheral encounters
between the world capitalist system and local, indigenous subsistence formations (social economies) where anthropologists have done most of their
work. It is in these peripheral (colonial and postcolonial) encounters between
a fully developed capitalist-commodity system of production and noncapi-
talist social formations that we find conflicts arising from moral ambigui-
ties between the commodity form (or fetish) and local forces and relations of
production. These conflicts are managed by indigenous beliefs and practices
in which the new forces and relations of production often appear demonic.
Some examples include the Luo people in Kenya, who believe that the monetary profits made in producing commodities for Europeans (e.g., tobacco
and gold) using Luo land and labor is "bitter money" that is barren, unpro-
ductive as capital (Shipton 1989). Some Bolivian mine workers (Nash 1979)
and Brazilian Cuaco Valley plantation workers (Taussig 1980) experience the
wage payments for their labors as a pact with the devil, which workers can
magically manipulate to increase their productivity and wages. One of the
devilish pacts involves secreting a peso with an infant undergoing baptism,
so the peso receives the holy blessing and promise of unending return instead
of the human infant, whose life is thereby secretly consigned to a mundane
mortality. The extra wages earned by such devilish means are barren and cannot be used as investment capital—they can only be consumed. We should
add to these scenarios the Rumpelstiltskin tales that tell something of the
experience of flax spinners and weavers during the European transition to
a commercially driven system of cloth production (Schneider 1989). (The
reverse scenario of the baptized pesos is the "spirit favors" distributed in
Dao Mao Temple ceremonies discussed earlier, where blessing the money is
in the public act of circulating and redistributing it, which gives the money
procreative powers.)

The interpretation of scenarios of secret bargains with demonic forces in
exchange for monetary wealth that is tainted with immorality and sterility—
or just its opposite, as in the Dao Mao ceremony, in which money mediates a
collective relationship between the community and its spirits—can go much
deeper and in multiple directions. Suffice it to say here that people on the historical cusp of shifting into the capitalist mode of production may and often
do perceive a negative life-force (the animosity in the human social animus)

in the capitalist commodity because they have not been fully socialized into the *ideology* of the capitalist form; but can still see it as an immoral (invisible, private) force with which they are nonetheless willing to make a secret (invisible, mystical) pact, albeit with the realization that it costs them dearly in long-term tolls on their way of life and longevity.

More importantly, the analysis of these transitions should recognize the connivance or complicity of the subordinate relations of production with the dominant mode in the overall process of transition (or, in dynastic China and Vietnam, the normalizing of this process as the prototype of a highly developed feudal formation). As Terrence Turner reminds us, precapitalist relations of production are also exploitative and where people are recruited from these modes into the capitalist mode, as on Cuacan sugar plantations, the analysis, to the extent that it seeks a Marxian insight, must consider how the dominant mode of exploitation employs the indigenous relations of exploitation that survives at the domestic level. The analysis should view the whole peripheral situation, the world of plantation labor and the world of domestic labor, in its economic and biological dimensions, as a single mode of production/reproduction and exploitation.

The point that Turner emphasizes here and that Munn emphasized with Gawa, and that I have emphasized throughout *Burning Money*, is the necessity for a holistic analysis of a social formation in all of its productive and reproductive relations. In appreciating the exploitation in different modes of production and social formation, I also insist on the necessity of appreciating that these different modes entail different kinds and levels of alienation and very different ways of ameliorating or assuaging or otherwise managing them in the process of fetishization, from footbinding and burning money to the baptism of money and embittering of money, that is, the process of avowing the presence of a human animus or life-force (benign or malignant or a bit of both) that is not actually present but, in its virtuality and effect on behavior, might as well be. Where the capitalist mode of production is not fully matured, among the Luo of Kenya, the Cuacan Valley peasants of Brazil, and early modern European peasants, we might propose that the commodity fetish is often realized as a negative life-force working unseen; whereas otherwise, in its maturity, it is reified as a force of nature, which when understood (by economic science) is considered a force for human progress.

The Chinese money-burning custom can also be seen as a fetishization, in this case, of a protracted historical formation based on *agrarian* forces and relations of production. The money burning custom was a sacrificial offering that upheld this agrarian formation by the very people whose sacrifice of labor power made the whole thing possible. The ritual was a gigantic money-laundering operation that turned the monetary wealth of the carnal world into a kind of spiritual wealth that indemnified lives on both sides of the lifeworld with the kind of fortune and productivity and longevity that was valued by the agrarian-based social and cosmic formation. This was a form of mystification such that the artifice recognized the human hand in the process. I have argued that this process belonged to an advanced feudal formation; further, in the current historical encounter this advanced feudal formation is suffering its final collapse against the onslaught of the European and now the global capitalist system, thanks to the mediation of a communist party. Although the money-burning custom retains old forms in the encounter, there are newer forms that Chinese label "exotic," "new-wave," and "shocking" and many otherwise regard as the haunting of some demonic force.

On its face, the money-burning custom is a simple, common, taken-for-granted practice that becomes ever more complex the longer it lasts and the longer we stop to reflect on it. It is many things to many people—virtually whatever one wants to make of it: ostensibly and most commonly, it sends replicas of things valued in this world to the other world in ways that are highly self-referencing and self-producing, not to mention self-benefiting as sacrifice. This requires an enormous pile of paper cut from an endless scroll, which is turned into palls of smoke and shrouds of ash, an irritant and a pollutant of the physical environment, widely considered a serious fire hazard, a farce in the wake of the tragedy that was the communist's last hurrah, a burlesque of virtue and reason, an expression of pure value, a playful narrative, a commedia in the work of making ends meet, a serious canonical element in ritualizing the origins of our humanity and the nature of value and reality, a way of communicating with spirits, of indemnifying lives, of storing up, of saving for eternity, of giving material weight to the weightlessness of words, of realizing the essence of life in volitional obligations, of demonstrating and assuaging psychosomatic pains of regret and sadness, of teaching us something about value, of changing things of worldly value (exchange value, use value, labor value) into true value, spiritual value, human value. All said, paper money is an expression of the artifice—the *human* side of human nature, which is the obverse of the modern European emphasis on the *nature* side of human nature. Concern is more with the *genuineness* of artifice than the *reality* of nature. I warned the reader in my introduction that I'd be mindful of the risks, but I would not shy away from holistic arguments, of seeing a whole world in a grain of sand, so I will say once again that through its iconography and epigrams and ritual actions, the central message of the paper money custom and a lot of what passes as Chinese civilization is borne, folded, and burned.

A Postscript on the Grain of Sand

The long-dominant structure of the Chinese lifeworld saw little daylight between what is real (natural) and what is artificial or man-made. That which is real, that which is relevant, that which holds value, is man-made. The glare is seen between imperfection and perfection of workmanship in creating an *authentic world.* The purpose of work is not to change the world, but to live in it, to improve on "nature" by re-creating it in such a way that the illusoriness of the artifice, the workmanship of turning organic nature into social nature, itself becomes the great mystery, which is not to be explained away so much as appreciated. Whatever is real or has value is man-made. This is not uniquely Chinese. What is perhaps uniquely Chinese is the novel ways in which Chinese succeeded in manifesting this material spirit.

This is different from the Cartesian lifeworld of the West, which shows less and less regard for the authentic—or experiences it as nostalgia, the cost of living in a modern world—because it separates material and spirit essences in a constant struggle over how the two are related or which essence is preferable, powerful, and real. Modernity has increasingly favored that which equates a substantive, reductive nature to notions of the real (Newtonian-Darwinian nature); and this spurs continuous countermoves and challenges from the hoi polloi (with their genealogy of "intelligent designs") to the intellectuals (with their "postmodern turn"). The "postmodern turn" is in effect a return to the premodern minus its rituals and mysteries, "a desert of the real." It is "artifice" with neither art nor nature, since all three are conflated in a code or a matrix of signifiers, of simulacra, the ultimate alienation, from which there is no exit, only endless acts of "resistance" in the spirit that says since I cannot change the world, I will keep the world from changing me; but there is no "me" as in the older modern or premodern formations. The postmodern "me" is a product brand, or, seeking a more "authentic" brand, a tattoo, but now detached from its ritual and mystery, it lacks the aura of authenticity. No matter, for the brand or tattoo locates "me" in the matrix. Thus what Max Weber termed the "iron cage of bureaucracy" has morphed into a total global matrix. From a Marxian perspective these ways of experiencing and knowing the world—mystification, reification, and simulation—are shaped in modes of production/reproduction. Mystification is tied to a ritual mode of production/reproduction, which is concerned with the authenticity of the artifice, a preoccupation of social economies. Through historical processes of industrial-based rationalization, mystification is sublated as reification and tied to an ideological mode of producing/reproducing state-based capitalisms. With the mutation of state-based capitalisms into international corporate-based global capital, reification is simulated through semiosis. To the extent we want to view this in the totality of historical dialectics, we would have to say that thus far capitalist civilization has moved the human spirit toward an alienation of historic profundity. Our task is to understand how our notions of value are shaped by these modes of production/reproduction.

NOTES

Chapter 1: Chiasm

1. In the story "Spirit Calling," Lucy Chen (1961:17–18) tells how a family endeavors to call back the spirit of a mortally ill little brother, how they burn "gold paper ghost money" and beg the celestial powers to let the boy's soul return home. As they are calling, the boy's sister hears her inner voice explaining that this is pointless: "This is superstition so it is of no use; even if it is of any use it is only a small temporary self-comfort. But her throat was clogged up and her eyes were misted with tears. . . . The whole ceremony, the entire scene, floated in the midst of her tears. . . . The prayer ascended into the night sky, the sound of the bell floated into the distance, the gold paper ghost money became ashes, the white tiger and yellow charm intermingled and also disappeared."

2. That the practice is experienced so matter-of-factly and self-evidently does not mean that the devotees view it as simple. On the contrary, and especially in matters of ritual "symbolism," the devotee may find the answer to our questions otherwise inexpressible. The perception of the indigenous spokespersons of questions asked by the ethnographer is notoriously problematic, recognition of which goes back to the beginning of ethnographic field work (Rivers 1910:10). I elaborate on this point in chapter 4.

3. The eight-*reales* Carolus silver dollar, bearing the bust of the Spanish kings Carolus III and Carolus IV, was minted in Spanish American colonies from 1772 till the 1820s, when the colonies declared their independence. These portrait dollars became popular in the mercantile establishments of Treaty Ports in China, replacing the Chinese silver sycee. Although the Carolus dollar was replaced by the Mexican Eagle silver dollar, the Carolus dollars, variously modified by Chinese chops impressed into their obverse and reverse sides, which in Fuzhou virtually obliterated the original design on the coins, remained in common use throughout the nineteenth century (Forster 1998).

4. When he arrived in New York City, however, Hunter's paper money trail went cold. He writes that he could find no vendors of paper monies in New York City's Chinatown. This does not square with what I found to be the case in

my hometown of St. Louis, Missouri, during the nineteenth century. Reports of Chinese using paper monies can be gleaned from city newspapers of that period.

5. Zhao Dasao (a common address term) was a handsome, tall, broad-shouldered woman in her late forties, who claimed she had never been to school. The day we talked to her, she was barefoot, with mud from the fields still caked between her toes; she had been asked by village leaders to talk to us. "We" included myself (who refrained from joining the conversation) and two Chinese colleagues: my principal spokesperson and our local host and vernacular spokesperson. During our conversation, there was a small crowd of onlookers jammed in the low, dark room; they were mostly amused by our topic but also interested in our project.

6. Zhao did not remember who had received that dream, but said the neighbor's daughter had told her about it. "But why did he have no shoes to wear?" asked our interlocutor. Zhao responded: "How can anybody know about that? When he died he was [in effect] barefoot, wearing [cheap white] sneakers. Sneakers cannot be burnt to that side [rubber soles do not burn completely]; only cotton shoes can be burned to that side."

7. The ancestral hall in the center of the village was a ruin—only the foundation was visible. The temple ruin, which was barely visible, was on the edge of the reservoir along the road to the hills outside the village where the village buries its dead. Although we only inquired of a few older people, none distinctly recalled the identity of the divinity enshrined in the temple other than it was vaguely "Buddhist."

8. This was over a background of blue waters and flying cranes, signs of longevity. The picture was framed by an epitaph and a couplet. The epitaph across the top was "Fortune permeates the multitude" (*fúzéwànmín*); the sense of "permeate" is in the word for a nurturing rain (*zé*), the graphic portent of profusion and prosperity. Running down one side, the first part of the couplet read, "The renown of this generation is passed down to the present day" (*yīdài fēngliú chuán gǔjīn*); the other side read, "The accomplishment of a thousand years shines as the sun and moon" (*qiānqiū yèjì zhào rìyuè*). These are traditional eulogies.

9. After their deaths in 1976, the Great Leaders, Mao, Zhou, and Zhu, were apotheosized when people in many villages around China lit candles and incense in the hope of receiving the blessing of these now powerful spirits. There were widespread reports of the same fervor during the "Mao fever" of his hundredth anniversary in 1993.

Chapter 2:   Endless Scroll

1. Seven is a key number in both Taoist and Buddhist cosmologies and liturgies. Here we were standing in a Buddhist temple, talking to a Buddhist nun. And here, engraved on a plaque behind the incense and paper furnace, in the

format of a memorial tablet divided into two sections, was the Buddhist liturgy in a nutshell. The upper part of the tablet listed the seven manifestations of Buddhist blessings, which when murmured over and over save the soul from the awful fates of Purgatory: the *Rúlái* (1) of gaining nirvanic repose, to stop the infernal anguish; (2) of avoiding terror, to afford everlasting happiness; (3) of quenching the awful thirst; (4) of beautifying the body, to prevent it from turning ugly; (5) of giving the shriveled body access to food and air and preventing food from turning to iron or some other metal; (6) of many treasures, to prevent destitution; (7) of avoiding the punishment meted out to those who engaged in vicious professions during their lives. Below these *Rúlái*, on the lower part of the tablet, is reference to the miserable manifestations of human mortals, flanked by the terms "males above," "females below."

2. Groot (1969: 1:1, 1:78) describes the *kùqián* in late-nineteenth-century Amoy: During the funeral "great quantities of white sheets with parallel rows of small scalloped incisions . . . have been previously purchased by the family in yellow parcels containing one hundred each. Every sheet of this so-called "treasury money" . . . is an imitation of regular rows of metal coins; so it is easy to calculate that each parcel represents a considerable amount of currency in the next world." In Taiwan, Hou (1975:18) divides the *kùqián* between funeral money, which is often burned in enormous lots, and money for the restoration of destinies, which is burned to prolong the life and fortune of the living after an illness, to guarantee numerous offspring, etc. These come in several subtypes and varieties and include money with a leaf of gold-colored foil on the outer package to signify that this string of cash is destined for the celestial treasury and a plain-foiled leaf for the money that goes to the bank in purgatory. Typically, these Taiwan subtypes are further divided based on décor and inscriptions to differentiate ever finer destinations. This elaboration of distinctions in these elementary forms of paper money has metastasized in the forms of perforated papers that I have found in places as far apart as Quanzhou and Chengdu. For instance, "white cash" is now sold next to the same papers dyed yellow (hence "yellow cash") and red ("red cash"). This is an example of the hypertrophy of forms that is so rampant today. The same terms are used in everyday discourse to refer to all kinds of real payments, from cash handed to children to cash for gambling debts and sexual services; whether the paper money cash has any such connotations might be judged against the findings reported in chapter 8, but in any case the matter requires further study.

3. In a therapy known as "coining" that is popular in China and Southeast Asia, a piece of Chinese cash is rubbed over the skin of the afflicted person.

4. An old sign on shops vending paper monies was a string of circles (see Hunter 1937). This logo is still widely used in advertising. The charmed cash is replicated in the gold-colored plastic and attached to the baubles that people

suspend from their rearview mirrors. Among the more remarkable ones are those that were popular during Mao's centennial in 1993, in which portraits of the Great Leader were attached to gold cash, and First Treasures (*yuánbǎo*), to be discussed below.

5. There are also historical periods when the hole was round, which does not lend itself quite so dramatically to this interpretation. The square, after all, implies structure: i.e., the earth offsets and gives structure to the round, amorphous infinite cosmos. The graphs on the cash during different dynasties were interpreted in ways that augured the fate of the dynasties that minted them (see *Guqian zhi chen* 2008).

6. Chinese would recognize the English expression "squaring the circle" (bringing order out of chaos), but Chinese would insist that the essence of that which exhibits order and structure is circular, nascent, inchoate, and in continuous interaction. Another mundane and concrete expression of this notion is the round-shaped festive table, which expresses the cosmic equality of those seated in a circle even though there is something very "square" about the seating arrangement, which reflects the worldly structure or incipient violence of unequal social positions. The round banquet table is not just a Chinese notion; Marcel Mauss (1990:83) ends his essay *The Gift* by discussing the way the round table of Arthurian legend was designed to be an all-inclusive table where "the highest placed will be on the same level as the lowliest . . . around the common store of wealth," thus obviating the envy that formerly caused banquets to erupt in bloodshed.

7. From the lowest piece of Chinese architectonics (the copper cash) to the loftiest piece (ground plans of imperial temples), the interplay of encircled and squared spaces are laid out, from my observations, as an *imago mundi* modeled on the interdependence of "the mathematically expressible régimes of heavenly bodies and the biologically determined rhythms of life on earth," a sort of "astrobiology" (see Wheatley 1971:414). The four imperial temple walls and altars at the four quarters around the imperial city in Beijing (Sun, Heaven, Moon, and Earth), where emperors annually rectified the imperial with cosmic order through grand sacrifices, appear to be laid out by permutations of encircled and squared spaces. The Sun altar to the East, with its circular walls (Heaven) enclosing a square altar (Earth), replicates the Sun's circulation across the diurnal sky, which is comparable in shape, motion, and function to the square-holed cash's circulation through this world and the other. The Heaven altar to the south is the mirror opposite of the Sun; here, circular altars are surrounded by square walls, replicating an Earth-centered celestial sphere in which, to paraphrase Wheatley (1971:417), the seasonal sacrifice constituted mankind's contribution to the regulation of cyclic time. To the west and north, the Moon and Earth altars are square and enclosed by square walls, thus replicating natural rhythms of life on

Earth. These are my own superficial observations, which yield completely to anything that architectural historians might add or subtract.

8. One is an old euphemism for fetishized money, which is not voiced so often nowadays: *kŏngfāngxiōng*. This plays on a word for money, *kŏngfāngxiōng* (lit., "square-holed money"). But here the *kŏng* for "hole" is replaced by the same *kŏng* that refers to Confucius' name, and the term for elder brother (*xiōng*) replaces the word for money (*qián*). Thus: one who pretends to cultivate true value (the reference to Confucian virtue) instead depends on (as one does an elder brother) a thing (i.e., money) that is as empty of true value as the square hole in the center of the old cash. Another, more common idiom for becoming fixated on money or entangled by desire for it is "to fall into the eye of the coin" (*diàojìn qiányănr lĭ*).

9. *Yuánbăo* has many meanings. The conventional dictionary definition is "a gold or silver ingot." The term can be traced to the Yuan dynasty's shoe-shaped unit of silver, which was worth fifty taels. But its literal meaning, "first treasure" (Scott 2007), has the advantage of not being tied to a particular material referent other than its mystical significance as a "treasure trove" or "vessel" of "uncountable value" that comes in many different shapes, not only shoe-shaped ingots.

10. For example, nineteenth-century Amoy residents burned huge lots of silver paper, which they referred to as "coffin paper," the ashes from which were interred with the coffin (Groot 1969: 1:25, 1:31–32).

11. The simple dichotomy of Big and Little Silver papers differentiate the family spirits from nonfamily spirits. The silver paper that circulates through the Hong Kong diaspora exhibits this simple distinction based on size of foil. In Taiwan, according to Hou (1975), the distinction between Big and Little Silver is signified more by the presence or absence of décor. The Big Silver may be decorated with lotus flowers, while the Little Silver bears only the leaf of foil. The Lotus Silver is reserved for the ancestral spirits. However, these two subsets of Big and Little are each divided into three subtypes, according to Hou's analysis, and it is here that size of foil is definitive. The Big Lotus Silver and the Little Silver have more or less the same foil sizes, called Big Silver, Number Two Silver, and Middle Silver (Hou 1975:25). I say "more or less the same scale of foil sizes" because the differences, based on Hou's table (1975:25), are measured in fractions of centimeters. Hou does not indicate how these sizes are measured, but in all likelihood they are averages with considerable standard deviations from a sample, as is my experience with measuring sizes of paper monies. Thus the silver for family and ancestors makes more or less the same distinctions based on size of foil as the silver for nonfamily spirits. A family spirit receives more or less the same amount of silver as a nonfamily spirit of commensurate status except for the addition of the lotus emblem, by which the one is designated "Big" and the other "Small." The lotus is emblematic of immortality; it stands for the promise of fellowship with eternity through the family and its line of descent, a promise

that payments of silver cannot vouchsafe for other spirits. It seems that silver offerings are attended by notions of commonality and equity, in contrast to the attention to hierarchy and sumptuary rules that become important in offerings of gold papers.

12. Hou formulates these three subdivisions in what is otherwise a bewildering assortment of gold papers, each of which has its own designation, the terms for which are often as obscure to native spokespersons as to the investigator: Triad gold includes Topmost Supreme Gold, Supreme Gold, Three Agents Gold, Large Longevity Gold, Longevity Gold, and Small Longevity Gold. Decorated gold includes Celestial Gold, Ruler Gold, and Basin Gold. And undecorated gold includes Gold of Percentage, Three-six Gold, Horse Longevity, Two-five Gold, Blessing (with happiness) Gold, and Small Gold.

13. The division of labor within the village reflected a division of labor regionwide, in which other villages specialized in the manufacture of other commodities like shoes, etc. While the household work unit was the primary production and accounting unit, the village was the unit of manufacture that disseminated the knowledge and made the connections with outside markets.

14. Near the village entrance there was a shop housing large electric paper-cutting machines. Here huge rolls of the coarse yellowish paper made from bamboo in northern Fujian were carried off trailers to the adjacent room to be cut to size and distributed to the various village workshops.

15. Traditionally, the reddish-yellow paste and dye were made from local resources: paste was made from sweet potato starch, and a reddish-yellow dye was made by boiling the branches of a variety of gardenia (*huáng zhīzi*). There was one workshop in Xu village that specialized in the manufacture of the dyes.

16. Traditionally, the stack of tightly pressed tinfoils ate up the bulk of production costs; in the old household-based workshop where labor was family, the tinfoil was 90 percent of the production cost.

17. We can appreciate how the message changes but the motif remains the same from a gold paper made in another village in the region during the 1930s. A gold-foiled paper from Yunchuan village of the 1930s was stamped with two woodblocks. The top one read, *"The Office of Heaven bestows fortune" (tiānguān cìfú)*; the bottom read, "Let male members and material wealth flourish" (*dīng cái wàng*) (Cheng 1999).

Chapter 3: Origins

1. Karl Marx cited a practice, reported in Aurangzeb's court at Delhi, in which the non-Muslim merchants secretly buried their money deep in the ground in the belief that the money they hide during their lifetime will serve them in the next world after their death. Marx interpreted this kind of behavior as rooted in

the abstract and mystifying nature of the money form, not to be confused with its tangible manifestation as coin or cash (quoted in Graeber 2001:101).

2. Other than immolation by fire, Chinese and others have used such means as casting valuables into streams or exposing things to the elements atop mountains or poles. One of the original ways of transmitting the value of paper things was by fluttering them in the wind, as indicated in the Tang dynasty poem by Bai Juyi at the head of this chapter.

3. Archaeologists of ancient China distinguish between two kinds of grave goods: goods that were used by the living before being interred with the dead, and goods that were made in order to be interred and were never used by the living. These latter goods are the *míngqì* (Dr. Lei Hongji, personal communication).

4. I have collected about twenty versions of folktales concerning the origin of paper money or the origin of the paper money custom.

5. Chinese have a complicated history of making woven and beaten fabrics from fibers of silk, wood, and bark, some of which long precede the official advent of paper in the imperial workshops of the Eastern Han dynasty. Historical references to exactly what innovations Cai Lun was credited with bringing to the paper craft are sketchy. They suggest that his innovation was the use of new materials like hemp and ramie fibers. Mulberry tree bark and rattan fibers were also among the early materials used to make paper, although mulberry and other tree barks were undoubtedly used long before the Eastern Han to make beaten fabrics. Made into paper, mulberry bark is often referred to in references to the kind of paper being used to make paper money and also real-world commercial money. In the mid-Tang dynasty the use of bamboo fiber further refined what was by then a paper-making industry. Grasses other than bamboo, like rice straw, were used to make cheaper, coarser grades of paper (also used for paper money), although I have no certain historical dates for these.

6. The reader may wonder why Cai Lun, the inventor of paper, in the other accounts could not sell his supply, given that it was presumably of finer quality. If asked, the storyteller would simply explain that the lack of demand was due to the conventional use of silk and bamboo surfaces for holding the written word, plus the fact that printing had not yet been invented. This configuration of factors resonates with the actual history of paper and printing and the advent of paper money.

7. The significance of the name Mo is a little ambiguous. It either conveys the sense of a brother who never existed or evokes the sense of an eldest brother who is of no consequence. However we interpret the name, eldest brothers are often depicted as the misfits of the family and typecast as the least capable in the cohort of brothers, whereas older brother's wife is depicted as the up-and-coming, necessarily conniving matriarch of the family. The eldest brother role embodies the succession of generations, a process fraught with competing responsibilities

and contradictory demands. The liminal position of eldest brother in Chinese family structure is comparable to the liminal position of women, whose filial obligations are torn between two different families and ancestries. But traditionally, wives go through rites of passage (from footbinding to marriage rites) that not only bridge these gaps in the social structure but also reincarnate and revitalize women as wives, mothers, and matriarchs. I might also add that in European folktales, the hero is often a youngest son, the only clever one among his stupid brothers (Langer 1951:157).

8. Compare the compulsion of Chinese to burn something to assuage deep feelings of grief, regret, or anger to the Ilongot of the Philippines, who feel compelled to take heads to assuage such feelings (see Rosaldo 1989).

9. I was told this story by Professor Yuan Tongkai, who heard it in Lanzhou in 1995 from his friend, the main protagonist.

10. Groot (1969: 2:719) refers to the many legends that can be found in books and in living people that tell how human spirits have begged paper money from the living, or have expressed their gratitude to those people who generously endowed them with it. "Further they contain stories of spirits who, assuming a visible shape, have spent money which turned into paper or ashes immediately afterward."

11. Groot (1969: 2:712) quotes a passage from *New Book of the Tang Dynasty* crediting Wang Yu, an educated spirit medium, with the first use of paper money in the ancestral sacrifices entrusted to him by emperors Xuan Zong (712–756) and Su Zong (756–762). The passage concludes that "during the Han dynasty and in subsequent times money had been placed in the tombs at every burial, and in later ages the country people had gradually replaced such money by paper in worshipping the manes of the dead." The same passage is rendered differently by Dudbridge (1995:54): "grave coins were used in burials from Han times, but in later generations the vulgar custom progressively used paper cash in dealing with spirits." The original text uses *zàngqián* (burial money) to refer to the money placed in tombs at every burial from the time of the Han dynasty. The literal translation of "grave coins" removes the sense that *zàngqián* is real-world current money, naming it as a special kind of money made for offerings to the spirit world. A recent newspaper report refers to a few lead-based coins found in an archaeological site as "either privately cast currency or *míngbì* [otherworldly coin] produced no later than 916." This article captures the excitement over excavating a thousand-year-old coin that was cast officially by (presumably) the Min kingdom (modern Fujian). According to the exuberant reporter, this coin is "the earliest circulating legal lead-based currency in the history of our country, even in the world." The other metal coins found were privately cast and therefore may have been used for deposits with the dead (*Xinmin wanbao* 1996).

12. Woodblock printing may have begun in the Sui dynasty (581–618), but by the Song dynasty (960–1279) it was a commercial enterprise (Fang et al. 2000:234).

13. The *Ming bao ji* is a collection of ghost stories authored by Tang Lin (601?–660), who was a high official at the end of the Sui (581–618). Some of these stories feature references to the use of paper money for supplicating spirits. These are among the earliest such references, according to Hou's book. According to the introduction in a modern edition of *Ming bao ji* (Tang 1992), which includes punctuation marks, the original manuscripts were lost, and no record of them has been found in China. The modern editions come from the discovery of old manuscripts discovered in a Japanese temple, the earliest of which is dated 889–897. Most Japanese and Chinese scholars agree that this manuscript was copied by Japanese from an original Tang dynasty manuscript. The *Ming bao ji* was one of numerous Tang dynasty manuscripts that Japanese Buddhist acolytes and students brought back to Japan on their trips to China during that period.

14. The four characters embossed around the square hole could be read vertically and horizontally as *kāi yuán tōng bǎo* or clockwise as *kāi tōng yuán bǎo*.

15. When paper currencies were once again common in early-twentieth-century China, "different currencies marked different communities of users who were distinguished socioeconomically and politically. . . . Money marked difficult and sometimes dangerous socioeconomic and political boundaries" (Notar 2004:129).

16. According to one Chinese encyclopedia, paper money developed as a cheap substitute for interring real valuables, and its development dovetailed with the growing popularization and increasing number of occasions for making offerings to family spirits on the part of the common people. Desire for economy is also evidenced in the folktales about Cai Lun, which tell how cheaper grades of paper were used as offerings to bring deceased family members back to life (see Feng 2004).

Chapter 4:   Liturgy

1. Pioneers of the structuralist approach include Lévi-Strauss in France and Edmund Leach (1976) in Britain. The structural approach is also known in broader terms as semiotics (the study of signs), which has a broad intellectual sweep that extends well beyond anthropological structuralism (e.g., Barthes 1968, 1982).

2. In Honolulu, for instance, expatriate Chinese go to the seashore, to places like Ala Moana Park's Magic Island, where, facing their ancestral land, they burn paper offerings.

3. In classical Confucian texts such as *Chu Hsi's Family Rituals,* the only materials were incense and food (Ebrey 1991).

4. The importance of sequential order is generally true of all ritual. Writing about sacrificial rituals, Hubert and Mauss (1964:28) wrote: "We must point out an essential characteristic of the sacrifice: the perfect continuity that is necessary to it. From the moment that it has begun, it must continue to the end without interruption and in the ritual order. All the operations of which it is composed must follow each other in turn without a break." Reading *Chu Hsi's Family Rituals* (Ebrey 1991), I am struck by the importance and sense of linear timing or the syntax of ritual acts. Also, the Taoist rituals for funerals and communal salvations follow parallel and exacting sequences (Schipper 1993:75).

5. Schipper (1993:78) describes the finale of funeral services in Taiwan, in which the Taoist spirit master narrates classic stories about paragons of filial piety rescuing their parents from Purgatory, and explains that the sequence of stories exhibits a crescendo of comedy, with the last one becoming "the occasion for especially bawdy word plays. The somber rites are dissolved in laughter."

6. E. E. Evans-Pritchard (1967:231) went further: "In Nuer ritual the meaning of symbolism is generally at once evident to ourselves, at any rate in its main import, for there is an intrinsic relation between the symbol and what it stands for." "Since we at once perceive the meaning of the symbolism of the ritual action we may suppose that Nuer also perceive its logical fitness to its purpose; and, indeed, it is often certain that they do so, for if asked to explain what they are doing they interpret the symbolism of a rite in terms of its purpose. But there is a deeper symbolism which is so embedded in ritual action that its meaning is neither obvious nor explicit. The performer may be only partly aware or even unaware that it has one. Interpretation may then be difficult for a person of alien culture, and the door is open for every kind of extravagant guesswork to enter. Nevertheless, if it be rash in such circumstances to put forward symbolic interpretations of ritual acts, or features of them, we are sometimes compelled to make the attempt, . . . by the very emphasis given to them by the culture we are trying to understand" (1972:232–233).

7. The liturgical or magical effect of words (Malinowski 1965) refers to the illocutionary power of words to do things. In ritual contexts, the difference between words and burning incense, for example, melts away: both are symbolic acts in which their "doing" intends an effect on the world, whether by simply affirming a hopeful or wishful attitude in the world of the performers, what Ahern (1979) calls a "weak illocution," or by changing the objective conditions of the world itself, a "strong" illocution. From my point of view it is important to emphasize that to the extent the Chinese lifeworld is rooted more in ontology than epistemology, the distinction between subjective effects and objective effects of an illocutionary act pales as a salient issue. But to the extent that we make these distinctions between "weak" and "strong," we need to appreciate how they form an intertwining or continuum. Coming back to the words, we

should note that the illocutionary power of ritual words often depends on the fact that the words do not belong to ordinary language (see Gennep 1960:169; Tambiah 1968). When ritual words are spoken in vernacular or translated into vernacular, they often seem to lose their mystery and their effect on emotion and feeling. One of the Taoist priests in Honolulu insists on using the classical words in his incantations and admonishes the local Cantonese businessmen for composing their ritual recitations in the vernacular Cantonese, thus implying their need to employ the Taoist priest if they want their ritual services to be effective.

8. The number of candles is always two, but the number of sticks in a cluster of incense varies between two and three: Most rites employ two candles and three sticks of incense. Funerals usually burn two incense sticks. Burning three incense sticks draws the attention of more than recently deceased familial members. A rationale for these numbers is that even numbers signify closure, exclusivity, and finitude, which is the nature of a life-ending rite (a funeral). Odd numbers signify openness and unending amplitude, which is the nature of life-continuing rites (e.g., ritual services), which often include nonfamily spirits.

9. Sometimes the rational answer suffices perfectly for "why" questions. Apart from the obvious reason that people would not want to tote around and display large sums of real money, the real money does not possess the same capacity for semiotic manipulation that is apparent in food offerings. Real money is limited by its denominational finiteness and by its general-purpose function. When paper facsimiles of real paper currencies are introduced, although only recently and with little acceptance in Taiwan, some of the problems of reification become apparent. I address this issue in chapters 7 and 8. Also, as I will show later when I reconsider the whole of the ritual service, every item of the ritual service is in fact consumed, in the sense that it gives off heat. In this sense the paper money plays its part in the ritual service.

10. McCreery's observation is overly general in view of the anthropology of feasting and of Chinese feasting in particular: when an object of value, whether money or food, intrudes into or mediates a relationship, it functions both to unify and to separate. Feasts are fraught with undercurrents that run counter to appearances of unity and hospitality. In China, it is the communion that re-creates the social asymmetries of the participants sitting around a festive table (Kipnis 1997:46–57). Seating arrangements may be used to communicate unpleasant decisions; sitting in the seat of honor may bestow a dubious distinction; in political contexts it may be a prelude to betrayal. "A Taiwanese dinner party is a seemingly informal affair that operates under very formal rules. Even in the village, feasts are rarely simple expressions of hospitality" (M. Wolf 1968:53).

11. McCreery's contrast between food and money is unsettled in several ways. One is the occasional use of real money and unreal or paper replicated food items in offerings. Another, more significant aspect is the custom of concealing gifts

of real money in red packets (*hóngbāo*). McCreery's assertion that money signifies the restoration of social distance seems to be based on the function of money in market transactions, which enables immediate exchange and freeing from further obligation. But real money is also used as a gift between the living, in which case it is concealed in a red charm-like packet. In my view, the red cover in effect takes the edge off any sense of immediacy, anonymousness, and finiteness that the bare face value of real money conveys. Furthermore, the paper money offered to spirits is not concealed to disguise its divisive quality. Already "charmed," it is usually displayed in the most conspicuous manner possible. In other words, paper money does not convey necessarily the same "general-purpose" leveling, separating, and rationalizing function as real currency.

12. These three and five phases or "energies" are salient in Taoist cosmology and ritual architectonics (see Schipper 1993: esp. 105–107). I am not aware that Taoist exegesis explicitly views the common ritual service in the way I am proposing. I assume that my analysis is implicit in Taoist exegesis. But, more to the point, I am using the "three and five" sequence of *yīnyángwǔxíng* as an analytic derived from native Chinese thinking, for as Kristofer Schipper (1993:35) states, "Everyone in China knows the correspondences of these five phases in the spatio-temporal continuum of the Tao." Thus my attempt to elevate *yīnyángwǔxíng* as a general analytic is a cultural borrowing quite apart from its articulation in any specific native exegesis.

13. Lucy Soothill (1931:106) described the final rite of a paper boat procession that sought to escort the illness demons (especially smallpox and cholera) beyond the city walls of 1880s Wenzhou: "The people who formed the procession returned to the city. But before stealthily entering the gates, they carefully blew out the lights in every lantern, lest the evil spirits should again come creeping back with them. Once inside, with the big gates shut and barred, they relit their lanterns, and went home rejoicing in the relief that again the demons of sickness and death were exorcised from their homes and the city." Also, see James Frazer's *The Golden Bough* (1920), especially chapter 62, "The Fire-Festivals of Europe," and section 8 on "The Need-fire." Also, we need much more study on the relationship between ritual fasting and feasting.

14. From the *Baihutang de Lun* (Comprehensive Discussions in the White Tiger Hall), which dates back to 80 CE, we learn the different meanings of the four spiritual essences by the way they manifest the vitality of four phases of *yīnyáng*. Seminal essence (*qíng*) is connected with the idea of quietness, calm, sedateness, and tranquility; *qíng* is the vitality of emission and generation under the greater *yīn* and thus corresponds with the transforming power of water, which leads to pregnancy and life. Earth-bound soul (*pò*) expresses the idea of a continuous pressing urge on man, governing the emotions. It is under the vitality of the lesser *yīn* (the transforming power of metal) and governs the emotions.

It is connected with the idea of brightening, for with the emotions the interior (of the personality) is governed. Ethereal soul (*hún*) expresses the idea of continuous propagation, unresting flight; it is the vitality of the lesser *yáng*, working in humankind in an external direction, and it governs the human nature (*xìng*). *Hún* is connected with the idea of cultivating, for with the instincts, the evil weeds in man's nature are removed. Mental essence (*shén*) is connected with the idea of "entrancement"; it is the vitality that is under the greater *yáng* and thus corresponds to the transforming power of fire, which sets all things in order (paraphrased from Needham 1972:ii, 87).

15. Victor Turner (1967b:94) writes of the reaggregation phase as a point of consummation, and Mikhail Bakhtin (1990) writes of how the point of consummation is an aesthetic experience.

16. I believe that the ritual process of the ritual service is the ritualization of Chinese alchemy.

17. The *Oxford English Dictionary* gives as the first, albeit obsolete, definition of taste: "The sense of touch, feeling (with the hands, etc.); the act of touching, touch."

18. Many families picnic at the gravesides of deceased loved ones. The most unique sharing of the picnic feast I have seen was by an extended family at the Linyi cemetery in Honolulu, which left the remains, eggshells, fruit rinds, and peels neatly spread over the top of the grave.

19. I have always been struck by how a whiff of smoke brings back the most intense memories, especially the whiff of burning plant fibers (even fossilized plant fibers such as coal), and how these are associated with intense memories and longings for conviviality and reunion (Blake 1999). I know I am not alone in this experience; I find confirmation from other folks all the time. I also think that what seems to be a panhuman practice of "sharing tobacco" is a manifestation of this sensibility.

20. "Tobacco is not consumed in the raw state, as are some foods like honey, nor exposed to fire to cook, as is meat. It is incinerated, so as the smoke thus released can be inhaled" (Lévi-Strauss 1973: 2:17–18).

21. "Only tobacco worthy of its name unites attributes that are generally incompatible" (Lévi-Strauss 1973: 2:29, 61).

22. Each process leaves visible remains, excrement and ash, which become semantically entangled in processes of restoration and regeneration. "Brown gold" is a term by which one Chinese vernacular signifies the value of excrement as money (Han Suyin 1965:32–35)! Han gives a beautiful description of the semantic and material interconnections among Sichuan's tributary and commercial economy, tobacco growing and consumption, the revenues of public cloacae, and the restoration of soil fertility for spring planting. Conversely, the ash of paper money often contains residues of tinfoils that are reconstituted into real

exchange value, and the ash of certain charmed papers may be swallowed for the purpose of restoring a person to health. (The charmed ash of incense may also be used in this way.) In other words, the decomposed residues of food and paper money—i.e., garbage, compost, excrement, and ash—possess real, regenerative values, contrary to their appearance in the world of mundane appearances. Each, in its remains, constitutes a material trace.

23. According to the statement accompanying U.S. Patent 4550363, for a "candle simulating light bulb cover," "it has not been possible hitherto to produce an acceptable imitation of a candle flame, and to produce a bulb which emits a 'flickering' light. The illusion thus created, however, has been a very poor imitation of a real candle." The patent is for a cover that is handmade and painted, which is prohibitively expensive and unmarketable at this time. See http://www.freepatentsonline.com/4550363.html (accessed October 10, 2008).

24. A fuller rendition of the semiotics must go on to develop the paradigmatic shifts in what thus far is only the generic categories of the syntagm. That is to say, the syntagmatic chain, viewed in its temporal linear manifestation, is subject to shifts in paradigmatic meanings by substitutions of different sizes of incense sticks and candles and combinations and permutations of foods and paper monies. These shifts increasingly entail aspects of self-referencing in the performance of the liturgy.

Chapter 5:   Ideology

1. The term "cash nexus" originated with Thomas Carlyle (1840:58, 61, 66) and was used often by Marx and his followers. It refers to the relationship of persons connected by market ties alone. However, my study suggests that the Chinese lifeworld is a "cash nexus" quite apart from a society that is ruled by market ties, even if we restrict the concept of money to minted coins: Polanyi concluded in his study of ancient Greece that, "broadly, coins spread much faster than markets. While trade was abounding and money as a standard was common, markets were few and far between" (1957:84). This was also true of ancient China. I therefore distinguish between "monetization" and "commoditization." The former may exist outside the modern market, while the latter (*pace* Appadurai 1986) is a phenomenon of the modern market. Money in the form of coin or cash has multiple functions; the coin or cash has always had talismanic properties, and these were especially salient under ancient and medieval conditions.

2. Even where the gift of money takes the form of paper money, as in Groot's account of funeral practices in nineteenth-century Amoy, we read that funeral-goers brought gifts of coffin paper (*guān tóu zhǐ*) to express condolences; the quantity and value of each gift of coffin paper (presumably the retail price!) was duly set down in a special memorandum book, "it being highly desirable for the family to be able to calculate after the rites are over, how large a quantity

of sacrificial articles ought to be sent to each visitor in return" (1969: 1:31, 1:233).

3. Brown, writing as a historian, warns against the feudal construct as an ideal type because it tends to ignore historical features that do not fit the typology. But this argument cuts both ways. Alfred Kroeber (1957:286), who advocated the "historical approach" for anthropology, found historiography wanting to the extent it was "forever attached to its phenomena instead of advancing from them to systematic generalization, abstraction, and theory." Ideal typologies allow us to see things that would otherwise remain hidden, in addition to giving us a comparative basis for explaining and, yes, envisioning history. Max Weber's (1964) discussion of feudalisms based on ideal types is a good example of Kroeber's admonition. Lukács went even further, expressing regret that such an all-encompassing mind as Max Weber still failed to exhibit "even the shadow of a genuine universalism" (1980:126). Obviously, we need a methodology that encompasses both the historian's cautions and the social scientist's search for general explanations even at the level of historical totalities.

4. "Community of goods" is another term I use guardedly. For me, the term simply refers to an economy based on the moral order, as opposed to a moral order based on the economic system (as in modern capitalism, where a pervasive and expansive market system or pricing mechanism governs the allocation of all goods referred to as commodities). The locus classicus of a community of goods may be Acts 2:44, which refers to the way the primitive Christian church allocated resources: "All who believed were together and held everything in common." The community of goods as the original state of human nature was widely assumed by Roman ecclesiastics, most pointedly expressed in their support for mendicant orders as well as by their eschatological opponents in uprisings of the dispossessed and disaffected (Cohn 1970). China offered a parallel set of assumptions in the Mandate of Heaven: compensative justice, emperor as parent of the people, perennial recollection of a Golden Age based on the ancient well-field system and occasional attempts to reinstitute it. At the interpersonal level, it took the shape of the round banquet table (see note 10 in chapter 4), and of course it comports with the shape of the cash money itself. Roundness (sharing) and squareness (structure or hierarchy) mutually interact to keep the moral order of things in balance.

5. If we go with the conventional definition of "commodity"—anything that is *traded* (e.g., Appadurai 1986)—then we lose the significance in the historical shift from feudal to capitalist formations and hold with the convention that value comes from trade or circulation of things. The Chinese feudal formation seems to have recognized that true value comes from labor, not exchange, as it kept merchant capital separate from peasant production—this is an essential feature of a feudal mode of production. As I read Marx's *Capital,* the labor process

is a unity of man and nature, an anthropological term belonging to a species-nature. The commodity is a unity of use-value and exchange-value, a historical term belonging to the capitalist mode of production. Precapitalist formations need terms that are more in keeping with their modes of producing value. For example, Marx (1906:197) glosses the production of "use-values" with "goods" (virtually synonymous with the labor process itself). For Marx, the commodity is a type of good in which the production of surplus value (i.e., "surplus labor time") is realized in a system dominated by market exchange and circulation (capital). I suggest that we keep the term "good" for the general production of use-value, and restrict the term "commodity" to the kind of surplus value or profit that the capitalist mode of production depends on. Let goods refer to useful things that are simply made under various modes of production and work regimes and contributed under obligation or duress or traded as need be, as when a peasant brings a sack of rice to market to trade for a sack of salt, even if money is used as the means of exchange.

6. For example, the feudal mode of production in Europe was always "a complex unity" in which various regimes of labor, although ideally serf, could include slave or free-holding peasant, depending on the nature of the state formation. Of course, the ideal type of the feudal mode was based on the labor of serfs in northern France (Anderson 1974). In China, freeholding peasants who could not pay their debts could at times have their wives and children sold into slavery (Peng 1994: 2:533). See also Watson 1976, 1980, and 1998 on slavery in China. The modern capitalist mode of production in the United States, before 1865, employed slave labor in the industrial, cotton-gin-based agricultural section of southern states.

7. The succession of imperial governments and their official and semi-official local agents invented all kinds of ways to increase agricultural output, tax revenues, and patronage. One of numerous examples comes from Franz Schurmann's reading of the Yuan dynasty history (Song 1956). For example, in 1270–1271, the government promulgated fourteen regulations concerning agriculture and sericulture. Having established the village-based agricultural units called *shè*, the first regulation pointed out that the head of the *shè* is a man advanced in years and well versed in agricultural matters who is to instruct and supervise the agricultural population. The third regulation reads: "The *shè* leaders are to investigate from time to time . . . and encourage and admonish. . . . Those that do not follow instructions are to have their names recorded and submitted to the . . . official inspectors . . . for punishment. Those that do not treat their fathers and elder brothers with appropriate respect or who are perverse . . . are to be [dealt with] likewise. . . . If at the end of the year they have not amended their ways, . . . they . . . are to be inducted into the labor force (i.e., corvée) of the *shè* in question" (1956:51–52). In another edict (1281–1282), the government explicitly defined

and differentiated the duties of the *shè* leaders as semi-official appointees charged with raising the standard of living of those over whom they were appointed, while the village heads were agents of the state on the village level and charged with tax collection. "However, as one article of the decree indicates, *shè* leaders tended to directly exploit the people under them by interfering in the collection of taxes and taking a portion of the taxes for themselves" (1956:44). This illustrates how Chinese imperial authorities, at this point in time, regulated the extraction of labor power at the same time that they disciplined the labor process by enforcing the social relations of labor on the basis of kinship norms. (See Lukács 1971:56 for a Marxist generalization of this process.)

8. This point cannot be overstressed—the TCP was geared to an agenda that did not countenance the accumulation of capital for economic expansion. Western observers (including Marx) had difficulty trying to fathom this elementary difference, as so many have tried to explain why China "failed to modernize."

9. David Graeber's generalization (2001:86) is pertinent: "Insofar as state structures . . . succeed in legitimizing themselves, it's almost always by successfully appealing to the values which exist in the domestic sphere"; although defenders of the Confucian model might be more guarded, or in the olden days might have been dumbfounded by Graeber's further assertion that these domestic values "are, of course, rooted in those much more fundamental forms of inequality, and much more effective forms of ideological domination—most obviously gender."

10. The divining blocks are two crescent-shaped wooden blocks with a round and flat surface used to divine yes/no/maybe answers put to spirits. Dropped on the floor, they fall in one of three juxtapositions: two flat sides up signifies indifference; two round sides up signifies "no"; one flat side and one round side up signifies "yes" (cf. Ahern 1981:45–48).

11. Some of my readers may fairly ask me why I didn't simply ask the woman what she was doing or thinking. My answer is that I did not want to interrupt what I perceived was her concentration; or even after she was finished, I would not intrude on her reverie of success with a very intrusive hard-to-fathom question for which I would likely receive an unreflective naive-sounding rationalization. In any case, I felt that what I could see was patently self-evident.

12. Natural properties of commodities "claim our attention only in so far as they affect the utility of those commodities, make them use-values. But the exchange of commodities is evidently an act characterized by a total abstraction from use-value. Then one use-value is just as good as another, provided only it be present in sufficient quantity." In the next paragraph, "If we make abstraction from its use-value, we make abstraction at the same time from the material elements and shapes that make the product a use-value; we see in it no longer a table, a house, yarn, or any other useful thing. Its existence as a material thing

is put out of sight" (Marx 1906:44). Marx goes on to argue that use value is not the only thing abstracted; so is the value of the labor put into making it. All the forms of labor that are embodied in the object of use value "are reduced to one and the same sort of labor, human labor in the abstract" (1906:45). And again, Marx's famous quip: "So far no chemist has ever discovered exchange value either in a pearl or a diamond" (1906:95).

13. Following Poulantzas 1973; Boudon 1989, especially part 1:24–26; Gouldner 1976:30; Habermas 1970:99; Howard 1988:178; and others, I adopt the unconventional notion that ideology is a condition of the modern system that emerges around disputations over the nature of reality and objectifications of nature. To put a finer edge on it, ideology is the discursive practice of the capitalist mode of production—it is the discourse of capitalism—that more or less inscribes itself in the lifeworld of participants. As such, ideology reifies the lifeworld largely by a hegemonic rhetoric of science and reason conveyed through the principal institutions sponsored and protected by the nation-state (Lukács 1971). The claim that ideology is particular to capitalism means that other modes of production employ other means of reconciling their contradictions and reproducing themselves (e.g., ritualism and mystification). I glean from Marx and Engels, *The German Ideology*, that the more necessary a discursive practice is to sustain and reproduce a mode of production (e.g., bourgeois economic theory), the more ideological it is. The less directly pertinent the discursive practice is (e.g., religious beliefs), the less ideological it is. Ideology should not be confused or conflated with worldview, myth, magic, ritual, religion, or science. Ideology does include science, but only to the extent that science becomes increasingly rhetorical or, as Raymond Boudon (1989) professed, bad science. Ideology is as new to history as the capitalist system it sustains is. As a discourse, ideology may be doctrinaire in various forms of state capitalism (communism, fascism, neoliberalism) or implicit in the everyday speech of these modern formations.

14. Comparing gift economies with the market economy, David Graeber (2001:224) makes almost the same point: "Mystification, if that's what it is, happens to a surprisingly limited degree. Mauss clearly overstated his case here: Kwakiutl coppers, kula armshells, Maori war clubs, and the like were *not* normally seen to have their own minds and purposes; in fact, the striking thing is how much more likely one is to run into blatant subject/object reversals in flipping through the pages of the *Wall Street Journal*—where money is always fleeing one market to another, bonds are doing this, pork bellies are doing that—than in participants' accounts of the operations of a gift economy. Great mystifications do normally exist in such societies, but for the most part they lie elsewhere." What I am suggesting is that we restrict the term "mystification" to the way the things in gift economies cloak exploitation in ritual, while using the term "reification" as the basis for ideological cloaking in the capitalist economy.

15. György Lukács (1971:58), following his teacher Max Weber, stated that "status-consciousness—a real historical factor—masks class consciousness; in fact it prevents it from emerging at all."

16. My preference for the *yīnyáng* dialectic happens to concur with the analyses of Hegel and Marx, although minus their negative spins. Hegel saw Chinese civilization as the human *Geist* in its original (historical) form, i.e., altogether sensual and uninformed with subjectivity. Marx saw Chinese civilization formed by an "Asiatic mode of production" in which the state and society remain undifferentiated.

Chapter 6: Sacrifice

1. Angela Zito (1997:228, n. 2) states, "The character *jì* consists of two hands above a graph whose early meaning was 'omen' and whose later usages center upon ideas of showing, manifesting, and displaying. . . . I . . . use the term 'sacrifice' here although perhaps 'display' would be a translation less burdened by misplaced analogy." Zito's version is actually more useful to my interpretation of the nature of the offering, which "displays" the animal carcass rather than immolating the live animal, and also to my interpretation of the paper offering; but I cannot find any etymological basis for the "two hands" forming the upper part of the graph. The graph for "animal flesh" (*ròu*) and the other graph for "hand" can be traced to the Shang dynasty oracle bones. The animal flesh and the hand are above the graph *shì*, which is anciently referred to as "omen" or "spirit" and came to be thought of as that by which the spirits make themselves manifest, known, shown—i.e., that which constitutes the sacred space or altar.

2. Evans-Pritchard (1967:279–280) argued that among the Nuer and other cultures, the laying on of hands before the sacrificial killing signified that the animal should be accepted by God as a substitute for themselves.

3. For instance, Zito (1997:228, n. 2) notes that "while certain elements of the ceremony recall sacrifice as it appeared in anthropological descriptions (see especially Henri Hubert and Marcel Mauss, *Sacrifice* [1964]), the fit is not perfect. In their analysis, they generalized the Judaic sacrificial model to the Vedic to show fundamentally disparate realms occasionally connecting, but Chinese imperial rituals manifest a link between people and spirits or ancestors thought to be always there, merely invisible in daily life."

4. This note was made during the Chongyang Festival in Hong Kong, October 1999. During this festival, crowds of people repair to family graves to make their autumn offerings. The scene described here took place at the shrine for the tutelary spirit guarding the entrance of the Chaozhou section of the Wo Hop Shek cemetery near Fanling in the New Territories.

5. Groot (1969: 2:719) cites one tale whereby a local gentry named Sun in what is now Sichuan received requested information from a spirit in the nether-

world. Asking how he might reward the spirit, Sun was told that several hundred strings of a thousand cash would do. When Sun demurred, the ghost added, "Not in worldly copper or iron, but in treasures of paper." Then the spirit told Sun how to send it by burning, and added, "Wherever the fire has consumed it you must not stir the ashes, not poke therein, lest the cash be broken or pulverized."

6. S. E. Thompson (1988) elaborates the symbolic connection between pork and female fertility, and Gene Cooper (1998) describes how that symbolism is expressed in life-cycle passages that involve the exchange of gifts between affined families in eastern China.

7. The party secretary expressed interest in my research partly because she was responsible for my conduct while a guest in her village, but she also seemed to be interested in the "folk custom" and asked her own informed questions about the meaning of certain paper monies. I think her interest in the custom was based on a complex of motives: first, it is a common people's custom, and second, it absorbs so much creative energy that its value is dubious. At one point, one of the cohort of women was showing how to roll yellow paper to make bars of gold, and the party secretary turned to my local interlocutor and joked, "Have you ever seen such a thing? She just uses yellow paper to fold; when it's done, it's called gold bar," and turning to one of her cohort, she laughingly remarked, "This kind seems like a silver bar." I also think the party secretary was curious about why a foreigner would be interested in such a custom. She was nonetheless most obliging of my requests, and several times she interjected herself into the goings-on with a scolding tone to remind her neighbors that they were there to help me learn more about the paper money custom and not to teach each other the different folding techniques.

8. Liba.com offers various chat rooms and forums. The Web site explicitly appeals to the consumption and exchange interests of young families, with information on cars, real estate, weddings, childcare, etc. The Web site began in Shanghai but now includes many of the big metropolitan areas from around China.

9. The advantages of gleaning "data" from "virtual communities" are quickly compromised by some rather severe limitations, the most obvious of which is the lack of information on the social background of the "participants."

10. The boat signifies constant motion, coming and going with cargoes of goods. Some of the paper facsimiles of paper notes (see chapter 6) depict a sailing junk with the Chinese words for "a favorable wind all the way" inscribed on the sail. This notion of a boat delivering a cargo worth great fortune is also intoned in the American popular saying "When my ship comes in," which was also the title of a popular song sung by Eddie Cantor.

11. "If we have to sum up the meaning of Nuer sacrifice in a single word or idea, I would say that it is a substitution, *vita pro vita*. . . . Substitution is . . . the

central meaning of the rites" (Evans-Pritchard 1967:281–282). J. H. M. Beattie (1980:43) reiterates, "What one sacrifices is always, in a sense, oneself."

12. "Labour is, in the first place, a process in which both man and Nature participate, and in which man of his own accord starts, regulates, and controls the material re-actions between himself and Nature. He opposes himself to Nature as one of her own forces, setting in motion arms and legs, head and hands, the natural forces of his body, in order to appropriate Nature's productions in a form adapted to his own wants. By thus acting on the external world and changing it, he at the same time changes his own nature. He develops his slumbering powers and compels them to act in obedience to his sway" (Marx 1906:197–198).

13. This is a novel kind of "sacred violence" in the growing catalog of "types of violence," or perhaps it is akin to forms of sacrifice that go "beyond sacred violence," in the words of Kathryn McClymond (2008).

Chapter 7:   Ghost Bills

1. According to Elman Service (1971), "Cultural involution is a form of innovation that attempts to preserve an extant structure, solving its new problems by 'fixing it up.'" It is a conservative form of cultural change.

2. The real Chinese currencies of the 1920s often used Arabic numbers and English script, especially on the reverse side, to indicate face values and bank names.

3. Taiwan is a case in point. According to Hou (1975:16–17), the custom of using "Occidental" paper money began in the Shanghai region in the early nineteenth century, as this region "was very open to foreigners; they did not introduce it [Occidental forms of paper monies] to Taiwan until after 1949, the year in which many of the merchants of Shanghai fled to Taiwan. However, such money, utilized as it was by the Chinese merchants, hardly found favor by the Taiwanese. These [Taiwanese] have conserved a vast lot of the traditional paper money of which a deeper examination makes apparent the continuity with the different types of ancient monies."

4. These one hundred types are by no means the universe of typological variations, nor is this sample necessarily representative, since my decisions when obtaining specimens were guided more by an intuitive search for the anomalous and unique than by a list of random numbers.

5. The connotation of *tōngbǎo* is an endless flow of precious goods (*Xinmin wanbao* 1997).

6. Both of these billion-yuan certificates are on cheap tissue papers and roughly printed. I obtained them at Babaoshan (Beijing) and supposed they were a local product.

7. The syntax of the line *zhīwángdàdì móhē xī* suggests that *móhē xī* is the name of a reigning emperor; or *móhē* could be a transliteration of the Sanskrit

maha, meaning "great," which would presumably refer to *xī*, "west," whatever that means—the Occident or the Buddhist heaven or, in some satirical sense, both. I'm inclined to think these words are just bits of jargon strung together for the power of their rhyme, which is quite sufficient for a charm.

Chapter 8:   Burlesque

1. In 1995 an acquaintance of mine in Hong Kong received a dream from her deceased mentor requesting a computer; she was flabbergasted to learn that it would cost $1,000 HK—she had been expecting perhaps around $200 HK. Spending $1,000 for a paper computer seemed more expensive, or at least so we joked at the time, than simply buying and burning a secondhand computer. But she wasn't about to substitute the secondhand computer for the paper one for the simple reasons that it would be a used one and it would be harder to burn.

2. I have not yet come across the suggestion that such exotic offerings as the G-spot condom may be an "urban myth" or even a conspiracy to ridicule and destroy the paper money tradition. Perhaps one reason for the lack of conspiracy theories is that expressions of disgust at these exotic offerings can just as easily find refuge in the "traditional offerings" as in rejecting the whole custom.

3. The name *biànyí fáng*, from a medieval expression as a place of convenience and pleasure, carries the sense of a venerable business. The characters can also be pronounced *piányi fáng*, meaning a cheap place. The word *ānhuá* denotes the local identity of this particular restaurant.

GLOSSARY

bā	八
bā líng líng líng	八灵灵灵 [八靈靈靈]
báichāo	白钞 [白鈔]
báiqián	白钱 [白錢]
bái zhǐqián	白纸钱 [白紙錢]
bài xiǎorén	拜小人
bāo	包
bāofu	包袱
bǎo	宝 [寶]
bàofāhù	暴发户 [暴發戶]
biànyí fáng [*piányi fáng*]	便宜坊
cáishén	财神 [財神]
cáiyuán guǎngjìn	财源广进 [財源廣進]
cǎo	草
cǎozhǐ	草纸 [草紙]
chángqián	常钱 [常錢]
chāodù	超度
chāopiào	钞票 [鈔票]
chāopiào jīng	钞票经 [鈔票經]
chóudá shén'ēn	酬答神恩
chǔqián	楮钱 [楮錢]
chuānghuā	窗花
chuángshén	床神
dázi	答子
dà guìrén fú	大贵人符 [大貴人符]
dà shòu jīn	大寿金 [大壽金]
dà tiān jīn	大天金
dēngcǎo	灯草 [燈草]
dì	地
dìfǔ	地府

dìfǔ tōngyòng zhǐbì	地府通用纸币 [地府通用紙幣]
dìyù	地狱 [地獄]
Dìzàng	地藏
diàojìn qiányǎnr lǐ	掉进钱眼儿里 [掉進錢兒裡]
dié yuánbǎo	叠元宝 [疊元寶]
dīng cái wàng	丁财旺 [丁財旺]
dìngzi	锭子 [錠子]
ēmítuófó	阿弥陀佛 [阿彌陀佛]
ègǎo	恶搞 [惡搞]
fā	发 [發]
fācái píng'ān	发财平安 [發財平安]
fǎshī	法师 [法師]
fāngdìng	方锭 [方錠]
fāngtíng	方亭
fāngyuán hùyù	方圆互寓 [方圓互寓]
fó	佛
fú	符
fú	福
fúzéwànmín	福泽万民 [福澤萬民]
fùguì	富贵 [富貴]
fù hángzhǎng	副行长 [副行長]
G-diǎn tào	G点套 [G點套]
gòngyǎng	供养 [供養]
gǔpiào	股票
guānqián	关钱 [關錢]
guān tóu zhǐ	棺头纸 [棺頭紙]
guǐ	鬼
Guǐjié	鬼节 [鬼節]
guǐpiào	鬼票
guǐshén	鬼神
guìrén fú	贵人符 [貴人符]
hángzhǎng	行长 [行長]
héjiā píng'ān	合家平安
hóngbāo	红包 [紅包]
hútòng	胡同
huāyuán	花园 [花園]
huángbiǎozhǐ	黄裱纸 [黃裱紙]
huángzhǐ	黄纸 [黃紙]
huáng zhīzi	黄栀子 [黃栀子]
huǐhèn	悔恨
hún	魂

huó	活
jíxiáng	吉祥
jì	祭
jìlǐ	祭礼 [祭禮]
jiāshén	家神
jiàzhí	价值 [價值]
jiǎnzhǐ	剪纸 [剪紙]
jiǎo	角
jiào [teaching]	教
jiào guān jīng	叫关经 [叫關經]
jièdān	界单 [界單]
jīnchāo	金钞 [金鈔]
jīnshēng	今生
jīntiáo	金条 [金條]
jīn yuánbǎo	金元宝 [金元寶]
jīnzhǔ	金主
kāi tōng yuán bǎo	开通元宝 [開通元寶]
kāi yuán tōng bǎo	开元通宝 [開元通寶]
kǒng fāng qián	孔方钱 [孔方錢]
kǒngfāngxiōng	孔方兄
kùqián	库钱 [庫錢]
láishēng	来生 [來生]
lǐ [ceremony]	礼 [禮]
lì [profit]	利
lièshì língyuán	烈士陵园 [烈士陵園]
líng	灵 [靈]
lìnglèi jìpǐn	另类祭品 [另類祭品]
lù [deer]	鹿
lù [emolument]	禄 [祿]
mǎilùqián	买路钱 [買路錢]
máobiān xīqián	毛边溪钱 [毛邊溪錢]
Měijīn	美金
měinǚ	美女
měinǚ èrnǎi	美女二奶
ménshén	门神 [門神]
Mílèfó	弥勒佛 [彌勒佛]
míxìn	迷信
míxìn zhǐqián jī	迷信纸钱机 [迷信紙錢機]
mínqián	缗钱 [緡錢]
míngqì	明器
míng	冥

míngbì	冥币 [冥幣]
míng dū yínháng	冥都银行 [冥都銀行]
míngfǔ	冥府
míngguó	冥国 [冥國]
míng měi yínháng	冥美银行 [冥美銀行]
míng tōng yínháng	冥通银行 [冥通銀行]
mò (tuīzi)	磨 (推子)
nāmó ēmítuófó	南无阿弥陀佛 [南無阿彌陀佛]
niánhuà	年画 [年畫]
Niángniang	娘娘
pànguān	判官
pò	魄
pòqián	破钱 [破錢]
púsà	菩萨 [菩薩]
Pǔtōnghuà	普通话 [普通話]
qīxīng jīng	七星经 [七星經]
qípáo	旗袍
qì	器
qiānqiū yèjì zhào rìyuè	千秋业绩照日月 [千秋業績照日月]
qiánshēng	前生
qián	钱
qiánshén	钱神 [錢神]
qiánzhǐ	钱纸 [錢紙]
Qīngmíng	清明
qíng	情
quán {both}	全
quán {wellspring}	泉
quánqián	泉钱 [泉錢]
rènao	热闹 [熱鬧]
rén {human}	人
Rénmínbì	人民币 [人民幣]
rén {humaneness}	仁
ròu	肉
Rúlái	如来 [如來]
rúyì	如意
sānjiào	三教
sǎnqián	散钱 [散錢]
sēngmào	僧帽
shāozhǐ	烧纸 [燒紙]
shāo zhǐqián	烧纸钱 [燒紙錢]
shànggòng	上供

shàngxíngxiàxiào	上行下效
shè	社
shén	神
shénfó	神佛
shēngyì xīnglóng	生意兴隆 [生意興隆]
shì	示
shì fēnkāi de	是分开的 [是分開的]
shòu	寿 [壽]
sú	俗
tàijí	太极 [太極]
tiān	天
tiāndì tōng bǎo	天地通宝 [天地通寶]
tiāndì yínháng	天地银行 [天地銀行]
tiāndì yínháng cúnkuǎnzhé	天地银行存款折 [天地銀行存款折]
tiān dū yínháng	天都银行 [天都銀行]
tiānfǔ	天府
tiāngōng	天公
tiānguān cìfú	天官赐福 [天官賜福]
tiānkù	天库 [天庫]
tiāntáng	天堂
tiāntáng dìfǔ tōngyòng	天堂地府通用
tiāntáng yínháng	天堂银行 [天堂銀行]
tōngbǎo	通宝 [通寶]
tōng míng yínháng	通冥银行 [通冥銀行]
tōngyòng yínháng	通用银行 [通用銀行]
tōngyòng zhǐbì	通用纸币 [通用紙幣]
tōutōumōmō	偷偷摸摸
tǔdìgōng	土地公
tuōmèng	托梦 [托夢]
wěizào pǐn	伪造品 [偽造品]
wén	文
wǔ	武
wǔlún	五伦 [五倫]
xiào	孝
xībó	锡箔 [錫箔]
xìng	性
xìng yòngpǐn	性用品
xìnjiào	信教
xiōng	兄
xīqián	溪钱 [溪錢]
xītiān	西天

Yánluó	阎罗 [閻羅]
Yánwáng	阎王 [閻王]
Yánwángyé	阎王爷 [閻王爺]
yáng	阳 [陽]
yángjiān	阳间 [陽間]
yángpiào	洋票
yèqián	夜钱 [夜錢]
yīběnwànlì	一本万利 [一本萬利]
yīdài fēngliú chuán gǔjīn	一代风流传古今 [一代風流傳古今]
yīfānfēngshùn	一帆风顺 [一帆風順]
yīkǒuqì	一口气 [一口氣]
yīzhǐ	衣纸 [衣紙]
yíshì	仪式 [儀式]
yìzhuāngyìxié	亦庄亦谐 [亦莊亦諧]
yīn	阴 [陰]
yīnjiān	阴间 [陰間]
yīnmíng	阴冥 [陰冥]
yīnqián	阴钱 [陰錢]
yīnyángwǔxíng	阴阳五行 [陰陽五行]
yín sì wú fú	淫祀无福 [淫祀無福]
yínxiāng	银箱 [銀箱]
yǒng shùn zhǐbó	永顺纸箔 [永順紙箔]
yǒuxiàn gōngsī	有限公司
yúlè jié	愚乐节 (娱乐节) [愚樂節 (娛樂節)]
Yùhuáng	玉皇
Yùhuángdàdì	玉皇大帝
yuán	元
yuánbǎo	元宝 [元寶]
zànglǐ	葬礼 [葬禮]
zàngqián	葬钱 [葬錢]
záo chǔ	凿楮 [鑿楮]
zàoshén	灶神
zhēn yínzhǐ	真银纸 [真銀紙]
zhèng zhuāng jīn	正庄金 [正莊金]
zhèngzōng yuánbǎo	正宗元宝 [正宗元寶]
zhīwángdàdì móhē xī	知王大帝摩诃西 [知王大帝摩訶西]
zhǐ	纸 [紙]
zhǐbì	纸币 [紙幣]
zhǐmǎ	纸马 [紙馬]
zhǐqián	纸钱 [紙錢]
zhǐshén	纸神 [紙神]

zhǐzhā	纸扎 [紙扎]
zhōng	忠
zhōngjīn	中金
zǔxiān	祖先
zuōfang	作坊

REFERENCES

Ahern, Emily Martin. 1973. *The Cult of the Dead in a Chinese Village.* Palo Alto, CA: Stanford University Press.

———. 1979. The Problem of Efficacy: Strong and Weak Illocutionary Acts. *Man,* n.s., 14 (1): 1–17.

———. 1981. *Chinese Ritual and Politics.* Cambridge: Cambridge University Press.

Aijmer, Göran, ed. 1987. *Symbolic Textures: Studies in Cultural Meaning.* Gothenburg Studies in Social Anthropology 10. Gothenburg: Acta Universitatis Gothoburgensis.

Amin, Samir. 1980. *Class and Nation: Historically and in the Current Crisis.* Trans. S. Kaplow. New York: Monthly Review Press.

Anderson, Perry. 1974. *Passages from Antiquity to Feudalism.* London: Verso.

Appadurai, Arjun. 1986. Introduction: Commodities and the Politics of Value. In *The Social Life of Things: Commodities in Cultural Perspective,* ed. A. Appadurai, 3–63. Cambridge: Cambridge University Press.

Bachelard, Gaston. 1988. *The Flame of a Candle.* Trans. Joni Caldwell. Dallas: Dallas Institute.

Bakhtin, Mikhail M. 1981. *The Dialogic Imagination: Four Essays.* Ed. Caryl Emerson and Michael Holquist. Austin: University of Texas Press.

———. 1990. *Art and Answerability: Early Philosophical Essays.* Ed. M. Holquist and V. Liapunov, trans. V. Liapunov and K. Brostrom. Austin: University of Texas Press.

Barthes, Roland. 1968. *Elements of Semiology.* Trans. Annette Lavers and Colin Smith. New York: Hill and Wang.

———. 1982. *A Barthes Reader.* Ed. Susan Sontag. New York: Hill and Wang.

Bataille, Georges. 1977. *Death and Sensuality: A Study of Eroticism and the Taboo.* New York: Arno Press. (Orig. pub. 1962.)

Baudrillard, Jean. 1981. *For a Critique of the Political Economy of the Sign.* Trans. Charles Levin. St. Louis: Telos Press. (Orig. pub. 1973.)

———. 1993. *Symbolic Exchange and Death.* Trans. Iain H. Grant. London: Sage.

————. 1994. *Simulacra and Simulation*. Trans. Sheila Glaser. Ann Arbor: University of Michigan Press.

Beattie, J. H. M. 1980. On Understanding Sacrifice. In *Sacrifice,* ed. M. F. C. Bourdillon and Meyer Fortes, 29–44. London: Academic Press for the Royal Anthropological Institute of Great Britain and Ireland.

Beijing chenbao. 2008. *Fandian Qingming lihe daizhe zhiqian mai, youguan bumen ze cheng ciju weifa* [Qingming Gift Boxes with Paper Money Were Sold in a Restaurant and Condemned as Illicit by the Relevant Department]. *Beijing chenbao* [Beijing Morning News], April 2. http://www.ce.cn/bjnews/zonghe/200804/02/t20080402_15034792.shtml (accessed July 20, 2009).

Belk, Russell W. 1983. Worldly Possessions: Issues and Criticisms. *Advances in Consumer Research* 10:514–519.

Benjamin, Walter. 2010. *The Work of Art in the Age of Mechanical Reproduction.* N.p.: Prism Key Press. (Orig. pub. 1936.)

Bergson, Henri. 1914. *Laughter: An Essay on the Meaning of the Comic.* Trans. Cloudesley Brereton and Fred Rothwell. New York: Macmillan.

Binswanger, Ludwig. 1941. On the Relationship between Husserl's Phenomenology and Psychological Insight. *Philosophy and Phenomenological Research* 2 (2): 199–210.

Binyon, Laurence. 1917. *The Cause: Poems of the War.* Boston: Houghton Mifflin.

Blake, C. Fred. 1981. *Ethnic Groups and Social Change in a Chinese Market Town.* Honolulu: University Press of Hawai'i.

————. 1994. Foot-binding in Neo-Confucian China and the Appropriation of Female Labor. *Signs* 19 (3): 676–712.

————. 1999. An Epistle on Patriarchy. Unpublished manuscript.

————. Forthcoming. Lampooning the Paper Money Custom in Contemporary China. *Journal of Asian Studies.*

Block, Melissa. 2008. Thousands Feared Dead as Earthquake Hits China. *All Things Considered,* National Public Radio, May 12. http://www.npr.org/templates/story/story.php?storyId=90380404 (accessed May 12, 2008).

Boas, Franz. 1897. *The Social Organization and the Secret Societies of the Kwakiutl Indians: Report of the U.S. National Museum for 1895.* Washington, DC: U.S. Government Printing Office.

Boudon, Raymond. 1989. *The Analysis of Ideology.* Trans. Malcolm Slater. Cambridge, UK: Polity Press.

Brown, Elizabeth A. R. 1974. The Tyranny of a Construct: Feudalism and Historians of Medieval Europe. *American Historical Review* 79 (4): 1063–1088.

Brown, Joseph Epes. 1971. *The Sacred Pipe: Black Elk's Account of the Seven Rites of the Oglala Sioux.* Baltimore: Penguin Books. (Orig. pub. 1953.)

Bücher, Karl. 1919. *Arbeit und Rhythmus.* Leipzig: E. Reinicke. (Orig. pub. 1896.)

Burkert, Walter. 1987. The Problem of Ritual Killing. In *Violent Origins: Walter Burkert, René Girard and Jonathan Z. Smith on Ritual Killing and Cultural Formation,* ed. Robert G. Hamerton-Kelly, 149–191. Palo Alto, CA: Stanford University Press.

Carlyle, Thomas. 1840. *Chartism.* Boston: Charles C. Little and James Brown.

Cataldi, Sue L. 1993. *Emotion, Depth, and Flesh: A Study of Sensitive Space; Reflections on Merleau-Ponty's Philosophy of Embodiment.* Albany: State University of New York Press.

Cave, Roderick. 2002. *Chinese Ceremonial Papers: An Illustrated Bibliography.* Risbury, UK: Whittington Press.

Chai, Ch'u, and Winberg Chai, eds. 1967. *Li Chi (Book of Rites).* Trans. James Legge. New Hyde Park, NY: University Books.

Chen Dachao. 1997. *Zhiqian (xiao xiaoshuo)* [Paper Money (short story)]. *Renmin ribao* [People's Daily], overseas ed. July 21.

Chen, Lucy Hsiu-mei. 1961. Spirit Calling. In *New Voices,* trans. Nancy Chang Ing, 3–22. Taipei: Heritage Press.

Chen Shihlun. 2010. The Culture and Economy of the Show Truck Business in Taiwan. Unpublished ms.

Cheng Hau Ling. 1999. Handcrafting, Offering and Selling *Jin.* Unpublished ms.

Ch'ü T'ung-Tsu. 1965. *Law and Society in Traditional China.* Paris: Mouton.

Codere, Helen. 1956. The Amiable Side of Kwakiutl Life: The Potlatch and the Play Potlatch. *American Anthropologist* 58 (2): 334–351.

Cohn, Norman. 1970. *The Pursuit of the Millennium: Revolutionary Millenarians and Mystical Anarchists of the Middle Ages.* New York: Oxford University Press.

Cooper, Eugene. 1982. The Potlatch in Ancient China: Parallels in Socio-political Structures of the Ancient Chinese and the American Indians of the Northwest. *History of Religions* 22:103–128.

———. 1998. Life-Cycle Rituals in Dongyang County: Time, Affinity, and Exchange in Rural China. *Ethnology* 37 (4): 373–394.

Day, Clarence Burton. 1940. *Chinese Peasant Cults: Being a Study of Chinese Paper Gods.* Shanghai: Kelly and Walsh.

Dean, Kenneth. 1988. Funerals in Fujian. *Cahiers d'Éxtrême-Asie* 4:19–78.

Détienne, Marcel, and Jean-Pierre Vernant. 1989. *The Cuisine of Sacrifice among the Greeks.* Trans. Paula Wissing. Chicago: University of Chicago Press.

Dongnan kuaibao. 2009. *Qingming jipin bangshang "mingpai"* [Qingming Offerings Labelled with "Brand Names"]. *Dongnan kuaibao* [South East Express News], April 3. http://press.idoican.com.cn/detail/articles/20090403502A42/ (accessed July 25, 2009).

Doolittle, Justus. [1865] 1966. *Social Life of the Chinese.* Taipei: Cheng Wen.

Dore, Henri. 1914. *Researches into Chinese Superstitions.* Trans. M. Kennelly. Shanghai: Tusewei.

Dou Hongmei. 2009. *Yang chaoshi "ruxiangsuisu" mai mingbi* [Since You Are in Rome, Do as the Romans Do: The Foreign Superstore Sells Otherworld Notes]. *Beijing ribao* [Beijing Daily], March 31. http://news.163.com/09/0331/09/55NM88O3000120GU.html (accessed July 25, 2009).

Douglas, Mary. 1973. *Natural Symbols: Explorations in Cosmology.* New York: Vintage Books.

———. 1980. *Edward Evans-Pritchard.* New York: Viking Press.

Duan Chengshi. 1975. *Yu Yang Tsa Tsu* [Yu Yang Miscellany]. Taipei: Taiwan Xuesheng Shuju [Taiwan Student Press].

Dudbridge, Glen. 1995. *Religious Experience and Lay Society in T'ang China: A Reading of Tai Fu's Kuang-i chi.* Cambridge: Cambridge University Press.

Durkheim, Emile. 1915. *The Elementary Forms of the Religious Life.* Trans. Joseph Swain. London: G. Allen & Unwin. (Orig. pub. 1912.)

———. 1938. *The Rules of Sociological Method.* Trans. Sarah Solovay and John Mueller. Glencoe, IL: Free Press. (Orig. pub. 1895.)

Dushi ribao [Metropolitan Daily]. 2009. June 25. www.metrohk.com.hk/printable.php?id=109930 (accessed September 7, 2009).

Ebrey, Patricia Buckley. 1991. *Chu Hsi's Family Rituals: A Twelfth-Century Chinese Manual for the Performance of Cappings, Weddings, Funerals, and Ancestral Rites.* Princeton, NJ: Princeton University Press.

———. 1993. *The Inner Quarters, Marriage and Lives of Women in the Song Period.* Berkeley: University of California Press

———. 1999. *The Cambridge Illustrated History of China.* Cambridge: Cambridge University Press.

Eco, Umberto. 1986. *Travels in Hyperreality.* Orlando: Harcourt, Brace & Company.

Eliot, George. 1913. *Silas Marner.* New York: A. S. Barnes.

Engels, Frederick. 1937. *Engels on Capital: Synopsis, Reviews, and Supplementary Material.* 2nd ed. Trans. Leonard E. Mins. New York: International Publishers.

Evans-Pritchard, E. E. 1967. *Nuer Religion.* Oxford: Clarendon Press. (Orig. pub. 1956.)

———. 1976. *Witchcraft, Oracles, and Magic among the Azande.* Oxford: Clarendon Press.

Fang Xing et al. 2000. Paper Making, Printing and Publishing. In *Chinese Capitalism 1522–1840,* ed. Xu Dixin and Wu Chengming, 228–239. English version ed. C. A. Curwentrans. Li Zhengde, Liang Miaoru, and Li Siping. New York: St. Martin's.

Fazhi wanbao. 2008. *Qingming jipin chuxin, xiaofan mupang doushou "tianguo shou-qiang"* [New-Style Qingming Sacrificial Materials Such as "Heavenly King-dom Hand Guns" Sold by Peddlers alongside the Graves]. *Fazhi wanbao* [Legal System Evening News]. *Sohu wang* [www.sohu.com], April 3. http://news.sohu.com/20080403/n256086157.shtml (accessed July 20, 2009).

Feng Feng. 2004. *Baixing minsu liyi daquan (Zhencang ban)* [Encyclopedia of Folk Rituals (Rare Editions)]. Zhongguo mangwen chubanshe [China Braille Publisher]. Online at the *Guojia shuzi wenhua wang* [National Digital Culture Net].

Feuchtwang, Stephen. 1989. The Problem of "Superstition" in the People's Republic of China. In *Religion and Political Power,* ed. Gustavo Benavides and M. W. Daly, 43–68. Albany: State University of New York Press.

———. 1992. *The Imperial Metaphor: Popular Religion in China.* London: Routledge.

Fine, Ben, and Alfredo Saad-Filho. 2004. *Marx's Capital.* London: Pluto Press.

Forster, Georg H. 1998. The Old Carolus Dollar and Chinese Chops: More First Hand Accounts. *Journal of East Asian Numismatics* (JEAN) 19 (winter). Online at http://www.chopmarks.com/info/forster-1.htm#* (accessed October 25, 2009).

Frazer, Sir James George. 1920. *The Golden Bough: A Study in Magic and Religion.* 3rd ed. London: Macmillan.

Gates, Hill. 1987. Money for the Gods. *Modern China* 13 (3): 259–277.

———. 1996. *China's Motor: A Thousand Years of Petty Capitalism.* Ithaca, NY: Cornell University Press.

Gennep, Arnold van. 1960. *The Rites of Passage.* Ed. M. Vizedom and G. Caffe. London: Routledge & Kegan Paul. (Orig. pub. 1908.)

Gernet, Jacques. 1962. *Daily Life in China on the Eve of the Mongol Invasion, 1250–1276.* Stanford, CA: Stanford University Press.

Girard, René. 1987. Generative Scapegoating. In *Violent Origins: Ritual Killing and Cultural Formation,* ed. Robert G. Hamerton-Kelly, 73–105. Stanford, CA: Stanford University Press.

Godelier, Maurice. 1999. *The Enigma of the Gift.* Chicago: University of Chicago Press.

———. 2002. Some Things You Give, Some Things You Sell, but Some Things You Must Keep for Yourselves: What Mauss Did Not Say about Sacred Objects. In *The Enigma of Gift and Sacrifice,* ed. Edith Wyschogrod, Jean-Joseph Goux, and Eric Boynton, 19–37. New York: Fordham University Press.

Gordon, Richard, Kathy Kline, and Daniel Sipe. 1984. *Small Happiness: Women of a Chinese Village.* Videorecording. Long Bow Productions. New York: New Day Films.

Gouldner, Alvin Ward. 1976. *The Dialectic of Ideology and Technology: The Origins, Grammar, and Future of Ideology.* New York: Seabury Press.

Graeber, David. 2001. *Toward an Anthropological Theory of Value: The False Coin of Our Own Dreams.* New York: Palgrave.

Gregory, Christopher A. 1980. Gifts to Men and Gifts to God: Gift Exchange and Capital Accumulation in Contemporary Papua. *Man,* n.s., 15 (4): 626–652.

———. 1982. *Gifts and Commodities.* London: Academic Press.

———. 1983. Kula Gift Exchange and Capitalist Commodity Exchange: A Comparison. In *The Kula: New Perspectives on Massim Exchange,* ed. Jerry W. Leach and Edmund Leach, 103–117. London: Cambridge University Press.

Groot, J. J. M. de. 1969. *The Religious System of China, Its Ancient Forms, Evolution, History and Present Aspect, Manners, Customs and Social Institutions Connected Therewith.* 6 vols. Taipei: Ch'eng Wen. (Orig. pub. 1892.)

Guangzhou ribao. 2008. *Guangzhou chuxian linglei jipin: Bieshu, xinyongka, anquantao* [Exotic Offerings Appeared in Guangzhou: Villa, Credit Cards, Condoms]. *Guangzhou ribao* [Guangzhou Daily], cited in *Beijing wanbao* [Beijing Evening News] April 1. http://villa.soufun.com/2008-04-01/1627036.htm (accessed July 25, 2009).

Gulik, R. H. van. 2003. *Sexual Life in Ancient China: A Preliminary Survey of Chinese Sex and Society from ca. 1500 B.C. till 1644 A.D.* Leiden: Brill.

Guqian zhi chen [Augury of Ancient Money]. 2008. March 24. http://news.artxun.com/huoquan-1320-6597928.shtml (accessed December 3, 2010).

Habermas, Jürgen. 1970. *Toward a Rational Society: Student Protest, Science, and Politics.* Trans. Jeremy J. Shapiro. Boston: Beacon Press.

Haikou wanbao. 2009. *Qingming jisi, huaqian yue duo yue xiaoshun?* [Does the More People Spend on Qingming Sacrificial Offerings Indicate Their Greater Filial Piety?]. *Haikou wanbaowang* [Haikou (Hainan) Evening News], April 7. http://www.hkwb.net/html/2009/04/07/96334.html (accessed July 20, 2009).

Hamerton-Kelly, Robert G., ed. 1987. *Violent Origins: Walter Burkert, René Girard and Jonathan Z. Smith on Ritual Killing and Cultural Formation.* Palo Alto, CA: Stanford University Press.

Han feng gu yun [Ancient Charm of Chinese Customs]. 2010. *Rui ping: Gei xianren shao "ernai," jituo de shi aisi haishi weixie?* [Critically Discuss: Does Burning a "Mistress" for the Ancestors Convey Mourning or Obscenity?]. Forum Xinhuanet.com, April 5. http://forum.home.news.cn/detail/74949353/1.html (accessed July 11, 2010).

Hansen, Valerie. 1990. *Changing Gods of Medieval China, 1127–1276.* Princeton, NJ: Princeton University Press.

Han Suyin. 1965. *The Crippled Tree.* New York: Putnam.

Harvey, David. 1982. *The Limits to Capital.* Chicago: University of Chicago Press.

He Bingdi. 1962. *The Ladder of Success in Imperial China: Aspects of Social Mobility, 1368–1911.* New York: Columbia University Press.

Heesterman, J. C. 1993. *The Broken World of Sacrifice: An Essay in Ancient Indian Ritual.* Chicago: University of Chicago Press.

Heidegger, Martin. 1962. *Being and Time.* New York: Harper.

Heilbroner, Robert L. 1962. *The Making of Economic Society.* Englewood Cliffs, NJ: Prentice-Hall.

He Youzhi. 1997. *Shou zhiding hui* [Picking Ashes of Paper Ingots]. *Xinmin wanbao* [New People's Evening News], January 6.

Hou Ching-Lang. 1975. *Monnaies d'offrande et la notions de trésorerie dans la religion chinoise.* Paris: Collège de France, Institut des hautes études chinoises.

Howard, Dick. 1988. *The Politics of Critique.* Minneapolis: University of Minnesota Press.

Hubert, Henri, and Marcel Mauss. 1964. *Sacrifice: Its Nature and Function.* Chicago: University of Chicago Press. (Orig. pub. 1898.)

Hui Jiyuan. 2009. *Qingmingjie qite jipin, shimin bu maizhang* [The People Don't Accept Qingming's Strange Offerings]. *Yingkou wanbao* [Yingkou (Liaoning) Evening News], April 2. http://press.idoican.com.cn/detail/articles/20090402809B22/ (accessed July 20, 2009).

Hunter, Dard. 1937. *Chinese Ceremonial Paper: A Monograph Relating to the Fabrication of Paper and Tin Foil and the Use of Paper in Chinese Rites and Religious Ceremonies.* Chillicothe, OH: Mountain House Press.

Husserl, Edmund. [1913] 1962. *Ideas: General Introduction to Pure Phenomenology.* Trans. W. R. Boyce Gibson. New York: Collier Books; London: Collier Macmillan.

Illich, Ivan. 1973. *Tools for Conviviality.* New York: Harper & Row.

Jameson, Fredric. 1988. The Vanishing Mediator; or, Max Weber as Storyteller. In *The Syntax of History*, vol. 2 of *The Ideologies of Theory: Essays 1971–1986*, 3–34. Minneapolis: University of Minnesota Press.

———. 1998. Postmodernism and Consumer Society. In *The Cultural Turn: Selected Writings on the Postmodern 1983–1998*, 1–20. London: Verso.

Ji Dongping. 2001. *Qingming jisi jing shao zhenqian* [How Strange that Real Money Was Burned for Qingming Sacrifice]. *Jianghuai chenbao* [Jianghuai Morning News], April 2. http://www.people.com.cn/GB/shenghuo/76/125/20010402/431229.html (accessed April 3, 2009).

Jin Peng. 2009. *Qingming jisi jing ke dingzuo zhihu "meinü"* [How Strange that Paper Pasted "Beautiful Ladies" Can Be Ordered for Qingming Offerings]. *Huan Bohai* news web, March 31. http://info.paper.hc360.com/2009/03/31091546455.shtml (accessed July 23, 2009).

Josephides, Lisette. 1985. *The Production of Inequality: Gender and Exchange among the Kewa.* London: Tavistock.

Kipnis, Andrew B. 1997. *Producing Guanxi: Sentiment, Self, and Subculture in a North China Village.* Durham, NC: Duke University Press.

Ko, Dorothy. 2005. *Cinderella's Sisters: A Revisionist History of Footbinding.* Berkeley and Los Angeles: University of California Press.

Kroeber, Alfred. 1957. An Anthropologist Looks at History. *Pacific Historical Review* 26 (3): 281–287.

Langer, Susanne K. 1951. *Philosophy in a New Key: A Study in the Symbolism of Reason, Rite and Art.* New York: New American Library of World Literature.

Leach, Edmund. 1976. *Culture and Communication: The Logic by Which Symbols Are Connected: An Introduction to the Use of Structuralist Analysis in Social Anthropology.* Cambridge: Cambridge University Press.

Lévi-Strauss, Claude. 1966. *The Savage Mind.* Chicago: University of Chicago Press.

———. 1970. *The Raw and the Cooked: Introduction to a Science of Mythology: I.* Trans. John and Doreen Weightman. New York: Harper Torchbooks.

———. 1973. *From Honey to Ashes.* Trans. John and Doreen Weightman. London: Cape.

Levy, Howard S. 1967. *Chinese Footbinding: The History of a Curious Erotic Custom.* New York: Bell Publishing Co.

Liao Gang. 1934–1935. *Qi jin fenzhi dazi* [Memorial to Prohibit Burning Paper]. In *Gao Feng wenji* [Collected Works of Gao Feng (Liao Gang)], vol. 1: 15–18. From the *Siku Quanshu zhenben chuji* [Precious Editions from the *Siku Quanshu*]. Shanghai: Shangwu yinshuguan [Commercial Press].

Lin Jianwei. 1996. *Popo tuomeng* [Grandma Entrusted with a Dream]. *Xinmin wanbao* [New People's Evening News], December 19.

Linsiting [Web site nickname]. 2008. *Zheli you ren hui die xibo ma?* [Does Anyone Know How to Fold Tinfoiled Paper?]. Liba.com, February 16. http://bbs.hz.liba.com/t_13_3724659_1.htm (accessed October 25, 2009).

Liu, Lydia H. 1995. *Translingual Practice: Literature, National Culture, and Translated Modernity—China, 1900–1937.* Stanford, CA: Stanford University Press.

Liu Sheng, Cui Fengqing, and Li Qingyun. 2002. *Taren menqian shao yinqian: Mingyu qinquan pei qianyuan* [Burning Otherworld Money to Ruin a Reputation Incurred a Penalty of Thousands of Yuan]. *Xinmin wanbao* [New People's Evening News], October 20.

Liu Wanping. 2005. *Mingbi zhiqian ye zaojia? You mixin shimin zhizhuo qiuzheng lingren tixiaojiefei* [Are Ghost Bills Fake Forms of Paper Money? It Is Ridiculous that a Superstitious Citizen Is So Pedantic in Verifying an Obvious Truth]. *Dahua wang–Shantou dushi bao* [Dahua Web–Swatow

Metropolitan News], February 3. http://news.sina.com.cn/s/2005-02-03/ 11165033022s.shtml (accessed July 19, 2009).

Li Xiang. 2000. *Cuo ba zhenqian dang mingbi, laohan shaole chungeng kuan* [Mistaking Real Money for Netherworld Notes, Old Man Burned Spring Planting Money]. *Changchun wanbao* [Changchun Evening News], February 25. http://news.sina.com.cn/society/2000-2-25/65312.html (accessed September 6, 2009).

Lukács, György. 1971. *History and Class Consciousness: Studies in Marxist Dialectics.* Trans. Rodney Livingstone. Cambridge: MIT Press.

———. 1980. Marx and the Problem of Ideological Decay. In *Essays on Realism: Georg Lukács,* ed. R. Livingstone, trans. David Fernbach, 114–166. Cambridge: MIT Press. (Orig. pub. 1938.)

Malamoud, Charles. 1996. *Cooking the World: Ritual and Thought in Ancient India.* Trans. David White. Delhi: Oxford University Press.

Malinowski, Bronislaw. 1958. The Role of Magic and Religion. In *Reader in Comparative Religion: An Anthropological Approach,* ed. William A. Lessa and Evon Z. Vogt, 86–99. Evanston, IL: Row, Peterson. (Orig. pub. 1931.)

———. 1965. *Coral Gardens and Their Magic.* Bloomington: Indiana University Press. (Orig. pub. 1936.)

———. 1984. *Argonauts of the Western Pacific: An Account of Native Enterprise and Adventure in the Archipelagoes of Melanesian New Guinea.* Prospect Heights, IL: Waveland Press. (Orig. pub. 1922.)

Mann, Susan. 1987. *Local Merchants and the Chinese Bureaucracy, 1750–1950.* Palo Alto, CA: Stanford University Press.

Marcus, George. 1995. Ethnography in/of the World System: The Emergence of Multi-Sited Ethnography. *Annual Review of Anthropology* 24:95–117.

Marx, Karl. 1906. *Capital: A Critique of Political Economy.* Vol. 1. Ed. Frederick Engels. New York: Modern Library.

Mauss, Marcel. [1923–1924] 1990. *The Gift: Forms and Functions of Exchange in Archaic Societies.* Trans. W. D. Halls. New York: W. W. Norton.

McClymond, Kathryn. 2008. *Beyond Sacred Violence: A Comparative Study of Sacrifice.* Baltimore: Johns Hopkins University Press.

McCreery, John L. 1990. Why Don't We See Some Real Money Here? Offerings in Chinese Religion. *Journal of Chinese Religion* 18:1–24.

Meng Genfang, ed. 2006. *Jumin menshang bei tieman "zhiqian," jingfang yi jieru diaocha* [Paper Money Was Pasted All Over the Door of a Resident, the Police Are Already Investigating]. *Xin'an wanbao* [New Anhui Evening News], January 5. http://ah.anhuinews.com/system/2006/01/05/ 001414739.shtml (accessed July 19, 2009).

Merleau-Ponty, Maurice. 1968. *The Visible and the Invisible.* Evanston, IL: Northwestern University Press.

Muller, Jerry Z. 2002. The Philosopher of Money. *Wilson Quarterly* 26 (4): 52–60.

Munn, Nancy D. 1986. *The Fame of Gawa: A Symbolic Study of Value Transformation in a Massim (Papua New Guinea) Society.* Cambridge: Cambridge University Press.

Murongqiubai. 2006. *Ruci huangtang de binzang guanli tiaoli* [Such Absurd Funeral Administration Regulations]. *Murongqiubai de rizhi* [Murongqiubai's Log], April 29. http://hi.mop.com/profile2.do?id=16280930 (accessed November 28, 2010).

Nash, June. 1979. *We Eat the Mines.* New York: Columbia University Press.

Needham, Joseph. 1954. *Science and Civilization in China.* Vol. 1. Cambridge: Cambridge University Press.

———. 1972. *Science and Civilization in China.* Vol. 5, Chemistry and Chemical Technology, Part II. Cambridge: Cambridge University Press. (Orig. pub. 1954.)

Notar, Beth E. 2004. Ties That Dissolve and Bind: Competing Currencies, Prestige, and Politics in Early Twentieth-Century China. In *Values and Valuables: From the Sacred to the Symbolic,* ed. Cynthia Werner and Duran Bell, 128–157. Walnut Creek, CA: Altamira.

Ortner, Sherry. 1995. Resistance and the Problem of Ethnographic Refusal. *Comparative Studies in Society and History* 37 (1): 173–193.

Peng Tong, Ouyang Jianjun, and Luo Qinbiao. 2005. *Haikou: Qingmingjie saomu baikuo doufu, youren shao zhenqian ji xianren* [People Sweeping the Graves at the Haikou Qingming Festival Ostentatiously Compete for Wealth by Burning Real Money to Sacrifice for the Ancestors]. *Haikou wanbao* [Haikou Evening News], June 4. http://www.hinews.cn/news/system/2005/04/06/000038754.shtml (accessed July 19, 2009).

Peng Xinwei. 1994. *A Monetary History of China.* Trans. Edward H. Kaplan. Bellingham: Western Washington University Press.

Pfänder, Alexander. 1967. *Phenomenology of Willing and Motivation and Other Phenomenologica.* Trans. Herbert Spiegelberg. Evanston, IL: Northwestern University Press.

Polanyi, Karl. 1944. *The Great Transformation.* Boston: Beacon Press.

———. 1957. Aristotle Discovers the Economy. In *Trade and Market in the Early Empires: Economies in History and Theory,* ed. Karl Polanyi, Conrad M. Arensberg, and Harry W. Pearson, 64–94. Glencoe, IL: Free Press.

Potter, Sulamith Heins, and Jack M. Potter. 1990. *China's Peasants: The Anthropology of a Revolution.* Cambridge: Cambridge University Press.

Poulantzas, Nicos. 1973. *Political Power and Social Classes.* Trans. Timothy O'Hagan. London: NLBand Sheed and Ward.

Qixing de boke [Blog from Qixing district, Guilin, Guangxi]. 2010. *Leiren de jisao fangshi neng bu neng shao yidian?* [Can There Be Fewer Appalling Sacrifi-

cial Offerings?], March 30. http://feilong2018.blog.163.com/blog/static/
121900655201023052328225/ (accessed July 11, 2010).

Qu Yunfei. 2005. *Shi mixin haishi courenao? "Guijie" lai shi "cunzhe" rexiao* [Super-
stition or Emulation? Bankbooks Were Well Sold on the Ghost Festival].
Jinri an bao [Today Safety Newspaper], Xinyang, Henan, August 22. http://
www.ha.xinhuanet.com/add/hnnews/2005-08/22/content_4936365.htm
(accessed August 22, 2005).

Radcliffe-Brown, A. R. 1958. Taboo. In *Reader in Comparative Religion: An
Anthropological Approach,* ed. W. Lessa and E. Vogt, 99–111. Evanston, IL:
Row, Peterson and Company. (Orig. pub. 1939.)

Radin, Paul. 1972. *The Trickster: A Study in American Indian Mythology.* New
York: Schocken. (Orig. pub. 1956.)

Rappaport, Roy. 1999. *Ritual and Religion in the Making of Humanity.* Cambridge:
Cambridge University Press.

Ricoeur, Paul. 1966. *Freedom and Nature: The Voluntary and Involuntary.* Evanston, IL: Northwestern University Press.

Rivers, W. H. R. 1910. The Genealogical Method of Anthropological Inquiry.
Sociological Review 3:1–12.

Robbins, Richard H. 1999. *Global Problems and the Culture of Capitalism.* Boston:
Allyn and Bacon.

Rosaldo, Renato. 1989. Grief and the Headhunter's Rage. In *Culture and Truth:
Remaking of Social Analysis,* 1–21. Boston: Beacon Press.

Saad-Filho, Alfredo. 2002. *The Value of Marx: Political Economy for Contemporary
Capitalism.* London: Routledge.

Sahlins, Marshall. 1999. Two or Three Things That I Know about Culture. *Journal of the Royal Anthropological Institute* 5 (3): 399–421.

Saint-Exupéry, Antoine de. 1984. *Airman's Odyssey.* San Diego: Harcourt Brace
Jovanovich. (Orig. pub. 1942.)

Sangren, P. Steven. 2000. *Chinese Sociologics: An Anthropological Account of the Role
of Alienation in Social Reproduction.* London: Athlone.

———. 2003. Separations, Autonomy, and Recognition in the Production
of Gender Differences: Reflections from Considerations of Myths and
Laments. In *Living with Separation in China: Anthropological Accounts,* ed.
Charles Stafford, 53–84. London: RoutledgeCurzon.

Sapir, Edward, and Tsan Hwa Hsu. 1923. Humor of the Chinese Folk (A Deer
and a Dream). *Journal of American Folklore* 36 (139): 31–35.

Schipper, Kristofer. 1993. *The Taoist Body.* Berkeley: University of California
Press.

Schneider, Jane. 1989. Rumpelstiltskin's Bargain: Folklore and Merchant Capitalist Intensification of Linen Manufacture in Early Modern Europe. In

Cloth and Human Experience, ed. A. Weiner and J. Schneider, 178–213. Washington, DC: Smithsonian Institution Press.

Schurmann, Franz. 1968. *Ideology and Organization in Communist China.* Berkeley: University of California Press.

Scott, Janet. 1997. Traditional Values and Modern Meanings in the Paper Offering Industry of Hong Kong. In *Hong Kong: The Anthropology of a Chinese Metropolis,* ed. Grant Evans and Maria Tam, 223–241. Honolulu: University of Hawai'i Press.

———. 2007. *For Gods, Ghosts and Ancestors: The Chinese Tradition of Paper Offerings.* Seattle: University of Washington Press.

Seaman, Gary. 1982. Spirit Money: An Interpretation. *Journal of Chinese Religion* 10:80–91.

Seidel, Anna. 1978. Buying One's Way to Heaven: The Celestial Treasury in Chinese Religion [book review]. *History of Religions* 17 (3–4): 419–431.

Service, Elman R. 1971. *Cultural Evolutionism: Theory in Practice.* New York: Holt, Rinehart and Winston.

Sexton, Lorraine. 1986. *Mothers of Money, Daughters of Coffee: The Wok Meri Movement.* Ann Arbor: UMI Research Press.

Shahar, Meir, and Robert P. Weller, eds. 1996. *Unruly Gods: Divinity and Society in China.* Honolulu: University of Hawai'i Press.

Shipton, Parker. 1989. *Bitter Money.* American Ethnological Society Monograph Series No. 1. Washington, DC: American Anthropological Association.

Simmel, Georg. [1907] 1978. *The Philosophy of Money.* Trans. T. Bottomore and D. Frisby. London: Routledge and Kegan Paul.

Skinner, G. William. 1964. Marketing and Social Structure in Rural China: Parts I, II, and III. *Journal of Asian Studies* 24 (1): 3–43; 24 (2): 195–228; 24 (3): 363–399.

———, ed. 1977. *The City in Late Imperial China.* Stanford: Stanford University Press.

Smith, Arthur H. 1894. *Chinese Characteristics.* New York: F. H. Revell.

Smith, W. Robertson. 1957. *Lectures on the Religion of the Semites.* New York: Meridian Books. (Orig. pub. 1889.)

Song Lian. 1956. *Economic Structure of the Yuan Dynasty* [chapters 93 and 94 of the *Yuan History*]. Trans. H. Franz Schurmann. Cambridge: Harvard University Press.

Soothill, Lucy. 1931. *A Passport to China: Being the Tale of Her Long and Friendly Sojourning amongst a Strangely Interesting People.* London: Hodder and Stoughton.

Spiegelberg, Herbert. 1975. *Doing Phenomenology: Essays on and in Phenomenology.* The Hague: Martinus Nijhoff.

Spiro, Melford E. 1996. Postmodernist Anthropology, Subjectivity, and Science: A Modernist Critique. *Comparative Studies in Society and History* 38 (4): 759–780.

Stafford, Charles. 2000. *Separation and Reunion in Modern China.* Cambridge: Cambridge University Press.

Staunton, Sir George Thomas. 1810. *Ta Tsing Leu Li: Being the Fundamental Laws, and Selections from the Supplementary Statutes, of the Penal Code of China.* London: T. Cadell and W. Davies. Reprint, Taipei: Ch'eng-Wen, 1966.

Stoller, Paul. 1997. *Sensuous Scholarship.* Philadelphia: University of Pennsylvania Press.

———. 2002. *Money Has No Smell: Ethnography of West African Traders in New York City.* Chicago: University of Chicago Press.

Strathern, Andrew. 1971. *The Rope of Moka: Big-men and Ceremonial Exchange in Mount Hagen, New Guinea.* Cambridge: Cambridge University Press.

———. 1979. Gender, Ideology and Money in Mount Hagen. *Man* 14 (3): 530–548.

Strathern, Marilyn. 1988. *The Gender of the Gift: Problems with Women and Problems with Society in Melanesia.* Berkeley: University of California Press.

Sun Xidan. 1989. *Liji jijie* [Collected Commentaries on the *Book of Rites*]. Vol. 1. Beijing: Zhonghua shuju [Zhonghua Book Company].

Tambiah, S. J. 1968. The Magical Power of Words. *Man* 3:175–206.

Tan Chee-Beng. 2006. Chinese Religious Expressions in Post-Mao Yongchun, Fujian. *Southern Fujian: Reproduction of Traditions in Post-Mao China,* ed. Tan Chee-Beng, 97–120. Hong Kong: Chinese University Press.

Tan, Taylor Lauren. 2003. Qingming and the Significance of Burning Money. Unpublished ms.

Tang Lin. 1992. *Ming bao ji.* Beijing: Zhonghua shuju [Zhonghua Book Company].

Taobaowang [Taobao Internet (store) home page]. 2010. http://shop57566375 .taobao.com/ (accessed July 19, 2010).

Taussig, Michael T. 1980. *The Devil and Commodity Fetishism in South America.* Chapel Hill: University of North Carolina Press.

Thompson, E. P. 1991. *Customs in Common: Studies in Traditional Popular Culture.* New York: New Press.

Thompson, S. E. 1988. Death, Food and Fertility. In *Death Ritual in Late Imperial and Modern China,* ed. J. L. Watson and E. S. Rawski, 71–108. Berkeley: University of California Press.

Tiexue Net. 2009. *Jintian mai de chao jiong mingbi! Jinlai dai hao bileizhen, zai tiantang douhui bei lei de jingcai pinglun* [Today I Bought Extremely Shocking Otherworld Currencies! Bring Your Lightning Rod to My Chat Room, You'll Be Struck by the Lightning Even If You Are in Heaven, Some Interesting Comments]. Beijing ICP Certificate Number 050083, Beijing ICP

Record 09067787 Police file 1101080496, March 27. http://bbs.tiexue
.net/post2_3449459_1.html (accessed July 25, 2009).

Turnbull, Colin M. 1961. *The Forest People.* New York: Simon & Schuster.

Turner, Terence S. 1977. Transformation, Hierarchy and Transcendence: A
Reformulation of Van Genep's Model of the Structure of Rites of Passage.
Secular Ritual, ed. Sally F. Moore and Barbara G. Myerhoff, 3–24. Assen,
the Netherlands: Van Gorcum & Co.

————. 1986. Production, Exploitation and Social Consciousness in the
"Peripheral Situation." *Social Analysis: Journal of Cultural and Social Practice*
19:91–115.

Turner, Victor W. 1967a. Symbols in Ndembu Ritual. In *The Forest of Symbols:
Aspects of Ndembu Ritual,* 19–47. Ithaca, NY: Cornell University Press.

————. 1967b. Betwixt and Between: The Liminal Period in *Rites de Passage.* In
The Forest of Symbols: Aspects of Ndembu Ritual, 93–111. Ithaca, NY: Cornell
University Press.

————. 1969. *The Ritual Process: Structure and Anti-Structure.* Chicago: Aldine.

————. 1974. Passages, Margins, and Poverty: Religious Symbols of Communitas. In *Dramas, Fields, and Metaphors: Symbolic Action in Human Society,*
231–271. Ithaca, NY: Cornell University Press.

Tu Weiming. 1994. *The Living Tree: The Changing Meaning of Being Chinese Today.*
Stanford, CA: Stanford University Press.

Tylor, Edward. [1871] 1958. *Religion in Primitive Culture* [originally *Primitive
Culture,* vol. 2]. New York: Harper.

Veblen, Thorstein. 1953. *The Theory of the Leisure Class: An Economic Study of Institutions.* New York: New American Library. (Orig. pub. 1912.)

Vu Tu Anh. Forthcoming. *Dao Mau Religious Practices: Soft Power and Everyday
Lives of Women in Contemporary Vietnam.* PhD diss., Department of Anthropology, University of Hawai'i.

Wallace, Anthony F. C. 1956. Revitalization Movements. *American Anthropologist*
58 (2): 264–281.

Wang Fuzi. 1998. *Binzang wenhuaxue—Siwang wenhua de quanfangwei jiedu* [The
Cultural Studies of Funeral: The Comprehensive Interpretation of the
Culture of Death]. Vol. 2. Beijing: Zhongguo shehui chubanshe [Chinese
Society Publisher].

Wang Li. 2004. *Jipin yu xiangwu: Zhiqian yu chuantong sangzang fengsu xintai
jianlun* [Offerings and Propitious Objects: Paper Money and the Psychological Attitudes toward Traditional Funerals]. *Guangxi minzu daxue xuebao*
[Journal of Guangxi University for Nationalities] 6:108–111.

Wang Xinling. 2004. *Meinian jisi shaozhi haozi shu qianwan yuan, Shenyang
quancheng yanjin shaozhi* [Shenyang Consumes Several Ten Million Yuan
Every Year in Burning Paper for Offerings: The Whole City Bans Burn-

ing Paper]. *Liaoning wanbao* [Liaoning Evening News], August 24. http://www.people.com.cn/GB/shizheng/14562/2747318.html (accessed August 20, 2006).

Wank, David L. 1999. *Commodifying Communism: Business, Trust, and Politics in a Chinese City.* Cambridge: Cambridge University Press.

Watson, James. 1976. Chattel Slavery in Chinese Peasant Society: A Comparative Analysis. *Ethnology* 15 (4): 361–375.

———. 1980. Transactions in People: The Chinese Market in Slaves, Servants, and Heirs. *Asian and African Systems of Slavery,* ed. J. L. Watson, 223–250. Berkeley: University of California Press.

———. 1987. From the Common Pot: Feasting with Equals in Chinese Society. *Anthropos* 82:389–401.

———, ed. 1997. *Golden Arches East: McDonald's in East Asia.* Stanford, CA: Stanford University Press.

———. 1998. Slavery in China. In *A Historical Guide to World Slavery,* ed. Stanley L. Engerman and Seymour Drescher, 149–152. Oxford: Oxford University Press.

Weber, Max. 1964. *The Theory of Social and Economic Organization.* Trans. A. M. Henderson and Talcott Parsons. New York: Free Press.

Wei Huaxian. 2006. *Songdai silei wupin de shengchan he xiaofei yanjiu* [A Study of Production and Consumption of Four Kinds of Products in Song Dynasty]. Chengdu, Sichuan: Kexuejishu chubanshe [Sichuan Science and Technology Press].

Weiner, Annette B. 1992. *Inalienable Possessions: The Paradox of Keeping-While-Giving.* Berkeley: University of California Press.

Wen Yansheng. 1991. *Zhongguo gui hua* [Chinese Ghost Stories]. Shanghai: Shanghai wenyi chubanshe [Shanghai Art and Literature Publisher].

Werner, E. T. C. 1932. *A Dictionary of Chinese Mythology.* Shanghai: Kelly and Walsh.

Wheatley, Paul. 1971. *The Pivot of the Four Quarters: A Preliminary Enquiry into the Origins and Character of the Ancient Chinese City.* Chicago: Aldine.

Wilk, Richard R. 1996. *Economies and Cultures: Foundations of Economic Anthropology.* 2nd ed. Boulder, CO: Westview Press.

Wissler, Clark. 1906. Ethnic Types and Isolation. *Science,* n.s., 23 (578): 147–149.

Wolf, Arthur P. 1974. Gods, Ghosts, and Ancestors. In *Religion and Ritual in Chinese Society,* ed. Arthur P. Wolf, 131–182. Stanford, CA: Stanford University Press.

Wolf, Margery. 1968. *The House of Lim.* Englewood Cliffs, NJ: Prentice-Hall.

Xiao Gang, Zhang Song, and Lei Haoran. 2008. *Jinnian Qingming mudi bian cha huang juhua* [Yellow Chrysanthemums Were Placed All Over the Cemetery This Qingming]. *Chengdu shangbao* [Chengdu Commercial News], March

20. http://www.chengdu.gov.cn/moban/detail.jsp?id=183588 (accessed July 15, 2009).

Xie Haoming and Huang Jin. 2004. *Zhiqian cun "hequhecong"* [Paper Money Village "Where Does It All Lead?"]. *Jiangnan dushi bao* [Jiangnan Metropolitan News], April 6. http://www.jxnews.com.cn/oldnews/n935/ca643966 .htm (accessed July 25, 2009).

Xin kuai bao. 2005. *Qingming linglei jipin: Fenshao "ernai, weige" ji xianren* [Qingming Exotic Offerings: Burn "Mistresses, Viagra" to Memorialize Ancestors]. *Xin kuai bao* [New Express News], April 11. *Jinyang wang—Xinkuaibao* Web site, April 11. http://news.sina.com.cn/s/2005-04-11/01346345065 .shtml (accessed April 5, 2008).

Xinmin wanbao [New People's Evening News]. 1996. *Qiannian qianbi chong fang yicai: Ji Quanzhou faxian de Minwang fading qianbi* [Thousand-Year-Old Coin Again Releases Radiant Splendor: A Legal Coin of the Min King Found near Quanzhou]. November 22.

———. 1997. *Bao wen qian* [Money Cast with the Character for Treasure]. August 21.

Xu Dixin and Wu Chengming, eds. 2000. *Chinese Capitalism, 1522–1840.* English version ed. C. A. Curwentrans. Li Zhengde, Liang Miaoru, and Li Siping. New York: St. Martin's.

Xue Li, ed. 1994. *Zhonghua minsu yuanliu jicheng* [Collection of the Origin of Chinese Folk Customs]. Vol. 2, *Liyi sangzang juan* [Ritual and Funeral]. Lanzhou: Gansu renmin chubanshe [Gansu People's Publisher].

Xu Hualong. 1998. *Guixue quanshu* [The Anthology of Ghost Studies]. Beijing: Zhongguo huaqiao chubanshe [Overseas Chinese Publisher].

Yang Kechang. 1995. *Song wangfu "chuguo youji"* [Sending Deceased Father "on a Trip Abroad"]. *Xinmin wanbao* [New People's Evening News], February 4.

Yan Yunxiang. 1996. *The Flow of Gifts: Reciprocity and Social Networks in a Chinese Village.* Stanford, CA: Stanford University Press.

Yao Lingxi. 1941. *Cai fei jinghua lu, shangjuan* [Quintessence of Picking Radishes, Vol. 1]. Tianjin: Tianjin shuju [Tianjin Book Store].

Yin Hong. 2006. *Qingmingjie: Cong "muji" zhi li dao qingya ji you* [Qingming Festival: From "Tomb Sacrifice" Ritual to a Refined Way of Memorializing]. *Guangming ribao* [Guangming Daily], April 4. http://www.gmw. cn/01gmrb/2006-04/04/content_398505.htm (accessed December 11, 2010).

You'a. Baidu.com. 2010. [Have it! Baidu.com online store.] *Sanwei kongjiantao + G diantao, 5 + 5 zuhe zhuang—Shixian sanwei liti xuanzhuan xiaoguo* [Three-Dimensional Condom + G-Spot Condom, Five + Five Piece Set— Achieves Three-Dimensional Whirling Effect]. http://youa.baidu.com/ item/b86a51321a7eca348230ed8c (accessed July 10, 2010).

Zhang Xueshan, and Zhang Chunsheng. 2002. *Zhongguo chuantong lisu* [Chinese Traditional Custom]. Tianjin: Baihua wenyi chubanshe [Hundred Flowers Art and Literature Press].

Zhou Kailing. 2000. *Laozi Qingming shao mingbi, xiao'er mofang shao zhenqian* [Dad Burns Netherworld Currency on Qingming, Son Mimics Him by Burning Real Money]. *Yangzi wanbao* [Yangtze Evening News]. http://news.sina .com.cn/society/2000-4-12/81135.html (accessed July 20, 2009).

Zhou Xin. 2009. *Huangzhi mingbi xianshen chaoshi, shimin renwei qiantuo* [Yellow Paper and Otherworld Cash Show up in Superstore, Citizens Regard It as Inappropriate.] *Jinghua shibao* [Jinghua Daily News (Beijing)], March 30. http://news.163.com/09/0330/02/55KBM2S200011229.html (accessed July 20, 2009).

Zhu Ling, ed. 2006. Organizers of Funeral Stripteases Detained in E. China. Xinhuanet, August 23. http://news.xinhuanet.com/english/2006-08/23/ content_4999002.htm (accessed April 24, 2010).

Zito, Angela. 1997. *Of Body and Brush: Grand Sacrifice as Text/Performance in Eighteenth-Century China*. Chicago: University of Chicago Press.

Zu Xian, ed. 2006. *Linglei jipin huayangfanxin, wenming jidian renzhongdaoyuan* [Exotic Offerings Keep Reinventing Themselves: Civilized Manner of Sacrifice Has a Long Way to Go]. *Yinzhou xinwen wang* [Yinzhou News Web site], April 3. http://www.yznews.net.cn/gb/node2/node572/node579/ userobject1ai16034.htm (accessed July 20, 2009).

INDEX

Ahern, Emily Martin, 15, 80, 106, 224n7, 231n10
Aijmer, Göran, 79
alchemy, 3, 86, 101, 227n16
alienation, 109, 111, 169, 207, 209, 213, 214
Amin, Samir, 7
ancestor (*zǔxiān*): altar, hall, tomb, 22, 47, 57, 166, 184; and paper money, 23, 27, 28, 40, 45, 46, 57, 68, 71, 76, 166, 182, 183, 184, 185, 186, 188, 190, 219n11; regard for, 23, 40, 46, 182, 183, 184, 185, 186, 188; as spirits, 21, 22, 76, 104, 112, 233n3
Anderson, Perry, 102, 103, 230n6
animus: in commodities, 107, 108, 194, 204, 207, 208–209; in social economies, 200, 201, 202, 204–205
Appadurai, Arjun, 110, 119, 207, 228n1, 229n5
artifice, 21, 93, 105, 115, 119, 126, 172, 173, 180, 199, 210, 213, 214
authenticity, 105, 113, 115, 119, 121, 143, 174, 178, 199, 203; distinguished from realism, 49, 171, 172, 173, 178, 180, 203, 210; and ritual effectiveness, 31, 44, 72, 105, 133, 171, 173; of the fake, 180, 199; of the world, 213, 214. *See also* realism

Bachelard, Gaston, 6, 76, 84
Bai Juyi, 53, 221n2
Bakhtin, Mikhail, 6, 28, 227n15

BaMbuti, 204; *molimo*, 203
Bataille, Georges, 184
Baudrillard, Jean, 5, 14, 119, 168, 182, 184, 190
belief: concept of, 7, 19, 20, 21–22; about paper money, 13, 31, 57; suspension of, 4
Belk, Russell, 204
Benjamin, Walter, 6, 142, 173
Bergson, Henri, 158
Binswanger, Ludwig, 5
Block, Melissa, 12
blogosphere. *See* internet
Boas, Franz, 199
Bodhisattva. *See* Buddha
boisterous mood (*rènao*), 79, 86, 184. *See also* jocund mood
Book of Rites (*Liji*), 63–65, 72, 78, 80, 170, 199
brands and logos, 14, 35, 179, 186, 189, 190, 214, 217n4. *See also* corporation; exotic offerings
Brown, Elizabeth, 99, 229n22
Bücher, Karl, 125
Buddha: as Earth Treasury Bodhisattva, 155; as Guanyin, 30, 41, 80, 106, 134, 155; as Maitreya, 128; as Mílèfó, 41; not connected to paper money custom, 66, 133; and paper money custom, 23, 30–31, 38, 41, 45, 63, 66, 69, 71, 72, 128, 130, 131, 133, 136, 200; and paper money iconography, 131–132, 136, 149, 150, 152–155, 163–164; and print-

prophylactic functions of, 23, 54; specific examples of, 34, 41–42, 94, 130, 154, 217n4; type of paper money, 16, 28, 45, 154, 200

Cheng Yichuan (1033–1107), 68

chiasm (flesh of the world), 21, 24, 75, 82, 85, 87, 115, 122, 125, 165

children: afraid of family ghosts, 19; awareness of paper money, 10; as beneficiaries of paper money, 12–13, 34–35, 188; birth, maturation, and death of, 12–13, 34, 188; burning paper money, 32, 166–167, 177; consigned to a mundane mortality, 208; and folding paper money, 132, 133; importance of, 40, 42–43, 45, 94, 155, 184–185, 199, 202, 217n2, 234n8; and intercorporeality, 126, 202; in new urban folklore, 183; oracle power of, 11; recipients of lucky cash, 217n2; in the arms of Emolument, 42–43

Christian, 15, 18–19, 23, 24, 77, 139, 229n4

cigarettes, paper simulated, 179, 189, 190. *See also* exotic offerings

civilization, Chinese project of, 50, 94, 100, 101, 114, 115, 141, 166, 182, 194, 211, 233n16

Codere, Helen, 196

Cold Food, festival, 53

commoditization, 109; and decommoditization, 162; distinguished from monetization, 96, 111, 228n1

commodity: in capitalist periphery, 206, 208, 209; definition of, 229n5; distinguished from good, 99, 110, 204; fetish nature of, 108, 204, 207, 208, 209; as form of reification, 141, 204, 207; as germ of ideology, 108, 204, 207, 209; in modern capital, 96, 107, 108, 110, 113, 114, 141, 204, 205, 208, 209; paper money as, 73, 105, 106, 162, 165, 192–193, 206; in precapitalist formations, 99, 108, 110, 111, 204, 205; in regimes of values, 10, 124, 137, 165. *See also* capital; fetish

common ritual service, 3, 5, 76–93 passim, 117, 118, 226n12; compared to *Genesis,* 77, 89; as language of the senses, 79; shifting mood of, 5, 78–79, 184; ultimate sacred postulate of, 82, 84

commonsense, 20, 79, 84, 110, 115; in relation to magic, 115. *See also* lifeworld

communism: compared to the capitalist juggernaut, 196; as form of state capitalism, 232n13; and journalism, 171; paper iconography of, 24; and paper money custom, 15; realized in the *yin*-world, 104; and religion, 22, 171; as vanishing mediator, 113, 171, 210

Confucius: and paper money, 63, 67–75, 139, 154, 185, 186, 223n3; precepts and admonitions of, 5, 21, 63–65, 67–69, 75, 231n9; as statecraft (ritualized hegemony), 100–101, 113; used in word game about money, 219n8. See also *Book of Rites*

consecration: the act of, 117, 119; bloodless sacrifice of, 120; blood offering of, 121; the production of spiritual value, 119, 125, 165; the restoration of sensual value, 123–124, 127, 165; of sacred ground, 78; by touching, pressing, fanning, folding, 4, 86, 116, 123–124, 125, 128, 130, 165. *See also* folding paper objects; sacrifice

consumption: in balance with production, 111; economy based on, 14, 109, 180, 184; in Gawan society, 202; and paper money, 189; politics and poetics of, 7

convivial tools, 32, 203

Cooper, Eugene, 199, 234n6

corporation: based global capital, 214; brands and logos, 35, 186, 189–190; of Hell with limited liability printed on ghost bills, 153–154. *See also* exotic offerings

correlative thinking, 82

cosmic and compensative justice, 104, 229n4

ABOUT THE AUTHOR

C. Fred Blake received his Ph.D. from the University of Illinois at Urbana-Champaign. He is presently associate professor of anthropology at the University of Hawai'i. His teaching and research is concentrated on the lives of ordinary people in complex societies and how they make and remake their own histories. His particular cultural focus has been the historical formations of China and how the social order is reproduced in the common customs and how it also constrains and exacts tolls on the interpersonal lives of participants.

Production Notes for BLAKE / BURNING MONEY

Design and composition by Josie Herr with
text and display in Garamond 3

Printing and binding by Sheridan Books, Inc.

Printed on 50 lb. Natures Recycled Text, 440 ppi